TEXT IN ACTION

Cicely Berry
Foreword by Adrian Noble

First published in 2001 by
Virgin Publishing Ltd
Thames Wharf Studios
Rainville Road
London W6 9HA

10

A catalogue record for this book is available
from the British Library.

ISBN   9780753505410

Typeset by TW Typesetting, Plymouth, Devon

MIX
Paper from
responsible sources
FSC   FSC® C018179
www.fsc.org

Penguin Random House is committed to a sustainable future for
our business, our readers and our planet. This book is made from
Forest Stewardship Council® certified paper.

Printed and bound in Great Britain by Clays Ltd, St Ives plc

Vurgin - 2001 - £15.99.

Also by Cicely Berry

Voice and the Actor
Your Voice and How to Use It
The Actor and the Text

Contents

Acknowledgements

Because this book is about the work I have done over the years and how it has been able to develop, I would like to acknowledge my gratitude to the following:

Gwynneth Thurburn, who was Principal of the Central School of Speech and Drama from 1942 until 1967, for both her wisdom and her encouragement;

The Royal Shakespeare Company, first under the leadership of Trevor Nunn, then Terry Hands, and recently Adrian Noble, who have not only given me the opportunity to explore and develop the work, but have also supported that development;

Jeffrey Horowitz, Artistic Director of Theatre For A New Audience in New York, for organising the ongoing series of workshops that have given me the opportunity to further the work with directors.

And lastly, to Edward Bond, whom I have quoted frequently. The quotations are simply thoughts that I have heard him express at one time or another during workshops or rehearsals – or simply over the phone – which always put something into place for me.

Foreword

Cicely Berry will enter the rehearsal room quietly, frequently unnoticed, and sit listening, head slightly to one side, or follow the text thoughtfully. Her comments are invariably unpredictable, and can be quite discomfiting to the director and the actor. Why? She has an extraordinary knack of cutting the crap and focusing on the essential challenge of a scene, or a speech, or a characterisation. Her honesty, her intuitive understanding of actors and their processes, and a profound study of technique and methodology have made her one of the most influential figures not only at the RSC, where she has worked for the last 30 years, but in world theatre.

This is an important and invaluable book because in a brilliantly clear and practical way it addresses the central question of classical theatre: how to bring alive the world of the play through its language. This is much talked of and seldom properly addressed. She brings to bear on her subject the natural curiosity of the explorer and the patience in explanation of the good teacher. But more than anything else, she illuminates, as only an artist can.

Adrian Noble
Artistic Director, Royal Shakespeare Company

Introduction

There are four quotations/thoughts going round in my head which all seem to resonate with theatre now. First, a line from Thomas Kyd's *The Spanish Tragedy*:

Where words prevaile not, violence prevails

We, the Royal Shakespeare Company, were working on this play in the Swan Theatre in Stratford, and every time I heard this particular line it came out and hit me. It seemed so truly relevant to now, the year 2000 AD, yet it was written around 1585.

For in this day of Internet technology, management jargon and minimal communication, our whole way of relating to one another is in the balance. Managements run courses on staff communication as if there were some kind of science to it, and I think in a sense we are controlled by the people who have the right jargon. But perhaps this has always been true to some degree, and it is simply that technology has taken over and bent the rules – an Internet hierarchy rather than a societal or political one.

But that jargon cannot express feelings or what goes on in the imagination for it is only concerned with the literal, and therefore I believe we have created a two-tier world where those who are computer-literate and speak the right jargon – or should I say, make the money – set the rules, and those who want to enquire imaginatively into the nature of being, and who often have a fuller understanding of what is going on around them, become the underclass. There is a deep divide between those who can only see things literally, and those who have a deeper imaginative awareness and resource.

If we do not/cannot express our inner selves, how do we know what we think or what we feel? How can we have any philosophy or viewpoint? For it is in the expressing of our thoughts and intuitions that we can recognise them and deal with them – and take action. But if we cannot express these ideas and thoughts, the result can only be silent anger.

And here I want to digress for a moment to think about the written language. I am particularly interested in the area of dyslexia, and how this problem or this gift, whichever way you look at it, can also affect the way we express ourselves.[1] If you have dyslexia in any form it affects your ability to read and write, a proficiency on which your intelligence is judged, and you are deemed slow and unintelligent – all the things guaranteed to destroy your self-esteem. No matter that you have a different area of intelligence – a different mind's eye – you are profoundly affected and demoralised by the status quo judgement. How then can you express yourself with any authority? No wonder it is estimated that 52 per cent of offenders in prison are dyslexic, plus 80 per cent of drug addicts. Yet Einstein was dyslexic, as were Churchill and DaVinci, and in every NASA space station there is one dyslexic, specifically because they are regarded as having a different, and perhaps more encompassing, view of space.

But what I am also saying is this: when we read words they take us into a different area of awareness than when we speak them, for when we read our brains are being used to interpret what we read so that our imagination is not as free as when we are speaking them aloud. And this is why the actor, having learned the words off a printed page, must be given time to explore them verbally, for they will reach the imagination in a different way.

But now to the business of the book. I want to explore the speaking of text in 2000, although I am aware that it will be out of date by 2010, for fashions/modes of speech are constantly changing and we have to continually redefine what is required

---

[1] An excellent book to read on this subject is *The Gift of Dyslexia* by Ronald D. Davis with Eldon M. Braun.

of the actor. But because this book is about our awareness of, and response to, language, and how we adjust to both classical and contemporary writing, perhaps it will still have some value. I hope so.

Every play has a very specific world, and it conveys that world through the language: by this I mean not only through the meaning of the words but also in their sound, in the shaping and rhythm of the speeches, the images, and the spaces in that language. This is just as true in modern vernacular writing – the shaping of the language has to be found, or should I say heard, and that can sometimes prove more subtle than in heightened poetic writing.

But in Shakespeare, or indeed any highly poetic drama, the writing is much more extreme, and the modern actor must connect with the extravagance of the image yet make it sound as if spoken for now.

Gallop apace you fiery-footed steeds,
Towards Phoebus' lodging . . .

These are words with which we are all familiar – Juliet waiting for Romeo on her wedding night. The richness of the language in this speech tells us something of the extremity and heat of her love for Romeo, but we need to hear that heat and passion as if it is being spoken for now and not in some far-off, archaic time. The dynamic of that language has to be present in the actor at the moment of speaking.

And I suppose it is this very personal connection which the actor has to make with the language which has continually interested me. For this connection goes far beyond the literal meaning: it is the meeting between the intention of the character and the imagination of the actor which is then released into the word – and this has many complexities.

The actor then has a difficult task: he/she must draw the listener in and energise the audience with the language, but not by making it 'beautiful'. We do not want the listener simply to appreciate it; we want him/her to recognise its necessity, its essence, and more than this, we want to awaken the desire to talk.

In the introduction to my book *The Actor and the Text*, I wrote the following:

It seems to me there is so often a gap between the life that is going on imaginatively within the actor in order to create the reality of the character he/she is playing, and the life that he/she gives the text which is finally spoken. It is as if the energy and excitement that an actor feels when working on a part is not released fully when he/she commits to the words, when he/she is bound by the language set down.

The Actor and the Text was addressed directly to the actor, setting out the exercises which I have found to be particularly useful when working on text – modern as well as classical. But since I wrote that book I have developed the group work more and more, plus I have done a number of workshops with directors, including a very productive ongoing series in New York, refining the original exercises and exploring new ways by which this work can be an integral part of the rehearsal process.

And so here I want to take the work forward and look at it from the perspective of the director as well as the actor: to look at how voice and text work can be layered through the rehearsal period in order to have a truly creative input. 'How we think is how we breathe' – Edward Bond said that to me one day – the spaces between thoughts, the very choice and sound of the words themselves: all these lead us to the person in the play, and to the play itself. Voice work should not be something that is done at the last minute to make the play 'clear' and the actor communicate 'better': it should be integral to the creative exploration of the play itself and of the character. The true exploration of the language should inform how we think, and how the character thinks.

My second quotation is from Heine Muller:

Now is the time to turn the theatre into a space
for the imagination.

Now a piece of theatre has to get at its truth, its centre, via an imaginative journey in an imaginative world: the director has to provide that world, and the actor has to make the journey happen. So, when working on a part, he/she is always having to move delicately between exploring the reality of the character and situation and making them clear, while at the same time being sensitive to the form and the sound of the language: for it is through this sound and form that the perception of the audience is engaged and made alert. The actor has to leave room for the audience to hear – to leave space for the imagination. This is a tricky balance.

My third quotation, and to me very important, is Rauschenberg:

I am mistrustful of ideas –
ideas are based on information you already know.

I think it is significant for this reason: as an actor you have, with the director, come to certain basic conclusions about the motive, the character, the story, in order to rehearse, and these surface out of one's own experience and ideas. Yet at the same time you must leave yourself open to be surprised – surprised at the discovery of what the words do to you when you speak them, and how the act of speaking them, how they sound in the air, may shift the meaning and alter your understanding of them. This can be very exciting.

My fourth quotation is from Edward Bond's poem 'On Leaving The Theatre' – the first two lines:

Do not leave the theatre satisfied
Do not be reconciled.

The role of the actor today is more important than ever: the more techno-speak takes over, the more we will disable our belief in language. Words have the power to disturb, surprise, delight and provoke, and they are happening in the moment – and between people. We must never forget this.

Two things about this book: I have called it *Text in Action* for it is about how we engage with the written text and make it active, and in so doing how our perception of the meaning can be changed. Secondly, it lays out the exercises, a number of which I have written about in *Voice and the Actor* and *The Actor and the Text*, and develops them in a way which is specifically focused on the rehearsal process itself. They are set out in a format which is designed to be used as an integral part of that process, and because that is essentially a collaborative one, I have written it with both director and actor in mind.

5

Just to keep everything in perspective, so that we do not get too solemn, I will complete the quotation from *The Spanish Tragedy*:

Where words prevaile not, violence prevails,
But gold doth more than either of them both.

Might this have some relevance to our present dilemma, our present society?

Part One
Language and Diversity

1 Hearing Language

Language resonates within us in deep and unexpected ways, and I believe that we cannot apprehend the full meaning of a text until we have voiced it aloud; voiced it with an understanding of its meaning, but without pre-empting either its emotional or its logical truth. This is not an easy thing to do. We have to be open to both its sound and its sense – we have to allow it to resonate within ourselves. I say this because I know there is something in all of us which responds to the sounds in language – whatever language it may be – as well as to its sense, and we must start by asking just how primal is that response.

'Who's there?' – the opening line of *Hamlet* and perhaps the most famous beginning of any English play, or indeed any play anywhere. Let us take a look at these lines:

BARNARDO	Who's there?
FRANCISCO	Nay, answer me. Stand and unfold yourself.
BARNARDO	Long live the King!
FRANCISCO	Barnardo?
BARNARDO	He.
FRANCISCO	You come most carefully upon your hour.
BARNARDO	'Tis now struck twelve. Get thee to bed, Francisco.
FRANCISCO	For this relief much thanks. 'Tis bitter cold, And I am sick at heart.
BARNARDO	Have you had quiet guard?
FRANCISCO	Not a mouse stirring.
BARNARDO	Well, good night. If you do meet Horatio and Marcellus, The rivals of my watch, bid them make haste.

[*Enter Horatio and Marcellus*]

FRANCISCO	I think I hear them. Stand ho! Who is there?
HORATIO	Friends to this ground.
MARCELLUS	And liegemen to the Dane.
FRANCISCO	Give you good night.
MARCELLUS	O, farewell, honest soldier
	Who hath relieved you?
FRANCISCO	Barnardo hath my place.
	Give you good night. [*Exit*]
MARCELLUS	Holla, Barnardo!
BARNARDO	Say –
	What, is Horatio there?
HORATIO	A piece of him.
BARNARDO	Welcome, Horatio. Welcome, good Marcellus.
MARCELLUS	What, has this thing appeared again tonight?
BARNARDO	I have seen nothing.

Hamlet, I.i.

Now obviously the initial question, 'Who's there?', is intriguing: to open with a question is a good rhetorical device, and our interest is kept by the spareness of the dialogue that follows. Now for the question: is this prose or verse? Some people will surely feel that it is a naturalistic opening, and therefore it is prose. But I believe it is written in verse, iambic pentameters; for if we speak those words out loud, observing the iambic metre, we will find that what arouses our interest are the spaces in the lines where no words are spoken. And it is those spaces that give us that sense of waiting and of suspense, and of words reaching across the dark, which take us immediately into the world of 'the other' – the mystery. And this is what resonates within us when we listen.

So let us look for a moment at the possibilities of that rhythm. If we take it that each line has five beats, consisting of one unstressed and one stressed syllable – 'te-tum, te-tum, te-tum, te-tum, te-tum' – you then become aware of the moments where there are no words – the silences.

BARNARDO	Who's there?	(4 silent beats)
FRANCISCO	Nay, answer me. Stand and unfold yourself.	
		(full 5-beat line)
BARNARDO	Long live the King!	

FRANCISCO	Barnardo?

BARNARDO	He. (this is one shared
	                            4-beat line, but there is
	                            a space somewhere)

FRANCISCO	You come most carefully upon your hour. (full 5-beat line)
BARNARDO	'Tis now struck twelve. Get thee to bed, Francisco. (full line)
FRANCISCO	For this relief much thanks. 'Tis bitter cold, (full line) And I am sick at heart. (2 silent beats)
BARNARDO	Have you had quiet guard?

FRANCISCO	Not a mouse
	                              stirring.
	                            (shared 5-beat line)

BARNARDO	Well, good night. (3 silent beats) If you do meet Horatio and Marcellus, The rivals of my watch, bid them make haste. (2 full lines)

I love the way the line 'Have you had quite guard?' hovers a moment before 'Not a mouse stirring'. You could say it poises. The lines that follow are regular five-beat lines, mostly shared. I have been rather didactic in that I have specified where the lines are shared etc., plus the number of silent beats, and I have done this simply to make us aware of an underlying dynamic in the rhythm which we have to hear first before we find the possible variations. As Peter Brook would say, there are a million ways to say one line, but we have to first find where the beat is because that is what gives it its electric energy and its suspense.

We will of course be looking in detail later at the whole issue of rhythm: how language and metre interact, and how the sense stress plays with the metre stress and syncopates with it. But just for now read the passage out loud to hear what is happening. Hear the possibilities.

Notice that language is demotic and ordinary, i.e. not poetic, yet it is defining what is unordinary in that situation. It does this through the shaping of the dialogue, finding the spaces yet keeping the rhythm of the line as a whole, giving you that sense of waiting and disquiet. And a few lines later when Barnardo asks, 'What, is Horatio there?', and Horatio answers, 'A piece of him', it is seemingly ordinary, but we as listeners have to know it has been said – we have to be allowed to remark it. What does 'A piece of him' signify? Unease?

Our expectations have already been aroused so that when, a few lines later, Marcellus asks, 'What, has this thing appeared again tonight?', that first word suspends a moment in order for us to take in 'this thing' – the mystery. I wanted to start with this piece of text in order to open our ears to the possibility of suspense, of the silences which allow our imagination to work, and how these silences make us ready for what is to come.

Our imagination has been transported to that 'other' world: it does not have to be demonstrated by soldiers, military bustle and all that so often goes with this beginning. I heard Michael Billington put it exactly when he said 'visual reality is a decoy for the excitement of the argument'. What is being said here is exciting enough, for it challenges our idea of reality and of what 'the other' may be – and whether we believe. Bond says that there is a ghost in every play, and there is no doubt about this in *Hamlet*.

The point is there is something in the spareness of the language and the way it is spaced that intrigues and makes us want to listen. However ordinary, however demotic the dialogue is, it is there to define something: and this goes for contemporary writing in exactly the same way. It defines by its very form, and we have to be able to notice it, however thrown away or casual it may seem. It may not have a rhythmic beat, a metre, but it has its own very specific rhythm nevertheless.

We open the dialogue of this book with a question: how important is an awareness of rhythm for the actor today? How does it help us to find character and what does it tell us about the situation? I have purposely taken a piece which I believe is written in verse so that we can hear its spaces and its poises. But, as I have said, the rhythms of prose are just as defined and the spaces just as integral to the meaning, yet they are often more elusive and difficult to pin down.

So, the beginning of *Hamlet* is not poetic, i.e. heightened language, yet we respond to its emotional undercurrent, its hidden agenda. We could have taken a speech from *King Lear*, Act II, scene iv, where the emotion is overtly released into the sound and the language is most certainly heightened:

O reason not the need! Our basest beggars
Are in the poorest thing superfluous.
Allow not nature more than nature needs –
Man's life is cheap as beast's.

This is the premise – an enigmatic one because it makes us question the basic needs of life, and whether those basic needs are different for a king and for a beggar – but how those vowel sounds reach into his very soul. He goes on to argue this through with his daughters and ends with these words:

> You think I'll weep.
> No I'll not weep.
> I have full cause of weeping;
>   [*Storm and tempest*]
>   but this heart
> Shall break into a hundred thousand flaws
> Or ere I'll weep. O Fool, I shall go mad!

Because the language is heightened, we hear Lear's desperate need for understanding and solace in the sound as well as the sense. And it is precisely through the sustained rhythm and the length of those vowels that we apprehend something of the depth of his feeling. They resonate within us and we know that his heart is breaking. We are left with the question, where will he go?

We could of course have cited the most famous speech of all – 'To be, or not to be – that is the question.' Hamlet starts with this central question – the question for us all – and he argues this through in relation to his own dilemma, and comes to some sort of resolution – or non-resolution – which leaves us asking what will happen now. The ideas are interesting and of course crucial to the play, but they are made emotionally powerful by the way they are rhythmically spaced, how the thoughts get longer and gain momentum, so that the cadence of the speech works together with the argument on our subconscious ear – this is what gives it its emotional power.

The principle is the same for prose, as in the emotional power of the phrasing in the hostess's speech in *Henry V* when she is relating the death of Falstaff. The rhythm and spaces in the speech make it chilling.

So far we've considered Shakespeare, partly I suppose because his plays have always been central to my work in the Royal Shakespeare Company, but really because all the things one wants to say are palpable in his writing, for he was so in touch with the spoken word – its elegance, its roughness and its reality. He wrote the spoken word. However, what I am saying about the rhythm and shaping of language is as true for all dramatic texts – Kyd, Marlowe, Johnson – through Jacobean, Restoration to Shaw. The way the writing is shaped, the vocabulary used, the muscularity and sound of the language, all take us immediately into the world of the play: if the rhythms are jagged, with the thoughts knocking against each other, as it were, as in Kyd's *The Spanish Tragedy*, we know we are in a very harsh world – but then that can also be true of Bond and Barker and Rudkin. I think in many cases, particularly in Jacobean writing, the rhythm is more difficult to get hold of than in Shakespeare because the thoughts are denser and more complex, but once you grasp how the thoughts and the rhythm interconnect, it becomes very clear. The shaping and sound of the language is the bedrock of the meaning – that is why it is so powerful. Or, in a very different way, in the writing of Shaw, it is in the rhythm that we find not only the wit, but the underlying passion of the argument.

But what I find really interesting is that all this is as true for modern writing: though the rhetoric is seldom apparent in the same way for it is 'today's speak', the form and the rhythms are just as crucial to the meaning and content. What it evokes in the listener can be just as extraordinary and surprising as in more obviously extravagant text. Look at the beginning of *Waiting for Godot*:

Estragon:	Nothing to be done.
Vladimir:	I'm beginning to come round to that opinion. All my life I've tried to put it from me, saying, Vladimir, be reasonable, you haven't yet tried everything. And I resumed the struggle.
	So there you are again.
Estragon:	Am I?
Vladimir:	I'm glad to see you back. I thought you were gone for ever.

| **Estragon:** | Me too. |
| **Vladimir:** | Together again at last! |

Waiting for Godot, I.

Where are they? Our imagination is engaged immediately.

Because we live in a time which minimalises how we communicate our feelings, it does not mean that we feel with any less depth: it in fact makes the need to communicate our feelings much more desperate. 'Words are like the top of an earth-shift,' said Bond, and when we are working on contemporary plays we have to be aware of this. We have to be aware of the cry beneath the surface.

There is something therefore in the sound and the form of the language which holds our attention and which the actor has to find and then connect with the character. If the writing is naturalistic we have to hear that naturalism – yet it must be given room to define the situation. If the language is heightened and the imagery extravagant, the actor has to convey that extravagance yet sound in tune with the modern ear: we do not want 'museum-speak'. It must relate to now, which is not an easy task. For the actor is constantly walking a tightrope or, like the poet in Ferlinghetti's poem:[2]

> Constantly risking absurdity
> > and death
> whenever he performs
> > above the heads
> > > of his audience
> the poet like an acrobat
> > climbs on rime
> > > to a high wire of his own making

So, what is it that we want to hear, and is there some kind of collective chord that can be tapped into? I think there are three issues here which we need to address:

(i) As individuals, director, actors or members of the audience, we each hear text differently according to

---

[2] 'Constantly risking absurdity and death' – from the Collected Poems of Lawrence Ferlinghetti.

background, culture, age, class, taste etc. If this is so, can there be such a thing as a collective voice: by that I mean a sound which appeals to all of us irrespective of our differences – a sound that strikes that chord – a sound which is appropriate and fulfils both the writing and the needs of the listener?

(ii) To what extent are we conditioned by what we are educated to believe is 'good' speech: by this I mean of course received pronunciation (RP) here in the UK, or 'Standard Speech' in the US, this being a kind of mid-Atlantic sound. And because both these have such class, money, education implications, how much does this limit our response to language and its possibilities?

Before we even try to find answers to these questions I want to recount three pieces of work in which I have been practically involved during the last ten years – all very different. They are equally relevant to both director and actor, but I will be considering them from the practical perspective of the actor first – I think it will make it clearer that way. And along the way I will also be citing examples from other languages and cultures, for it is interesting to know that actors everywhere have the same pressures to deal with.

The first piece of work is grounded in rhetoric, and how we can be aroused by the form of a speech almost independently of its meaning. There is a very interesting, and I believe important, book by Max Atkinson called *Our Masters' Voices*,[3] in which he lays out certain forms in the building of a speech which will provoke a favourable response. He claims most applause is caused by a small number of rhetorical tricks. He says the following: 'An ability to speak effectively is one of the oldest and most powerful weapons in the armoury of professional politicians.' And he cites examples of those in the present century who had this ability; among them Lenin, Churchill, Kennedy and Martin Luther King. Some mix.

He goes on to list certain 'clap-trapping' devices: opening with a provocative statement or question, building up in threes, contrasts, using a certain amount of alliteration and assonance,

---

[3] *Our Masters' Voices* by Max Atkinson published by Methuen.

and ending with a question or a riddle. He then analyses a number of speeches from different politicians – Thatcher, Powell, Kinnock – and comments on their effectiveness: it is a fascinating book. But what is interesting for us to note is that the structures he describes are all intrinsic to the way Shakespeare built the whole of his writing – not just the passages we all remember.

When *Our Masters' Voices* came out in 1984, Gus McDonald, who headed the programme *World in Action*, decided to make it the subject of a programme in order to test out the theories Atkinson had put forward. To do this they enlisted the help of Ann Brennan, who was about to address the Social Democrat Party conference in Buxton. She was a new candidate, the wife of a London taxi driver, and this was to be her first public speech, so she was naturally very nervous. The format to the programme was to be this: Ann Brennan would tell Max Atkinson what she wanted to say in her speech and he, aided by speech-maker Joe Haines, would then put it into a form of words which they believed would catch the ear. Then I would coach her in it, which I did on the stage of our main theatre in Stratford.

When it came to the day of the conference, Ann, with six other candidates, was given four minutes to speak. The other speakers got through their speeches quite normally and were each given a due round of applause: they all spoke well and had very relevant, thought-provoking things to say. When it came to Ann's turn, however, she was only able to get through about half her speech in the allotted time because of the applause she received. At the end she got a standing ovation. In all fairness, although what she said was interesting, I do not think it was the content of the speech that won that reaction, for all the speakers had had interesting things to say; I believe it was the form of words – the oratory, or rhetoric, that she had been given as a tool – which she had learned to use. This, I think, says a lot about how we listen – and how we can be unconsciously manipulated by the sound of language.

The actor does not want to manipulate people – that would not be truthful – but he/she must be able to strike that chord in his/her audience and make them want to listen. For the writing itself has a shape and a sound which we must be sensitive to, and then hopefully pass on. Good writing resonates in both the speaker and the listener. I believe we all have the ability to hear it, but it has to be worked for.

Now to the other extreme – comedy. Is there also something common to the rhythm and cadence of speech which can provoke laughter? In 1998 I directed a production of *King Lear* at The Other Place in Stratford, to some critical success. My reason for wanting to direct perhaps the most profound and difficult of all Shakespeare's plays was to explore how to enter it through the language with the barest of visual setting.

During the period of the run I held a number of open workshops on the language of the play, always with members of the cast involved. One particular workshop focused on the scenes between Lear and the Fool. Maureen Beatty, who played Cordelia, was involved in the workshop and she brought her father, Johnny Beatty, a very famous stand-up comic in Scotland, along to the session. He had seen one of the performances of *Lear*, but very little other Shakespeare. However, when we started working on the comedy scenes in the workshop, Johnny was astonished by the realisation that the rhythms the Fool uses as he attempts to make Lear laugh were the same rhythms that he uses in his comedy routines in order to get his laughs from the audience, in fact, they were guaranteed to do so.

And I think this is both simple and profound, for so often in Shakespeare an audience laughs at the Clown/Fool without totally understanding the matter, because the jokes are so very much part of the period and therefore hard to figure out. Yet there is patently something in the rhythm to which we inevitably respond, and which makes us laugh – and what is more, this something in the rhythm has lasted over 400 years.

So, just how primal is this response? I think it is innate in all of us. Children love nursery rhymes. They love their anarchy and their rhythm and their rhyme – even more so when they go wrong! But the crucial thing that we must learn is this: the varying use of cadence and of rhythm has the power to stir feelings of sorrow, of anger and of laughter, and this is a powerful tool both for the writer and the actor. So often the actor feels under pressure to explain, describe, overstress the feeling, etc. (in other words, make it easy for the audience), but this obscures the rhythm of the language and in fact does just the opposite, for it makes it more difficult to understand.

The third piece of work I want to recount is centred round modern writing. In the last ten or so years I have held a number of workshops with writers, always with a group of actors involved. The work has focused primarily on the speaking of text, for in each of the sessions we have first worked on Shakespeare together, the writers joining with the actors, using exercises that I have evolved which are to do with finding the physical movement of the language, and how the thoughts move, plus different ways of connecting with the imagery. We addressed the following issues:

(i) How we listen to and hear language.
(ii) What we apprehend from its sound and imagery.
(iii) How much the speaking of the text changes our understanding of it.

We have then carried these questions through into modern writing, so that each writer worked with the actors on short scenes from their own texts, using the exercises which we had previously used with Shakespeare.

The exchange has always been extremely valuable and thrown up many questions. The writers have found it useful to hear their dialogue spoken aloud: it has given them time to hear their rhythms and language without the pressure of rehearsal, and also to hear how the actual voicing of it may change their perception of its meaning. They have made adjustments if they felt it necessary. It also made them realise some of the complex feelings and inhibitions an actor has when faced with a script not seen before, and so clarified for them the actor's relation to a text.

From the actor's point of view I think two very valuable things have been learned – the first being that however modern the text may sound, however naturalistic, it still has a specific shape and music or cadence. It has an exactness which defines both the intention of the character and the world he/she is in, and if you go against that rhythm – clash with it, one might say – it does not fulfil the writer's intention. So often I think the actor feels under pressure to lay out the meaning and the emotion, explain it almost, and in so doing he/she loses the spaces, the rhythms, the music of the text – the means by which the writer chooses to reveal the play.

19

I think this last point is central to all acting: having discovered the emotional centre, the action and motive, sometimes you have to let the words go. If the speaker fills them too much with his/her intensity they become didactic, giving us the result of a feeling or motive, so that the words cease to be active and open to question. Words can be open and light and still make the desired impact.

But even more interesting for the actor, and also oddly reassuring, has been the realisation from these workshops that the writer so often gets a thought or an image from 'somewhere else' – either from somewhere in his/her subconscious, or from an image in the air, something seen outside which has awakened a train of thought, and which in some way defines the bottom line of an idea. So often there is not a defined, logical explanation to questions about the text: it is not 'worked out' logically but seems to come from a response to some deeper, 'other' impulse, and it is only then that the mind starts to shape it and give it form. In other words, the image can be the power which unlocks the meaning or logic of the writer's subconscious intention.

I think what is important about all this is that it puts imagination at the centre of the actor's exploration. Yes, of course you have to make logical sense of a character's journey through the play, but it cannot be confined to that logic: an actor has to be free to respond to that 'other' within him/herself and that is what will make the result unique and interesting.

The pieces we looked at were seemingly unconnected pieces of work, each one looking at language from a different perspective, yet each tells us something about how language both impinges on the hearer, and evokes a response in the speaker:

(i) How a political speech can arouse us, arouse our feelings of anger, sorrow etc., not just by the cogency of its argument, but by its very rhythm and use of rhetoric.

(ii) How the juxtaposition of varying lengths of phrases, plus an awareness of suspense, can provoke laughter and/or tears.

(iii) How the very shaping of dialogue can influence, and even change, the meaning as we speak it.

We see that it is through the speaker's sensitivity to the spaces and rhythms in the writing, to its muscularity and varying syllable lengths, and to the way the cadence of a speech can lift the meaning through, that the listener will understand not only its logical surface 'sense', but will also apprehend the underlying spirit/motive of the word – the hidden agenda, if you like.

And here I want to digress a moment, for I believe this awareness is present in all languages – though with very different forms and sounds. I have worked in Hindi and other Indian languages, in Mandarin, and in most Europoean languages – particularly Portuguese, having been to Brazil a number of times. My work has mostly, though not totally, focused on Shakespeare: this means that I am familiar with the content of what is being spoken so that once I am in tune with the sound of a particular language I am able to recognise and apprehend so much through the changes in rhythm and cadence. I hear where the actor is in the text, and what he/she is trying to do with it. I can work in these languages in the same way as I work with English text: i.e. getting the actors to feel the muscularity of the language, finding the movement of thought, plus the changes of cadence between the lyrical passages and the demotic. The exercises work in all languages, though of course just how far you can go depends to an extent on the quality of the translation. Work on contemporary plays is of course very different, but it is also very interesting to find just how much one can apprehend about the whole, the meaning, just by listening.

I particularly remember a workshop I did with actors in Beijing. We were looking at Act I scene i of *King Lear* and finding how the characters related to each other through the language. In this scene Lear asks each of his daughters how much they love him, to which both Goneril and Regan reply effusively, though with obvious underlying hypocrisy, and they are awarded land accordingly. Lear then turns to his favourite daughter, Cordelia:

LEAR   – Now, our joy,
            Although our last and least . . .
            . . . what can you say to draw
            A third more opulent than your sisters'? Speak!
CORDELIA   Nothing, my lord.

LEAR	Nothing?
CORDELIA	Nothing.
LEAR	Nothing will come of nothing. Speak again.

King Lear, I.i.

Now Mandarin is a tonal language, altering meaning by means of changing tones, as well as by speech sounds, and its sound is so totally different from English, yet I will always remember how that one word, 'nothing', rang out in Mandarin. The sound of that word became so powerful not by stressing it or being loud, simply because the actor had found its right space. That space was particularly telling because it pointed up the antithesis between the word 'nothing' and the heightened extravagance of the protestations of love that Goneril and Regan had made in order to get what they wanted. I think every actor knows when that link is made between sound and sense – when the word and the motive come together, giving that sense of authority, of being with the word.

That was a digression, but I think an important one, for I do believe that there is something in a good piece of text in whatever language – in its form, in its sound – which the actor needs to tap into as part of the process by which he/she enters a character. We have to 'hear' that language to find where it takes us, and we have to let it resonate within us.

So what gets in the way? I think so often it is the need to present, the need to be 'ready', to be interesting, which puts pressure on the actor and as a result something of the mystery in the language gets lost. I do not mean anything esoteric by that, for the actors have to make clear the motives and reasons behind the text, but once these are found then we must let the words have their own energy. There is a fine line to be drawn between presenting an idea as a result, and/or allowing that idea to be discovered, for while we are speaking we are still open to change, and we want the listener to be open to it as well. For me, in Shakespeare, or any other play for that matter, there is never a full stop until the end of the play.

How we relate to our own voice is full of complexities – complexities involving accent, confidence, intrinsic sound – and most actors are well aware of these. But before we look at these issues in detail I want to think for a moment about how we make our initial encounter with the language of a play we are about to rehearse – how we read the words. For here we are not just dealing with the sound of the voice, or the pronunciation of the words: we are dealing with something much deeper than that, and that is to do with hearing what is happening in the language, plus being aware of what happens to us as we speak it.

Let me give you this scenario. As an actor, you first read a play on your own, and as you read it through to yourself you will probably hear it somewhere in your head. If it is a play you know, you will certainly have an idea of how it sounds or how you think it should sound, and you may want to read parts of it aloud to relish its texture and experiment with it. If it is a play you do not know, you will still hear it somewhere in your head as you read, and you may voice some of it to clarify it further for yourself. Whatever you do, that private voice inside you is hearing it – I like to call it that 'secret voice'. Later, everyone comes together as a company to read through the play, including the director and perhaps the writer if it is a contemporary play, and hopefully the theatre voice teacher. Although we all still have that secret voice somewhere inside us, we instinctively start to make sense of it, to make it sound intelligent, and immediately some of what we had originally heard vanishes. Yet even so that initial reading has a freshness about it, a sense of discovery, for how often I have heard actors say, at the end of a rehearsal period when the play is just about to go on, that it does not sound as good as it did at that first reading: some of the rawness and simplicity is lost. We go on to discuss the play, perhaps even argue about it, and in so doing we begin to come to conclusions about the story, the argument, character relationships and intentions, etc., and by reasoning it through we involve the literal/linear side of our brain. We talk about the imagery, the hidden meanings, the rhythm and form of it. We are talking about our imagination, not listening to it.

And now for the director's perspective, who also hears the play with his/her secret voice. For it is you, the director, who has initiated the project and who has brought the company together, and it is your concept of the play, its style and design, which will underpin the end product. And you have spent a lot of time developing your vision of the production, what it means, how one character relates to another, and how the choice of language backs that up, plus of course a very particular vision of the style and setting. But how do you hear the play, and how much is the speaking of the language central to your vision? Individual taste is also very much part of the issue.

In including the theatre voice teacher I used the word 'hopefully' on purpose, because I feel that the role of the voice teacher is central to all theatre work: indeed, that is what this book is about. But I also think that role is still not taken seriously enough by many theatre companies – it is seen as a luxury rather than a vital part of the work. I have also had difficulty in finding exactly the right term: I toyed with the idea of 'voice associate' but felt that was a little vague. I certainly eschewed the term 'voice coach' as for me that implies someone instructing an actor how to say something, and that certainly is not what it is about. The work of the voice person is about enabling the actor to get the best possible use out of his/her voice in terms of range, clarity and texture, plus – and this is at the core – opening up the possibilities of the text both in terms of the demands of the production, and also in terms of the actors' own imaginations – i.e. what will trigger that off. This requires expert knowledge of the voice and how it works, coupled with an understanding of how the individual actor connects with it. So 'theatre voice teacher', though fractionally didactic in inference, is what I have decided on.

Now, the scenario I have just laid out is obviously a very generalised one, but I wanted to alert us to our initial approach to a play and how we find a collective viewpoint. As we know there are as many ways into a rehearsal process as there are directors: some work in great depth on improvisational work and on interchanging characters, some do a great deal of background work, sending actors off in small groups to research various societal issues involved in the story, others enter a play through inventive and exciting movement work, while others work in a totally text-orientated way, making sure of the literal meaning, discussing ambiguities, references, nuances of rhythm and imagery, etc. All of these methods can be wonderfully inventive and will open up the imagination of the actor, but they seldom integrate with the action of the text: it is as if, spoken 'properly', the language will take care of itself. That is why, whatever the rehearsal process, it is essential that work on the discovery of the language should be layered through the whole rehearsal period in order not only that we inhabit it fully, but also to discover just how the act of voicing it aloud can widen and deepen our understanding. The deeper we are into rehearsal the more this work will illuminate the play for us.

Added to all this of course is the whole issue of what 'good speech' is – what is acceptable and what is not – and this rebounds on the audience. In the United Kingdom there has been a general consensus which has, through the years, resulted in what we know as Received Pronunciation (RP). This is difficult to pin down for it has been arrived at via the speech of the upper and educated classes, which is often rather stilted and lacking music: the first book on the pronunciation of English, the *English Pronouncing Dictionary*, written by Daniel Jones and published in 1918, was based on public school speech – i.e. what was acceptable at public school. However, 'good' speech has always been flexible with a broad compass, as it were, and has blended with an awareness of the different sound components in the language and how they contribute to its music: plus there has always been a history of good oratory among politicians, preachers and professional speakers. Everyone has a different awareness of the music in language, its cadence and rhythm, but of course the awareness of the actor has always been strongly influenced by the language he/she has to speak on stage – and in the end by Shakespeare and those Elizabethan playwrights, for how can you speak their language without an ear for its rhetoric and music? But fashions in language are constantly changing: for instance, if you hear a news broadcast of even ten years ago it seems curiously out of date, and I think we are now much more relaxed about the differing speech patterns throughout the country, and open to those differences. This, of course, has much to do with the pervasive influence of television (so perhaps television has its uses!) but also I think it is chiefly to do with shifting power and money structures – and the vagaries of fashion which are bound up with these.

However, RP still rules among the theatre-going public, and many directors require it for classical work. In contemporary text the dialect/accent is seldom a problem, for modern work is based much more specifically within a class or location boundary, and this has to be part of the exploration of the play. But in Shakespeare, for instance, the general requirement is that

Hamlet/Richard II are spoken in RP and the lower classes in whatever 'common' dialect is chosen. There are, of course, maverick companies who do not comply with this, and so often interesting things emerge: for certainly Shakespeare was not originally spoken in RP, rather something akin to West Country, with open vowels and the final 'r' sounds pronounced and a much more musical cadence. Yet at the same time we have to recognise that there is a certain clarity and exactness, perhaps universality, about RP, which is useful and which we must negotiate somehow. But it must be made appropriate for now, and it must embrace the muscularity and cadence of the language. And of course one of the skills of the actor has to be the ability to reproduce a diversity of accents/dialects, yet stay truthful to him/herself, and feel at home with them. It is not always easy, and I think it is a step forward that now RP is taught as an accent in drama schools rather than as the 'correct' way of speaking.

The situation has been much the same in the US as in the UK: 'Standard Speech' is taught in drama schools, a kind of cleansed New England sound which emasculates the language to some extent for we cannot place where the person is coming from. Unfortunately, the mainstream theatre-going public both here in the UK, and to a large extent in the US, want to hear classical text in standard speech, but, as I have already said, in Shakespeare's time there was no such thing as a standard speech as we know it now. It was an altogether broader, richer sound: it was not clipped and took its own time. I remember being invited to watch a rehearsal of *Macbeth* in a small community somewhere in the Blue Mountains in Virginia: I was taken aback with the richness and muscularity of the language – it sang to me. Newcastle – Blue Mountains? I think we should be open to it.

I would like to quote a paragraph from an essay by Stan Brown called 'The Cultural Voice':

Being understood by an audience is fundamental, if not the bottom line of speaking on stage. If this could be addressed solely through the adherence to one dialect or one prescribed way of uttering the sounds of the English language, the scope of voice and speech training would be more narrow than it is. The means or methods one employs in learning 'Standard Speech' must, in philosophy and application, support and acknowledge his/her personal contribution to the ever-shifting, diverse reality of human language. More specifically, the English language does not currently belong to one culture of people, therefore it cannot be represented truthfully in one dialect or 'Standard Speech'. Casting a generalised version of reality to portray universal truth is dishonest. The means or methods employed in learning and teaching 'Standard Speech' must support and acknowledge personal contributions and orientations to the ever-shifting, diverse reality of human language.

Stan Brown is currently Associate Professor in the Department of Theatre Arts at the University of Nebraska and works on both voice and text, and he has worked in several other university departments as Voice Specialist, so he has all the problems of American 'mid-Atlantic' speech to contend with. I think he brings a very wide perspective to the case – and he articulates it wonderfully. Stan is also black, so he has another music in his head. But I think the point he makes about 'the ever-shifting, diverse reality of human language' is wonderful – and will hopefully inspire us to listen with fresh ears.

I have said all this so that we realise how arbitrary our taste is, but at the same time how bound we are by it. Just a thought: if Caxton's printing press had been invented in Newcastle, and the base of power had been there rather than London, would we now be speaking a form of Northumbrian dialect?

But in the end I think we just have to be sensible about the whole issue of accent; while being open to it, we must also recognise the limits. For, yes, there is a sound which we need to hear and which appeals to us all: there are rhythms, there is a muscularity in the language we have to find and which satisfies the listener, and this can be slightly different for each speaker. In music we know when someone is off-key, or is not in the rhythm: in speaking it is much more subtle. But I do believe we all recognise when the speaking fulfils and satisfies. I purposely did not say 'when it is right' for that use of the word 'right' inevitably narrows our perception, and you can find cadence, muscularity and music in all dialects, including RP, which fulfils the text and satisfies the speaker. We just have to use our judgement as to what is right for the moment.

Just as some people have what we call 'a good ear' for music, others have it for the spoken word, and curiously the two do not necessarily go together: this is to do with the parts of the brain used for music and for speech being different. However, I do believe that an ear for the music of language, innate or not, is something that can be developed.

Perhaps we have to teach ourselves to listen: to listen to the text, to each other and to our own response. We have to sit down in our own voice, and not be too 'ready' to respond – we have to hear what we are responding to. There is a wonderful analogy for the actor which is to do with drumming, told to me by a black actor in the Company a little while back, about the difference between white drummers and black drummers – 'the white drummer simply beats out the rhythm, but the black drummer waits for the beat to come back to him'. Perhaps we should all learn to trust to do just that – wait for the beat to come back.

So, just as the actor is bound by his/her need to make the text clear and the voice sound 'right', so the director is bound by specific concepts about the text and his/her preferences about the sound of a voice. And we cannot just think our way out of this.

Now I believe there are quite straightforward and direct exercises which we can use to release us from these preconceptions, and perhaps allow us to hear something else: furthermore, the exercises will release energies and surprises in the language that make the speaking more dynamic and pinpoint subtleties of meaning which can only enrich our understanding. We must be open to the music, the rhythm, the rhetoric in the text, and we must not shy away from its physicality.

But to achieve all this there has to be trust – a collective listening within the Company for which you, the director, must take responsibility. It is important that you not only allow the time this process needs in order that the possibilities of the text be fully realised and heard, and the language truly inhabited, but also that you are involved in this process. It is worth that time.

And let us not forget that words are the antithesis of silence, thus by their very nature they are dramatic – they break the silence. But silence is also important for it makes us ready to listen. The value of silence is suspense – it sharpens the appetite of the hearer. It also releases speed and energy. It is only in the spaces that we hear the dilemma, and this is what sharpens our appetite to listen. We have to know 'Who's there'.

2 Past Voices – New Perspectives

I think it would be useful here to give a brief account of where I come from in terms of work on Voice and Text, and how this has developed. Although it is a private journey, I believe it reflects how the work has changed in the past 50 years, and yet still remains a very central part of the actor's skill. Perhaps most important, it reflects our changing theatre culture. But first, I want to put the work into its historical perspective.

In the updated version of *The Actor and the Text*, I wrote a chapter, 'Further Perspectives', in which I gave a brief history of how the techniques of voice teaching have changed over the last century because of the changing demands made on the actor. In the last century and in the beginning of this, voice work for actors was closely aligned to that of the singer – and indeed was usually undertaken by singing teachers. I believe the actor then saw his/her work in a much more public way: I do not think it was regarded as being declamatory, but it had a much more public air to it, and the music within the language was integral to the actor's speaking – that is what the audience came to hear. And I think they would have felt cheated if that quality had been missing.

I say this because from our modern perspective we perhaps wrongly classify that declamatory style now as being false, untruthful – I know I have thought so in the past – but perhaps it was not so to the actor or the audience of then, for always we have to find what is appropriate to the time. They wanted, and I think needed, a more public form of theatre, a sense of public enjoyment and involvement. This must not be confused with entertainment – that is, entertainment as we define it today, which is so often passive – because for them going to the theatre was an active community experience. And that heightened poetic sound of Shakespeare had its own truth which connected directly with the audience of its time. Certainly in the US in the 1700s and 1800s, Shakespeare was the most popular source of entertainment among the gold miners in the west as much as in the educated enclaves of the eastern states. His work was so well known that minstrel shows could parody him and everyone would know what the reference was.

What seems to me to be relevant is that Shakespeare was not regarded as 'high culture', something you had to be educated about in order to understand and to appreciate fully, as it is today: it was then about stories, a collective enjoyment and a verbal culture which brought all classes together. People understood it because they heard the language and could identify with it: they did not have to translate everything literally in their heads, for English is an inclusive language. Whereas other languages seek to confirm meaning, English, by the often very subtle changes of sound, can open up unexpected nuances of meaning and add layers to it. So it was the sounds and the rhythms and the cadence of the language that in the end affected them – made them laugh or made them cry – and allowed them to enter the imaginative world of the play. And we forget this: we think we have to know the literal meaning of every word, but this does not leave room for our intuitive response and understanding.

However, as always, times and fashions changed. I do not think Shakespeare had such a universal popularity in the UK as it did in America in those earlier times, for there was always so much new writing being performed and theatre was always very much alive, but certainly by the beginning of this century in both countries there began a deepening divide between 'high/ serious' theatre and 'popular' theatre – the latter meaning vaudeville here or minstrel shows in the US. So inevitably Shakespeare took on a different and more serious face and, most relevant to us now, a more 'cultured' voice.

Going along with this, more attention was paid to what I call the grammar of the writing – by this I mean the verse form, the iambic pentameter, the line endings, forms of rhetoric – for though the style was still declamatory it was perhaps becoming more considered for its intellectual content, and how grammar and content went together. However, there were some, like Elsie Fogerty, who founded the Central School of Speech Training and Dramatic Art in 1906 and William Poel, director and actor, who became noted for his vital and energetic productions of Shakespeare in the early 1900s, who were trying to mediate between this heightened style of speaking and a more naturalistic and personal expression. And so the speaking slowly began to change as more attention was paid to the nuances of meaning and literary allusions: it was becoming more finely drawn and perhaps more personalised – i.e. actors were starting to speak rather than declaim – but the music and shaping of the rhetoric was still central to the speaking.

But I suppose it was not until the mid-50s that styles began to change radically: there was a new realism at work with the writing of Miller, Odets and Williams in the US; and Osborne, Wesker and Pinter in the UK. These dramatists were not writing about the privileged classes – its sound was not Received Pronunciation here in the UK, or mid-Atlantic in the US – but about life on the streets and, most important from our point of view, there was a strong psychological import. This writing clearly demanded a different approach to acting, and this in turn subtly affected our approach to the speaking of the classics, for anything which might be perceived as declamatory in style was now no longer appropriate. So we tried to make it sound naturalistic, everyday, but in the process began to lose some-thing organic to the writing – that something which the form and cadence of the writing gives us. If we have, as I believe we do, a secret hankering for that music because it takes us somewhere else in our beings and enlivens our imagination, then we have to perform a balancing act between the two: and this is exciting because it keeps us on the moment and makes the language ever active.

However, what is relevant to us is that we were at a turning point, for that was when the psychology of character became central to the actor's research into the part. And in this we were strongly influenced not only by films, but by the whole ethos of American Method acting: this had taken a firm hold through actors like Brando and Pacino, and the training of the young actor changed accordingly. Now, I believe Brando was a great actor, one of the greatest, in fact, but he conveyed everything through his body and through his sound but not necessarily through the specific choice of language: the words were not there to define the situation, rather as an adjunct to it. This improvisational effect was very appealing, but the words in a sense became secondary. This of course works in film, but is not necessarily fulfilling in theatre, where the defining of the character comes through the specific word used. The writing may be very naturalistic, but that naturalism has to be perceived by the audience: it may be a mumble, but that mumble is defining something which is special.

So this whole new psychological approach may have added depth to the perception of character, but it made the job for the actor working in a large space more complicated: for how do you make those very personal responses big enough to reach a 1,500-seater auditorium? But most important for us is that it lost the societal and political perspectives. The psychological approach did not take hold in the UK to the extent it did in the US, but it still influenced us, and we became more centred in the reality of the character and character relationships than in the larger issues of social hierarchy and how that affects behaviour. This radically altered our relation to the sound of the writing, to its music, for the emphasis was on the self and not on the larger world of the play. In Shakespeare, or indeed any classical text, we know we have to find that balance between the reality of the language and its form and rhetoric – it is not an easy mix. But conversely, and this is what we often do not realise, there is also a mix to be found in any good writing, however modern: Tennessee Williams is not truly fulfilled if the rhythms of his text are not completely found or the language is not articulated specifically within its particular style, however much the body is telling us. All the contemporary writers I have worked with are meticulous about the phrasing and spacing in their texts, for it is endemic to the meaning.

So far this has been about theatre writing, but very soon television was to pervade our consciousness and take firm hold on our ears. It was to alter our whole way of listening to and perceiving language: slowly at first, but then by the mid-70s, its sound had come to be at the centre of our lives, and we adjusted how we spoke accordingly. I am not saying that we consciously copied it in any way, but it influenced our perception of speech and thus subliminally affected our own attitudes to what we wanted to hear. But of course what we hear on television is constantly changing – if you hear a news broadcast of just ten years ago for instance, it sounds strangely out of date and out of tune with the time. Language is alive to the moment, and the good thing about this is that we have become much more open to and accepting of variations within dialects. We are now without question taking the wonderful variety of accents we have in this country on board – and taking them seriously. But all these issues change our perception of how language should sound. So when we go to the theatre what do we want to hear? That is the central question and a complex one.

My own working journey went in parallel to this. I was lucky enough to go to a minor public school, which my father could ill afford, where one was not forced into being academic, and where poetry was spoken aloud in class. I also took elocution lessons, something which one now views with a certain distrust as it is linked with 'good' speech and Received Pronunciation, but for me it was a good thing in that it awakened my ear to the music of language, to the subtleties of rhythms and cadence, and gave me the chance to practise all this out loud. My passion for poetry had always been with me – I could recite the whole of 'Hiawatha' and 'The Ancient Mariner' by the time I was eight – and now this passion was being validated formally. I became increasingly aware of how the sound of language, the variations of pitch and tempo, could be used to awaken people's interest.

From this early grounding it was a natural progression that I would go to the Central School of Speech Training and Dramatic Art in London which was, with RADA, one of the most prestigious drama schools in the country. Gwynneth Thurburn had recently taken over from Elsie Fogerty, who, as I said earlier, had founded the school in 1906. It ran three courses – one for teachers, one for actors and one for speech therapists. Gwynneth Thurburn was an extraordinary woman who had an absolute passion for poetry and for life. Her passion for poetry was never sentimental for she was always going to the root of it – why it was written and the value of the word and the music. But more than this, I suppose we always take from someone the thing we most need, our reinforcement, and for me it was that she was a committed Socialist, and it was this which informed her sense of service and the democracy of her teaching. She was a very impressive woman, handsome with high cheekbones and, because she only had one eye, you were never quite sure whether she was looking at you or not. In fact, she was always looking, enquiring, expecting something different – and she trusted you to supply it. In other words, she taught you to listen to what the other person could give: and this gift, this sensibility, must not be underestimated, for too often in rehearsal results are confined to what we think we should hear and not to the possibilities of the moment, and this cages our response. She also had a great sense of humour, which kept everything in perspective.

I say all this because what I learned from her was integral to the way in which I was later to develop my work, and to my belief that language is not just an outpouring of the brain, but it is something which takes root deep inside one and 'has to go through you', as Edward Bond once said to me. But there was still a way to go before I came to that point in my work.

I finished my training at the Central School in 1946, and after working for two years in different schools, I went back to teach there. I worked mainly on the acting course, teaching voice – breathing, resonance, articulation, etc. – and diction classes. These classes, contrary to what their name implies, focused totally on the speaking of verse – verse of different styles and times – in order to develop the skills needed to tackle dramatic writing of all periods. They were about increasing one's sensibility to the sound of language. At this time I also worked privately with many actors – Peter Finch, Sean Connery, Anne Bancroft – who wanted to develop further skills because of some specific piece of work they were about to do. I also had my own studio in Drury Lane for actors. All this work focused on voice skills – breathing, relaxation, finding resonance, and clarity of diction – and although I always used text work as a means to put the work on voice into action, it was still about the technique of speaking text rather than connecting with its central motive. The focus was on the sound of language.

I have said all this because I believe it is important that we recognise just how much the way we relate to language is forever shifting. Now, in the year 2000, we express ourselves in a much more minimal way. What moves us, what touches us, is different, yet somewhere I believe we are still rooted in a verbal culture, and we in the theatre have to keep our ears tuned and listen out for what is happening in the language so that we get an active response from our audience – a recognition of the whole import.

I came to work at the Royal Shakespeare Company in 1970: I think it was the first time a company had employed a full-time voice teacher. It was a great time to start in the Company for it was at that bridging time when the focus on language, on Shakespeare, was radically changing from the declamatory to the personal and we were hovering somewhere between – maybe we still are. But certainly there was an emphasis on the language and how the actor was inhabiting it, bringing his/her own experience to bear on it, as opposed to the well-formed sounding out of words, yet still fulfilling the rules of metre and the rhetorical devices such as simile, antithesis, etc. This was the challenge, and looking back it seems that all my previous work had been a kind of preparation for this.

My brief from Trevor Nunn, who had, at the age of 29, just taken over as artistic director of the Company, was to look after actors' voices and to develop vocal skills. He was young and very sensitive to the needs of the actors, and he realised that increasingly actors needed to work on voice, both on the power and the range: the days of long apprenticeships for the young actor were over, and those with little experience were being asked to fill the main theatre space. So initially my responsibility was to make sure that each actor could fill the large space of the Main House without strain, and that they could respond to the needs of the text. The Swan Theatre had not yet been built and The Other Place had not yet been invented.

For me the change was a big one: my job was now part of the working process of a theatre company. I sat in on rehearsals and became involved in the productions and began to see where the actors needed to go specifically in terms of that production – and of the play itself. Although my first priority, as it always must be, was to see the actor was comfortable in the space they were working, I began to realise that it was the language that had to fill that space, and that this could not be done just by fuller volume and better diction, but by an involvement with the language itself. In our changing perception of language we no longer wanted to be bombarded with fine sound, we wanted to hear the specific definition of the language through the precise weight and vibration of the words themselves. And also what began to really interest me was just to what extent the actor needed to respond to the method of the director, yet somehow keep true to his/her own way into the play.

The three main directors at the time were Trevor Nunn, John Barton and Terry Hands, each with very distinctive, and very different, approaches: from my own learning point of view this could not have been better. To follow is a rather simplistic view of how each of them worked, as I perceived it then:

Nunn went into great detail with character and character relationships – not Method as we know it, but he rehearsed quietly and with great intimacy, getting the actor to feel personal contact with the character by bringing his/her own personal experiences to bear.

Barton worked very much through the text: getting the meaning crystal clear, and making sure that the actors observed all the points of rhetoric in the language – antitheses, alliteration, imagery, form and metre. At times there seemed so much to bring out that almost every word needed to be stressed.

Hands tended to rehearse by getting the sweep of the play right from the beginning. He liked the actors off the text as soon as possible, and he was always pressing for speed and energy. He felt that if the actors could relate to the whole sweep of the play and become familiar with it, then the subtleties of character would emerge – the very opposite in approach to Nunn.

I soon perceived that my job was more than the normal voice work, because it needed to relate to the particular rehearsal process directly. It had to mediate between the vision of the director – after all, it is the director's vision which makes the production particular – and the talent of the actor. So often the actor went along with the rehearsal process at the expense of their own identity, perhaps following so closely that they negated their own qualities – negating them instead of negotiating with them. And of course this still happens as much as ever.

For instance, because Trevor Nunn rehearsed so intimately, finding where the personal experience of the actor could identify with the character he/she was playing, it often became difficult for the actor to find this personal truth yet balance it with the size needed in order to encompass the space that had to be filled. It also made it difficult to find the size and extravagance of the language. With John Barton, the rigour with which he pursued the metre, the line endings, the antitheses, etc., was often inhibiting to the actor. The older actor could take it on board and use it in perspective, but some of the younger ones followed the rules so closely that it became a restrictive process – so I had to find ways of making them feel free while still observing the structures. And with Terry Hands, his insistence on speed and volume tended to iron out the actor's sensitivity to the language and make it generalised – it tended to iron out its texture and colour.

With each of these processes, I had to find a way to release the potential of the actor without damaging the essence of the work in rehearsal. This was important, not only because the work done in rehearsal was where the production was, but because one could not undermine the actor's trust in the direction being taken – that would have been divisive and destructive. I had to get each actor to enter the language on his/her own terms, while still being in tune with the overall directive, and so I began to find those exercises which would release them: finding the extravagance of the language quietly for Nunn; finding the freedom and surprise in the language for Barton; and finding the detail and texture in the language for Hands. So in a Nunn rehearsal I would take individual actors aside and find ways to make them discover the extravagance of the language; with Barton I would get them to do a task of some sort to take their mind off the pointing up of the rhetorical devices; and with Hands I would have to get them to speak very slowly and quietly so that they could discover the imagery and texture of the language in their own particular way.

From this I found ways to release the actor's own individual response while keeping the form of the work intact. This was my initiation, if you like, into the whole area of how the actor integrates the personal intention with the public form – and this was to develop. And what was so good from my point of view was that each of those directors valued the language and the text in a very special way and gave it time to be explored.

I then had the good fortune to work with Peter Brook. I think I can say that this was a turning point, for he somehow validated the work I had been doing, and made me go on to develop it further. From him I learned ways of passing on language (the essence of what I have called the 'collective voice'), and being in tune with each other. He released my own love of poetry, which had been my hidden source of passion. From then I knew my work was right – listening to and for each other – and I moved from amending and repairing to setting up and developing new ways of working. All the exercises could be done alongside the director but they were true to themselves. And by this time I was accepted and given my own space and time.

I found, not consciously at first, that the secret was to take the actor's mind off the speaking of the text. By giving them very simple tasks to do while they were speaking, it would take the pressure off, and they would get in touch with their own subconscious response to the text – yet they were still speaking with the rehearsal motive in mind. The task would be quite simple: I would throw a heap of books on the floor and they would pick them up and arrange them on the shelf in order of height. Or I would play noughts and crosses with them, or ask them to draw something, such as what they saw out of the window; or the first house they lived in. They were all tasks which they could do quite easily and required little thought, yet somehow it made them connect with the words and made them spontaneous, and in the process often threw up other and deeper meanings. These first simple exercises were the basis from which all the other work grew.

Not long after I joined the Company something happened which was to influence me deeply. Maurice Daniels, who was at the time responsible for all the complex scheduling of Company work, started to arrange visits into schools – the initial stages of an Education Department which was to grow and develop. But then it was just a simple matter of me going into a classroom, usually with a couple of actors, and working on scenes from the play the students were studying. The idea spread rapidly, and soon we were taking in youth groups, community groups, teacher groups, etc. By the mid-70s, when the Company started to expand considerably, both geographically and in the size and output of the Company itself, with residencies as far apart as Newcastle and Brooklyn, the education work spread with it, and more and more people were involved.

For my own part, I did countless workshops with a wide variety of groups, covering a whole spectrum of class, age and educational ability, from Newcastle to Leamington Spa, plus I ran my own teacher weekends in Stratford for English and drama teachers under the auspices of the Ministry of Education. My aim when I went into a workshop, whatever the group, was always to get those participating to feel something for themselves through the very speaking of the text out loud, and to open this up in such a way as to increase their understanding of the play, and to discover what was below the surface. All kinds of complexities would emerge, and they would recognise connections to their own world – and to themselves. This was not only exciting, but it made me look at text in a different way.

The groups were so very different, and this was the challenge. To some extent, of course, you could judge the need of a group beforehand – a group of teachers would respond very differently to a group of inter-city teenagers, be it in London or Brooklyn. But however much you prepared the session according to your reading of the particular level of response, you could never foresee their expectations or how they would react. One school group, for instance, could be very well prepared and interested in the work, while another would start out by being antagonistic. This had nothing to do with the standard of education they were at, but often to do with how the workshop had been set up: the cooperation of the teachers involved was very important. Or you could find yourself in a group that was much larger than had been anticipated, with not enough books to go round and nothing really prepared, so that everything you had intended to do went out of the window, and you had to think on your feet. But, determined to change their attitiude to the words on the page and to get them to hear the resonance of the language in all its complexity, something always emerged: the exercises always enlightened my own way of looking at text, and this in turn informed my work with actors.

39

The aim of course was first to make the groups feel they understood the text, to make it accessible, but then I wanted them to find its roughness, its anarchy, within the form. In other words, to release them from the responsibility of making literal and literary sense, and to find a deeper connection with their own world, their thoughts and feelings, through the very sound and form of the language.

Two workshops stand out particularly in my mind: they both were to have a profound influence on the way I was to think about text and how to work on it. I mentioned both briefly in the last chapter of *The Actor and the Text*, but I would like to describe them more fully now.

I was doing a series of workshops in London for the then Inner London Education Authority (ILEA): in this particular workshop I was looking at *Othello* with a group of upper-sixth-form boys. The teacher was noticeably uninterested, and the students even more so. They knew what it all meant, so what more could one do? I took the central scene where Iago, by his subtle inferences, ignites Othello's jealousy – and we get Othello's reaction, which is earth-shattering:

IAGO	Patience, I say: your mind perhaps may change.
OTHELLO	Never, Iago. Like to the Pontic sea,
	Whose icy current and compulsive course
	Ne'er feels retiring ebb, but keeps due on
	To the Propontic and the Hellespont,
	Even so my bloody thoughts with violent pace
	Shall ne'er look back, ne'er ebb to humble love,
	Till that a capable and wide revenge
	Swallow them up. Now, by yond marble heaven,
	In the due reverence of a sacred vow
	I here engage my words.

Othello, III.iii.

I asked them to read Othello's speech several times out loud together, and when I asked them what reactions they had to it they were clearly unmoved. They knew what it all meant but they were disinterested. Incensed, I got them to stand up, link arms and speak it again, this time pulling against each other as hard as they could. It was quite chaotic – desks went over, they fell against each other – and at first they thought it was funny, but then when we repeated the exercise they began to get involved with the words and started to commit to them, finding their physicality and force. Afterwards, one young man said, 'I see how he feels – he is drowning in his feelings.' And this is precisely where the character is at that moment; he is swimming against the tide of both his feelings and his reason. It could not have been more accurate. Othello is not describing an image, he is living inside it. Through quite rough movement, the group had found the centre of that image and just how intrinsic it was to Othello's psyche at that moment and how it led to his decision to kill Desdemona.

The second workshop was with a group of what I was told were 'low-ability readers', also in London. The play was *King Lear*, and we were looking at Edmund's soliloquy at the beginning of Act I, scene ii, which begins:

Thou, Nature, art my goddess; to thy law
My services are bound.

We read it several times together, making sure what it all meant, and as we read it and they began to feel secure with it, I asked them to kick something – a shoe or a book – on all the words which had to do with Edmund's anger, or sense of inferiority ('bastard', 'base', 'deprive', etc.). This we did a couple of times and then, because I could not ask one person to read it on their own – they were not confident enough for that – I broke it up into short phrases so that each person had something to speak. We spoke it in order several times, and then as they were beginning to enjoy the language, I got them to go to different places in the room and speak their lines again, this time substituting the word 'bastard' with their own words that had the same resonances of anger. The result was both unexpected and riveting: words such as 'black', 'poor' and 'ugly' were said in its stead, but the one which hit me particularly was the word 'ignorant' – the word of the outcast, the person of low esteem. They had truly understood the hidden agenda of the language. And as we worked further on the text and went on to other scenes, I realised that they understood so much more than I had expected: they understood it at the very level of the imagery, and that the ability to read easily did not necessarily go with the ability to understand the resonances of the language. In the ensuing discussion it was evident that these young people recognised how the logic of the imagery took them to the heart of the character, and to the character's self-disgust. I stress that at no time did the work become psychological in its inference, but simply through the physical exercises they were able objectively to find the sound and the force of those words, and gain confidence from speaking them. I have since come to believe that the ability to read easily can, if we are not careful, be a limiting factor in our investigation of the imagery.

Another exercise I was particularly fond of is one which I will call 'Tramps'. I would get those taking part to get into groups of three or four, and make a home for themselves using anything they could find in the hall or classroom around them. They were to make themselves as comfortable as possible, plus find their own possessions. We would be working on a speech from Shakespeare, perhaps a speech from *King Lear*, and each person would have their own line or phrase which they would keep repeating – those were all the words they could use. I would then go to each group separately and suggest that they steal things from one of the other groups, all the time speaking their own particular phrase. We would do this for five minutes or so while they invented ploys to get the better of each other, and then I would stop the action and we would read the whole speech again. So much would erupt – the anarchy of the language and the imagery, and the sense of the words belonging to them.

The point about these exercises is that they did not have to make their voices behave, i.e. sound intelligent, because they were not trying to convince anyone that they knew what it all meant. Simply by letting the words erupt, and through a sense of owning them, they found meanings which related to them as individuals. All this confirmed my instincts that we have to continually find ways for the actor to get behind the literal meaning and connect with the words at their very root. Certainly, as we will see later, exercises like these are useful collectively to break down barriers about the text. I think the bottom line is this: you set up a kind of game, but all games become serious and you want to win, and this unconsciously releases another sound in the voice, which is a more basic, primitive vocal response. Certainly it is always noticeable after this kind of exercise that the voices have an added depth, a different timbre – and actors are quick to hear this. But of course the work was to develop in other, much more subtle directions to reveal changes of thought, personal allegiances, etc. This was just the start of finding ways to make us feel the voice responding to the movement of our mind and the movement of our feelings.

Back to the theatre. Very soon after I joined the Company, in 1974, in fact, The Other Place came into being – a tin shed which had been a theatre store-room. The idea came from Buzz Goodbody, an extraordinary woman in her late twenties who had a vision of re-finding Shakespeare in a small space. Buzz had joined the Company as an assistant director and had worked for several seasons with Trevor Nunn and done her own productions of *King John* and *As You Like It* in the Main House. She did not want The Other Place to be a studio theatre, which she felt would narrow its boundaries. Rather, she wanted it to be a second auditorium, and the reason for its existence would be to develop a 'wider audience for classical theatre'. She was always questioning the purpose of theatre, and whether our work in the Main House was in a way atrophying what we were producing, simply by the scale of the productions. In her proposal she says the following:

So the starting points for the Second Auditorium are practical as well as ideological. The RSC is funded by the whole of society. We know why we play to an audience largely drawn from the upper and middle classes. We have to broaden that audience for artistic as well as social reasons.

Her choice of name for this theatre space, The Other Place, was significant in itself in that, besides being a quotation from *Hamlet*, it carried with it an underlying agenda, a sense that we were going to challenge established ways of presenting classical work without bringing down the level of professionalism and expertise. It was simply about taking an 'other' look, and making people feel that they could be part of this enquiry: I think it was upping the stakes and not lowering them. The *Hamlet* quotation comes from Act IV, scene ii. When asked where the body of Polonius is, Hamlet replies:

In heaven. Send hither to see. If your messenger find him not there, seek him i' th'other place yourself.

A nice irony.

The opening of The Other Place presented an exciting challenge for the Company and opened up a whole new range of work. And this range was huge, for it spanned the whole spectrum of drama from the Elizabethan period to the present – from Marlowe, Jonson, Ford and Shakespeare through Strindberg, Chekhov, Brecht, Bond, Brenton and Rudkin. For those actors alternating between the two theatres the challenge was twofold: first, there was the continuing challenge of pitching it right for each space, that is, finding the particular weight, resonance, muscularity which the space and the text demanded. The intimacy of the second auditorium could be misleading for the plays performed there, whether classical or modern, were without exception complex and dense in their writing, so the size of the language had to be honoured in the right way for that space. And secondly, the diversity of the writing was also a source of discovery, moving as it did between Shakespeare and Brecht, for instance, and this kept the actor alert to the differing rhythms and styles of writing, and how to serve them.

But this was not all, for even more important was the fact that the plays being performed at The Other Place were without exception rich and thought-provoking, and often political in content, and this impacted on the work in the Main House, giving it just that bit more edge and perhaps raising the stakes. There was certainly a sense of interaction between the two auditoria, and very often there was a linking theme, as in 1982, when we performed *King Lear* in the Main House and Bond's *Lear* in The Other Place. The links on the whole were by no means as obvious as that, but there was a sense of relish for the ideas and a sense of provoking thought which the actors took on board. And I think this relish was shared by the audience: when you can see Brecht's *Schweyk*, Charles Wood's *Dingo* and David Edgar's *Destiny* alongside *The Winter's Tale*, *Troilus and Cressida* and *Romeo and Juliet* in the same season, it is at once stimulating, and hopefully makes us hungry for the ideas which lie behind the stories.

The variety of texts being performed in both auditoria gave the actor the opportunity to discover not just the volume and pitch needed for each space, but how to find the size, richness and texture of a heightened text in a small space, and conversely, the lightness and agility of comedy in the big auditorium. In that first year, for instance, an actor could be playing in *King Lear* or Rudkin's *Afore Night Come* in the small space and *Cymbeline* or *Twelfth Night* in the Main House. Tony Church in fact played King Lear and then Belarius in *Cymbeline*. It was this rich interchange that was exciting: how to define the language in each space and fulfil its size and weight was a challenge to the actor's craft.

For me this was a leap forward for it expanded the nature of the work in no uncertain terms. First, it made me reconsider and re-evaluate the whole notion of how we reach an audience: the word for this then in use was 'projection', but that is not a useful word because it implies speaking 'up', which narrows our whole perception of the sound of the language. I came to realise that whatever space you were speaking in, the focus had to be on how the vibration of the language was carrying, and this was not so much to do with volume, or indeed articulating crisply, but about how the actor could make the language impinge on the ear. And this in turn was totally to do with finding the right spaces within the text, and being sensitive to the texture of the language – the varying lengths of vowels and consonants and how they react on each other, and the length and vibration of the consonants. It also had to do with pitch. And this awareness of the texture in the language had to be worked at and practised, so a great deal of work was done on verse, both classical and modern, to open our ears to what was happening in the text in order to get the facility to respond to this. It was crucial that in each auditorium, and without in any way slowing up the speaking, the text be given its required time in space.

The great variety of plays now being produced needed real focus on the variety of style within them, and Voice work had to take this on board. This is where the exercises of action and interaction in text began to evolve. I found working on Jacobean texts particularly illuminating: initially you have to pay great attention to the grammar of the thought, which is always convoluted, but once that has been found then the physicality of the text somehow leads you through it. But to find the line of reasoning through that complex text is difficult, and I found that exercises which centred on the shifts of thought very helpful. For example, moving at each thought change helped to clarify the through line of the argument. It is strangely more difficult than Shakespeare at the start, for the text is often convoluted and it takes time for the meaning to unravel, but once we have wrestled with the shape and syntax of that argument and are clear about its meaning, I think it is more straightforward, for in its very reasoning both the state of the character and the motive are somehow clarified. On the whole, the choices for the actor are limited, unlike Shakespeare where they are limitless.

But perhaps the greatest plus for me came from working with new texts and discovering just how diverse the writing was: how each writer heard the rhythm and form of the writing and just how much this was integral to the meaning. Contrast the spareness of Charles Wood to the dense writing of David Rudkin. My ears were opened. There was an exactness in the rhythm and phrasing which was integral to the meaning and kept one alert, plus it was always particularly interesting when the writer was present and one glimpsed a moment's insight into how they developed their work. So often modern writing takes you suddenly into unexpected places and you have to go with it, and it is always a challenge. Although Shakespeare has all that volatility and more, it has that strong rhythmic centre which we can all feel and which somehow keeps the actor on course – and perhaps unconsciously subjugates. Yet this very fact in itself made me question whether we had been seduced by that rhythm and form which we value so much, and that perhaps we had lost something of the anarchy and roughness within it. So each period of writing both reacted on and informed the other.

What really hit me was the way the exercises which had been developed specifically for classical text worked equally well for modern writing, in that they pointed up the rhythms and the changes of thought. Those exercises which were to do with physical restraint of some sort made the actor define the meaning that much more precisely, so that the text never became over-naturalistic, and the balance was kept. For always when we are speaking we are doing so against what is the opposite, so the words are always active. It was wonderful to find the roughness in the work of Bond and Rudkin, and in so doing to help clarify the meaning and the purpose in those dense texts.

This work between the Main House and The Other Place remained constant and continued through to 1986 when we opened the Swan Theatre. This did not change how we worked in the way that the opening of The Other Place had done because, although not as large as the Main House, it was still a large space (450 seats) for an actor to reach out and fill. Also, it was quite difficult acoustically; actors needed to be aware both of its height and of the fact that unless you were playing straight out, your back was always turned to a part of the house. The focus for me, therefore, had to be on the muscularity of the language to ensure that voices reached the top gallery, and so it was essential that time was given to the actors to experiment with the space and height, finding just how quiet they could be yet still reach every part of the space. This sense of reaching across a space is so much to do with how aware you are of the size and shape and therefore how you inhabit that space mentally. Because of its very shape and size, its perhaps comfortable roundness and the fact that actors can enter from different points of the auditorium, there is an inclusiveness in the space which I think quite patently influences the style of playing. Mostly large classical work is done there: *Titus Andronicus*, *The Jew of Malta* and *The Spanish Tragedy* were among the first plays performed there. There has also been some Chekhov and quite a bit of modern work. I remember particularly Peter Flannery's *Singer* which, because of its large canvas, worked wonderfully in the space.

All this work has continued, and has been a continuous source of discovery, for although I have worked on many of the plays a number of times, most particularly Shakespeare, of course, they are different each time. The actors are different, the director is different, the concept is different and, most important, the time is different. We are constantly redefining the language for now, and it is never the same. We are always finding new ways, new images to help illuminate the text, and these new ways arise out of the specific needs of the play and its particular vision.

There have been many other influences – work in other countries, other cultures – which have opened up different ways of working for me, and which I will list in the next chapter. But most important, this work has deepened my commitment to the politics of language, and our job in theatre, which is to open up its roughness and violence as well as the poetic values – for the poetry is in the truth. Yet we have to make people want to listen, and that cadence, that music, has to be found – and this is the balancing act. As Bond said, 'When theatre loses poetry it loses its centre.'

All this has been about how theatre reflects society and its changing perspectives: we must always be open to these changes, but some part of us must connect with the basic power of language, and thus how theatre can stimulate and make us think.

I have an uncomfortable feeling sometimes that it is almost impossible for us in the West to find the danger in those classic texts, for although we all have private difficulties and personal tragedies, we live in an ordered society and in general our lives are guarded against danger and hardship. How do we find that danger and volatility and sheer excitement in our theatre now? The plays are first and foremost about survival, and that is made plain by the dynamic of the language.

3 Other Cultures – Other Views

I believe it is important to remember that language belongs to us all, be it theatre or everyday life: this keeps the work on text real. I have worked a great deal in prisons, and although the physical work could not be done, as body contact is not allowed, there are always ways to challenge the text so that the speaker can experience its power. One way this can be done is by getting the group to argue with the person speaking, and this gives the speaker a dynamic to work against so that the muscularity of the words can be felt. The feeling of deprivation that is ever present in someone confined like this can charge the language in a very special way, and this quite clear enjoyment in speaking that language aloud confirms my belief that our education system should include the teaching of language in this way, for it needs to be experienced.

There is a power that the human animal gains when he/she can be precise over a feeling or a thought – a sense of their own dignity, their own autonomy – and this sense of power is the right of every citizen. When people realise that words are a tool that everyone can use, it gives both confidence and pleasure. Although in a workshop situation we may be dealing with a powerful and emotive text, the work itself is never psychological, it is always kept practical: getting the mouth round those words, their physicality, is the experience we are after and which we want to build on – a step towards being articulate. Language has evolved in the human species in the same way that our other skills have evolved, e.g. hunting, nurturing, growing food, all because of the need to survive, but systems of precedence and power erode the individual's belief in their right to speak in all kinds of ways – hence violence when we cannot use that right.

But now back to theatre, and I want to look at some of the work I have done with theatre groups in other countries, and how this has informed me.

Working in another country, another culture and another language is continually stimulating and enriches my own work in so many unexpected ways. I have worked with groups of actors and directors in countries as far apart, both in distance and culture, as Korea and Iceland, China and Brazil, and because of my association with the Royal Shakespeare Company, my reference point is the work that is done here in the UK on voice and on classical text. I suppose because we have been working on Shakespeare for so long, and because British mainstream theatre culture is predominantly a text-based one, it is widely felt that we know how to 'do' Shakespeare, or indeed any classical text, and that is the experience, the expertise, if you like, they want to bring into their theatre.

But of course this does not take into account how language is forever shifting, and therefore just how much our approach to text is continually on the move – all the things I have talked about already – or indeed how concepts and choices can put a different emphasis on the speaking, and I think this is the same in most countries. Therefore to work only on Shakespeare would be extremely limiting and so I make it quite clear that I want to interchange both classical and modern text, and certainly to work on material which is part of the culture of their own country – particularly new writing. I also think that in the majority of countries the work on voice, which is often very good indeed, is somehow kept separate from the work on text and from an involvement with language: so it is this connection between voice and text which has to be my focus.

The starting point always is with solid voice work – exercises on breathing, relaxation and resonance, for that need is common to all. Plus that way I can start to listen and to hear where their voices are in relation to their own language, i.e. the particular placement of the vowels and consonants, and the different speech patterns. But the way into the text work is much more complex, and one has to take time and listen for those other sounds. And of course traditions of acting are so very diverse: the whole relationship of theatre with movement, and with mime and dance, of theatre with stories, and of theatre with written text, particularly current writing, are entirely different in each culture, and this affects the very nature of the relationship between actor and text, and actor and audience now.

I am not going to attempt any analysis of all this here: it would not be appropriate nor would it add to the centre of the book which is about the bringing of text work into the rehearsal process, but I do remember a number of things at random, all of which have made me learn to listen, and which I would like to set down.

Wherever I go, and whatever the language, I always start the text work with Shakespeare: the plays are translated into all the major languages, and because they are universally recognised as great literature, they are more often than not translated by poets or well-known writers. Of course, the quality of the translation will vary, but it is usually very true and heightened and poetic, plus you can always rely on the instinct of the actors to select the best and most speakable translation. Also, because I know the content of the plays well, I can begin to hear and recognise this other text more easily: it helps to break the language barrier for me.

In 1980 I was invited by China's Ministry of Culture to lead a workshop for actors and directors from all over China. The reason behind the workshop was this: there had been a good solid theatre culture performing classical and modern plays since the beginning of the century and there had been a strong Russian influence bringing with it a Stanislavsky approach to acting and to actor training, and with interesting European drama being performed. However, the Cultural Revolution, beginning in 1967 and lasting until the mid-70s, put a stop to this: the only work allowed during this period was traditional Chinese theatre, i.e. music theatre and dance, all from the old era. But with the Cultural Revolution over, they could now return to the kind of work that they had been developing before the shutdown, thus incorporating European writing and styles. Of course, they still had to be careful regarding content, for that had to conform with the politics of the regime, but they could

51

use their art in a way appropriate for now. The Minister of Culture now felt that theatre had lost some of the knowledge, the practice that they had previously been masters of, and wanted to provide opportunities for them to regain some of that skill. They recognised these changes and wanted to invest in this kind of training: it certainly made an interesting opening for me.

Because the group came from all over China, their reference to language was very diverse. They were very respectful to me as a teacher, and it took me some time to get them to feel a freedom with the work, and this initially inhibited their involvement with the language. But for me I think Mandarin is the most difficult language I have worked in: its tonicity makes it difficult to pin down, and as changes of meaning come with changes of tone as well as with the specific speech sounds, there seems little which is recognisable to the European ear. The main text work was done on *King Lear*: we looked at about four key scenes, focusing on the relationships between the characters and listening to what was happening in the language. They had chosen the oldest translation as they felt it was truest to the emotional depth of the story. We worked slowly to find the thought changes and the changing political allegiances between Lear and his daughters, but very specifically through finding the exact words to express these feelings, and how the words affected them as they spoke them, particularly in that first scene where Lear is testing out his daughters' love for him. And when, after several days, we presented the work to a small audience, it was that first scene that I remember so vividly, where they had found both the reality of the scene and the formality of the language – the exact rhythm and music.

And it was this that struck home. I have repeated this story because it made me realise that, whatever the language, you can always hear when something is right, when someone hits the moment and is behind the word. We can discern something of the depth and feeling of the words by the space and resonance given to them: this surely is an area of collective understanding, something which transcends cultures.

And now in India, on a totally different tack: I worked in Delhi with a group of actors from all over the country, from different states with different languages – there are so many languages spoken. We were working on Shakespeare, but all in the Sanskritised Hindi text, and I soon realised how difficult it was for them to feel comfortable with this, and to be able to bring their own background and experience to bear on the language. It just did not contain the warmth, the humanity and personal references – the this-ness – of their own speech, and this resulted in a sense of alienation.

I remember one actor in particular, a very talented and well-regarded actor from the State of Gujuarat. He was working on a speech from *Hamlet* which he knew well, but I noticed that his voice was sounding slightly strangled, nor was it open to the possibilities of the language. He sounded curiously uncomfortable. I tried to get him to speak in his own state language rather than Hindi, but he resisted to begin with as Hindi is the officially accepted language and in its way carries a status symbol. I had to use a good deal of persuasion before he finally spoke it in Gujarati, and the difference was incredible. He immediately sounded 'at home' in his own voice; it was resonant and had its own authority. He was what I call 'sitting down' in his voice. And this again was a powerful lesson, for it means that in every society people can feel that there is a 'right' way of speaking, a 'better' way – be it in the language or in the dialect – which overrides the speaker's intrinsic vocal quality.

As I worked further with the group, we concentrated on resonance, and sitting down in the voice, and particularly singing out on vowels. This is always interesting in another language for not only is the shaping of the vowels different, but their placing in the mouth varies considerably. We worked a lot on the sonnets – these had to be in Hindi so they could all take part – but parallel to this we worked on poems written in their own languages, and in this way they gradually found a balance and a freedom and a resonance, whether speaking in their own state language or in Hindi, the 'received' language. Again, status rules in all languages, and has the power either to give freedom or to inhibit.

This mixing of languages has repercussions of the most complex and subtle nature in so many countries: it has to do with different state languages within one country, always with different political implications and undertones, and of course the politics are even more complicated in those countries which have been colonised. Even as near home as Canada, the French/English divide is always present: this divide is covertly linked to the need to retain one's cultural identity. Language is a weapon both for offence and defence.

In Zimbabwe I worked in English as this is the language common to all. Those taking part came from different acting groups from all over the country, and came from both the Zanu and Zapu nations, so relations were not that easy and it proved difficult to get a collective involvement. In the light of recent tragic events, this is not surprising. The Zanu people spoke Shone and the Zapu spoke Ndebele, but, because we were working in English, everyone was put on an equal level, plus it also meant that we had a good choice of texts to work on. The group was made up of actors and directors who mainly worked in small theatre companies attached to the poorer areas.

These companies got their own material together, with a lot of comedy and mime, and of course there was a strong tradition of story-telling, but they had little experience of working with scripted texts, and this was precisely what they wanted to focus on. They wanted their work to become more educational, so that they could open up ideas, help deal with problems, and perhaps be more of a political force, and to do this they needed more specific texts in order to focus clearly on the issues at hand. My job, therefore, was to bring the two cultural aspects together, so that they could bring their gift of story-telling to bear on the work on scripted material.

Again we started with poems, a mixture of their own and ones I gave them: Auden, Brecht, Yevtushenko, MacNeice, Neruda. We worked in a number of ways until they became familiar with them, and then they would split into pairs: I gave one poem to each pair and asked them to find a way of presenting it to the group, to dramatise it. This was a great way to bring together a facility with the text of the poems, which were all quite complicated, with their own rich sense of story-telling. And this in turn gave them a start into the work on scripted plays which is where they wanted to go. Because they had not worked through scripts, the tendency in their story-telling was to play variations of themselves, and this had to do only with a character/audience relationship, and not the relationships between characters, so there were many different facets to open out and discover. This visit taught me so much about cultural perspectives – I still have a vision of people walking great distances at an unhurried pace – and how we in the West are so influenced and caged in by time and space.

My visits to Brazil have been a special source of inspiration for a number of reasons: there are three different groups with whom I work. First, with actors from the main theatre companies, all of which have a classical repertoire so that the actors are familiar with Shakespeare, and have a similar work pattern to ours. So my job with them has been to share my work on both voice and text and, because many of them are El Globo actors – i.e. their main source of income is with El Globo television soaps – I have worked with them mainly on Shakespeare to heighten their awareness of the imagery and size of the language while at the same time keeping it true to themselves. There was always a search for the best translation, but on the whole they were good and captured the poetic texture in their rhythm and flow, which meant that the actors could experience the musical sound of the language as well as find the thought and emotion within the text. And because of the huge television output in the country, it was important to keep this work going in depth, and they were very committed to doing just that.

My visits have also been enriched by my association with Augusto Boal. Boal is possibly best known for the work he initiated in Forum Theatre, a process through which theatre can make people aware of their own rights as citizens. The actors first invent a situation which is recognisable to the audience and with which they can identify around their own lives. This scenario is then developed, complications ensue, and it gradually builds to a crisis, at which point a character called the Joker intervenes and asks the audience how they would seek to resolve the problems that have accrued. They wait for seven answers to be given which are then discussed. The problems are thus laid out very fully and the possibilities of how to solve them are listed clearly, and the audience then has to choose the action which they think will be most effective. The purpose is to heighten the awareness of the audience to specific social problems which surround their lives and give them a sense of their own right to challenge, argue and speak, and above all to make them realise that they have the power to change things.

And of course this work has spread to many different countries and has a powerful and ongoing influence. All this is a wonderful reminder of just how active theatre can be in people's lives.

However, the particular value for me has been to see the way Boal works with actors on text, and because of this I invited him over to the UK to lead a workshop with a group of actors in the Royal Shakespeare Company. He worked on *Hamlet*, using his methods of imaging desires and motives, of communicating the text through different parts of themselves, i.e. eyes, then faces, then bodies, before speaking the words. For me it is always exciting to see the actor find new ways to unlock the language and discover their own very personal connection with the extravagant and often huge imagery and feel its seismic movement within them. The workshop was a great source of inspiration to our actors; they felt re-sensitised by it.

But perhaps my greatest joy in Rio has come from the work that I do with the group 'Nos de Morro' in Vidigal. Vidigal is one of the slums situated high up on one of the hills which surround this beautiful city, and is basically run by the drug cartels – police do not venture there except in armoured cars. The group was started in around 1984 by Guti Fraga, a successful actor, who had a vision of working with these young people from the streets to do serious theatre work, and he gave up his career to do just that. He was very insistent that no drugs should be brought into their space, and that they would leave their problems outside so that their room would become a space for work, and for the enjoyment of that work. But he did not want the work to be a way merely of filling up their time and educating them to some extent; he wanted to make them into a serious theatre company, working on good plays. He wanted the work to be professional in every sense so that it would be respected. In fact, the group was built on respect: he respected them, and he required that they respect each other, the work and the whole purpose of their aims. I went there first in 1997, when the work had been going for about twelve years. By all sorts of means Fraga had got some money together and the group had built a small theatre in the sub-structure of a school which seated 30: it was very small but beautifully planned, with proper entrances and exits and a small lighting board. There was also a properly fitted out dressing room. I remember watching my first performance there - adaptations of three eighteenth-century Portuguese short stories - and I was knocked out by the elegance and grace and clarity of the performances. It was an amazing evening: it said so much about their joy at being able to express themselves, and how that is part and parcel not only of self-confidence but of survival.

At the time they were preparing work on *Hamlet*, which they were going to perform later in the year, and so we did a lot of work on the beginning scenes, breaking them up with exactly the same kind of exercises I would use with trained actors - whispering the first scene to find the spaces in the language, pulling Hamlet back from the Ghost, telling the Player King's story as a group. They enjoyed them all and immediately made it part of their work in a totally professional way. I have been back several times, and every time I am amazed by their hunger for work on language, and their measure of understanding. Somehow Guti Fraga has managed to harness all the energy which they would normally use to combat their frustrations and difficulties, which are manifold, and redirect it into the creative process of their work. The group has now been recognised by the city and is being given a certain amount of funding, and some of the young actors have been taken on by television. Even so, it is still hard work to keep it all going. The discipline, concentration and commitment he has asked of them has paid off fully; plus it proves just how democratising language can be. And all this in view of the Statue of Christ - El Cristo. It should be a lesson to us all.

My other experience in Rio was of taking part in a Third World Theatre Conference, where representatives from theatre companies from a number of different countries in Africa and South America came together to talk and present their work. The purpose was to get them together with representatives from the World Bank, the Ford Foundation and UNESCO in order to get support for the great work of educating people that these theatre companies do. Talking with people who worked for UNESCO, I began to see the whole Western idea of nationhood in a different light. The concept of a nation state is a European one which cannot embrace ethnic or tribal divisions; it has to unify them under a democratic state; but it is the democracy that divides. And this reflects so much on the whole question of language.

In Bogota, Colombia, I found a different reference to the voice work in that they keep it very separate: by this I mean that, although there is much good voice training done, I think it comes from a singing perspective and this does not necessarily connect with text in performance. Their theatre has a very broad spectrum of work, and there has been a lot of exchange with European directors, Grotowski in particular. All this was perhaps more movement-orientated and was inventive and free, but they found it difficult to bring this freedom into their work on text. So we began by working on the sonnets, moving with the changes of thought, and so getting a freedom with the language. We then worked on the story of the Player King, both from a technical point of view, and then by telling the story moving round the space, and this they found very liberating.

One had to break through the idea that there was some sort of mystique in the way to train the voice, a right way, for this led to tension, which in turn made them hold their sound in the throat and so lose the richness and cadence in the language. However, when they realised that you had to find your own freedom and trust your own instinct, they really started to explore the sounds and textures in the language with exciting results.

In Seoul, South Korea, I found that the sound of the language itself was something I had to deal with: it sounded to me a much more stressed language, more emphatic, and that stress so often came from the throat. This gave the language a more literal sound which, to my ears, did not open up the possibilities, and so we worked quite a bit on whispering through text. They soon found that they could lift their voices through and allow the sounds to lengthen, and to hold the feeling. At one point one of the voice teachers said he thought that English theatre was dry, but I soon realised that it was because we did not emphasise language in the same way, and this he took to mean that it was less passionate. However, once we started to work on scenes from *Hamlet*, letting the sound of the language carry the meaning, they found a different emotional strength, and in fact the teacher retracted his statement. It was a wonderfully warm and generous group to work with, and so open to the possibilities of language.

Both these workshops made me very alert to the fact that the sound of a language can influence the resultant meaning and intention, and as listeners we are all in danger of pre-judging intention by the very sounds and patterns that are set up. And this poses questions about how much the sound pattern is intrinsic to the nature of the culture and to what extent the sound pattern influences the way we think.

And now to Europe – Poland, Iceland, Croatia, Russia, plus a number of forums in other countries. I suppose in Europe one expects the language to have much the same actor/text connection as in the UK, but strangely I think it is not so, for the emphasis is on the sound of the voice rather than an involvement in the language. For one thing, the written text does not play such a central role, for the work encompasses so many different styles involving movement, mime etc., and is perhaps more innovative than English theatre in general. Also the styles of presentation are very diverse – Brechtian objectivity at one end, and a Stanislavskian involvement with character and emotion at the other.

But when it comes to text-based work – classical text, for instance – the interesting thing is that Europeans are not afraid of ideas, and here perhaps it is the other side of the coin from the US. They are interested in the size of the ideas, and they are not afraid of their philosophical content or of the form of classical writing: the readiness of the audience to take this on board is intrinsic to their view of theatre.

In every European country I have visited the voice work is very good indeed and is taken very seriously. However, work is always necessary to get the actor involved with the language, for as I hear it it is often that little bit more stylised and perhaps presented, and this leaves little room for ambivalence. It is of course wrong to generalise; all I would say is that one has to continually negotiate the actor's involvement with language against the style and possible formality of the presentation. So the work needs to open out the flexibility, make contact with the imagery, and give the actor that sense of confidence and trust in his or her own voice to find out just how far to go.

All this work in other countries has been of untold value in that it keeps one's ear open to other possibilities, other perspectives. But crucially I suppose it makes one continually question what the centre of voice work is, for how the actor deals with text is organic to the style and politics of a production:

Is it to tell a story objectively?
Is it to get people involved in the language?
Is it to satisfy and fulfil the character's/actor's emotions?
Is it to make the audience feel and think?
Is it to take them into that 'other' world?

The balance is different in every case, but it is vital that the director takes these questions on board at the start of a rehearsal period, for the actor's involvement with language can be every bit as creative as his/her involvement with the movement of the body. But I do believe the purpose has to be defined.

And of course the work with the Company here in the UK has developed, not only in rehearsal, but in workshops with directors and writers, plus constant work on verse and the whole construct of heightened language.

I just want to mention the workshops with writers and actors because they are always magic in some way. While the writer and the actor often have a fragile relationship in a rehearsal setting, and may even feel threatened by each other, when they get together they discover that they share the same creative landscape which is not necessarily a logical one. You always learn something about the imagination and where it can take you.

A workshop starts in the same way as any other, with initial work on Shakespeare text and how we find ways to inhabit it. We then divide into groups, with each writer working with two or three actors on his/her own scenes. Many points have come up at different times. If, as one writer said, writing is an act of identity, how does the actor find that identity from a written text? Is there less form, less tension and counterpoint in a modern text? Actors often want to change a script to make it more familiar with what they already know, but a playwright hears his/her own text and phrasing in a very particular way. How organic is it to the meaning? One writer said that she does not necessarily know what the story is about until she can look at the scene structure.

This meeting point gives the actor a sense of freedom to explore the language without pinning it down to logic – allowing the words to take you to that other place. For the writer, who works in seclusion, it gives him/her a chance to explore his/her work actively with others. They are so often surprised how different exercises, quite simple ones like echoing words around the character in a scene, can add to their ideas: and more than once, after a workshop, a writer has gone back to re-work a scene or part of a play in the light of the exploration that has been done.

But the work that has been of greatest significance for me took place with directors in New York. I have worked regularly in the US for over twenty years, working in university drama departments plus small groups of actors all over the country, and I feel very at home with their approaches to acting and to text, both classical and modern.

In a way this does not seem like another culture. The language is the same – on the surface, at least – and because the whole theatre culture goes back to the same roots, leaving out for the moment ethnic diversities, there is so much that links us. And of course, not the least of those links is Shakespeare and the great American actors, e.g. Edwin Forrest, so traditionally it has run parallel to English theatre over quite a long period of time.

But, as in the UK in the mid-50s when theatre began to change quite radically, so change occurred in the US. With the beginning of the Studio, and the training of US actors in an Americanised Stanislavsky approach – the 'Method', as it has become known – the whole American style of acting changed for good. It became much more personalised and the investigation into the feelings and motives of a character became central to the acting process. And what is really interesting to me now is to look at the interaction between our two approaches: that is, the bringing together of the UK tradition bedded in the spoken word, with the 'Method' work of the US actors and its focus on the inner emotional drive. In broad terms – argument v. emotion. This is perhaps a simplistic definition, but it identifies clearly two different ways of entering a text. This has been brought to fruition for me by the work I have been able to do in the last few years with the New York-based 'Theatre For A New

Audience' – a series of three-week workshops with directors and actors.

Each workshop has consisted of six to seven directors plus about eighteen actors: prior to the workshop each director chooses two scenes which they want to work on, and these scenes are provisionally cast in advance.

We begin the workshop with a brief talk about the changing fashions of language, and how this affects the modern actor working on classical text today, then we go straight into collective work. I then talk through the other exercises – there is simply not time to work through them all in detail – and then the directors go off for two days with their cast and start work on the scenes they have prepared. I visit each group and, if appropriate, suggest exercises which might be helpful.

At the end of the two days the groups reassemble and show their pieces of work. We then talk about that work and the approaches used, plus the exercises that contributed to the result. We finish by exploring other exercises which might be appropriate. This process is then repeated in the second half of the workshop on a new set of scenes.

This work is not in any way about limiting or changing a director's approach to his/her work in rehearsal: the exercises are simply meant to reinforce and support their particular methods and open out other possibilities of the text and its meaning. For we have to keep remembering that English is an inclusive language, and we have to listen for what it can tell us in the very changes of rhythm, and changes in sound and texture. The hidden benefit from the work is that it creates a sense of trust between the actors and the directors, i.e. a trust which comes from discovering something together. Although most of the work is focused on Shakespeare, we also work on Jacobean texts in the same way, and these prove enormously useful, pointing up in more stark ways how we can be involved in language and make it active. For over-emphasis on feeling makes the language passive, and we end up describing our feelings rather than finding our way through them to an active solution, and this can lead to sentimentality – the prerogative of the rich!

All this has given me the opportunity and the time to test out the work in a professional way; moreover, it has given me enough time to see how the exercises could support the differing needs of both actors and directors. But what has been particularly gratifying for me is their recognition that these ways of working on language, inhabiting it, if you like, by finding its physicality, goes parallel to their 'Method' way of finding the want and the motive in the character. But more, it releases the argument/the reasoning, and clarifies the thoughts and makes them enjoy the speaking of those thoughts. It made the words the discovering element, for if you fill the words only with the feeling of the character there is no discovery left.

I have talked at some length about this work in other countries because, with the increasing interest in cross-cultural exchange, I think it is important that we recognise and meet those differences, and we do not blur over them or pretend they are not there. Interesting results can only come from the true meeting of cultures without any loss of identity.

From all these different workshops and experiences, plus from my work in the Company, there are certain seminal points that continue to inform me:

(i)   When the actor is truly on the moment, how the words can transcend cultures.

(ii)   Being on the moment - waiting for the drum-beat to come back to you - you allow yourself to hear your thoughts.

(iii) The need to be at home in your own voice. Sitting down in it - whatever language, dialect, you may be using.

(iv) Hunger for language - we are still a verbal culture. Enjoyment of eloquence - this has nothing to do with education.

(v)   Inclusiveness of the English language - hearing what is happening under the text.

(vi) Gold miners - their love of Shakespeare. They understood through hearing it - they listened with their imagination.

(vii) Roughness and gentleness together.

(viii) Words are always active - the need to survive prevails.

(ix) Catching the moments which are outside time. Reaching out to the existential moments - these are exciting.

(x)   'When theatre loses its poetry it loses its centre' - Bond

63

But of course, theatre is always provocative and interesting, or at least should be, and so the actor's job is to keep the text active, to keep listening for what is there, to contact the imagery and give the sense of confidence and trust in the voice. See how far you can go and above all use your own instinct.

Where is the wisdom lost in knowledge:
Where is the knowledge lost in information.

T.S. Eliot

Part Two
Uncovering the Layers

4 About the Exercises

Now for the practical part, the reason for the book: ways of working on text in a rehearsal context. I am calling it 'Uncovering the Layers' for it is about the sounds, the spaces, the choices which are there in the text, often hidden, and which are intrinsic to finding the world of the play and the world of the character.

Someone once said to me, 'The more we see the less we imagine.' We so often forget this, for we do not trust that the audience can be excited by the interaction of sound and meaning, and how one reinforces the other. Also, we do not take into account how selective our ears are, for when we listen we are not simply picking up the literal meaning, we are probably perceiving as much via the sounds and tones of what we are hearing.

Every piece of writing is expressing something very specific simply by the choice of language, its sound and rhythm, be it heightened or demotic, extravagant or minimal: and because both actor and director want to make everything as clear as possible, and rightly so, the focus at the beginning of rehearsal has to be on the meaning and the implications of situation and motive. There will be talk about the choice of language and how it bears on character and the underlying statement of the play and its style, but we are still talking about it and therefore pre-empting how it should be spoken. And because our focus is upon the meaning of the whole, we hear the words only as part of the grammatical sense: we hear clumps of words but not the words themselves.

To repeat what I said at the beginning, this then is a plea for time to be given during rehearsal for work to be done on both voice and text in order to open our awareness of language, and to give the actors time to explore the rhythms and textures of a text together: this not only gives a freedom to the work, but also fosters a group trust in the language itself. I have set out the group exercises in detail, but once the principles are laid then different exercises, or parts of them, can be layered through the rehearsal process so the work becomes central to the actor's entry into character. The later exercises, those on specific texts, focus on the rehearsal process itself: their purpose is simply to free the language from the restraint of 'making sense', so that the actor can discover its unexpectedness and how it is always erupting and changing the situation, changing the moment. It is about the inevitability of the words, for words to the actor should be as inevitable as breathing.

The work itself falls roughly into four sections:

Section One

Chapters Five and Six – group work on both voice and text. This work needs to be led if possible by the voice person attached to the theatre, but if this is not possible, then by the director or a senior actor. Initially the work needs to be given a good long session so that the principles can be laid clearly, but subsequently it can be done in short sessions, perhaps at the beginning of each rehearsal day. It is important not only because it helps the individual actor to centre the voice and make him/her ready for the space they will be playing, but also it gives a confidence in the voice so that the balance is found between voice and muscularity, and this prevents the actor feeling the need to push. If the voice is pushed, the life of the text gets lost. The collective work on language focuses the actor on listening to what is happening in the text, and on finding the moments to respond and to pass the language on. It is about keeping the language active.

Section Two

Chapters Seven and Eight – basic work on text and structure. Here the focus is on the subtext of a play and how the writing is structured, and how this informs both character and content.

Section Three

Chapters Nine to Eleven – these are about exercises which can be worked on specific scenes in rehearsal in order to heighten and inform both motive and situation.

Section Four

Chapter Twelve – this is about exploring space. It is important that work is done in the performance space itself prior to opening, so that the work done in rehearsal is kept intact.

Because how we work on voice and how we work on text interact so closely, we are always dealing with a complex mix of both subjective and objective responses by the director and the actor. So here I want to lay out the different perspectives and issues which surround the work.

THE VOICE ITSELF

What is intriguing is that we all have differing perceptions of the voice: what a good voice is, what attracts us about a voice, how people communicate with each other and with us, all of which is influenced by our own background, culture, age, class, and above all, taste. And perhaps taste is the big issue, not only because it is such a random factor, but also because it is impossible to pin down because it inevitably changes with the times. But what is particularly pertinent to the actor's work is that, as individuals, we each have a different awareness of the music or cadence in language. Just as some people have an ear for music, so others have a sharper sense of the poetry in language, its rhythm cadence, and how much this can affect both the listener and the speaker.

Now this subjective response, which we call taste, has been conditioned from a very early age – what we first heard, our relationship with our family, how verbal the family was, etc. And what makes it even more complex is that in the theatre we are dealing not only with the director and the actor and their collective approaches to text, but also with the listener, the audience, each one of whom has a different expectation of what they want to hear – but in the end, of course, it is the actor who has to deliver and make the choice. All this aside, there is very definitely something in the voice which potentially has the power to capture the interest of the listener – a vibration, a resonance that draws us to listen, if we can tap into it. And this resonance, this vibration, irrespective of accent or dialect, commands a collective response.

And here I want to talk a little about what I call the private voice: as individuals we have a very personal connection with our own voice, for it is the sole means by which we can communicate our inner self to the outside world. Therefore, any criticism of it or the way we speak is akin to criticism of ourselves and can profoundly affect our confidence. If, for instance, we are told to 'speak up' or that we cannot be understood for whatever reason, we immediately close up inside and do not want to go on: we lose confidence. Also, because we hear our own voice via the bone conduction in our own head we never hear it quite as others do, hence our disbelief when we hear our recorded voice. This is further complicated by the fact that we cannot quite separate ourselves, or I should say how we perceive ourselves, from the perception we have of our own voice – in other words, we can never be totally objective. All this is going on under the surface, for we do not consciously think about it, nevertheless there is that awareness within us which shapes the way we use our voice – the public versus the private.

There are a number of factors in our early years which inform not only the way our voice develops but also how we think of it through life:

(i)   Our enjoyment of early sounds.
(ii) What we inherited from our family, i.e. their response to language, plus how they communicated with each other.
(iii) Beginnings of social awareness – going to school, etc.
(iv) A growing awareness of your own voice, plus its effect on other people – whether you were listened to or not.
(v)   An awareness of sound – a natural 'ear'.
(vi) Anatomical development of the vocal muscles and resonating spaces.
(vii) Articulacy, confidence in expressing yourself, clarity.

All these points may seem incidental and unimportant to the actor who has in part to think of his/her voice as an instrument, yet they are all part of the growing process which makes a person's voice unique, and when training the voice and discovering its range and strength we must not let an overall wash of exercises blot out that individuality, that vulnerability, that uniqueness. Plus I want to stress that for me none of the above points have a psychological connotation, they are totally a matter of circumstance, of how we develop, and they happen in everyone's life.

These are the layers, then, that the actor is dealing with: finding the private imagination, the secret voice, and making it public. But what in the end makes us, the audience, want to listen is the actor's depth of feeling, passion and desire for truth – and this requires real vocal skill.

This is why I start the whole practical section of the book with group voice work which I call 'sitting down in the voice': it is a way for the actor to find the confidence within the group, and a way for the director to hear and experience the needs of both actor and text. For the work is not just about finding good relaxation or about breathing deeply, it is about taking that moment to feel the breath connecting with the centre, and with the whole self – the past and the present. It puts us in touch with both our power and our vulnerability, and it is important that this is shared around the group. I also think it is important for the director to do this work so that it is seen as central to the creative process of rehearsal, and not something which will just make it 'better' – and perhaps also to experience these discoveries within him/herself, something which takes courage to do. Making the voice public is not easy – it costs.

COLLECTIVE WORK

I started this book by talking about how language resonates within us, and though we cannot give a logical reason for this we know that words and sounds and rhythms carry more than their literal meaning, more than their space on the page. We looked at the opening lines of *Hamlet* and particularly at the spaces those lines need in order to excite the curiosity of the listener and to take us into that other world. But this as always needs trust – trust both in ourselves and in the text – and to get this we need to find out just how the sound of the language connects both with the meaning and with us. By doing this group work, telling stories collectively, or passing text around, we can explore both the extravagance and the simplicity of the text. But more than that, we hear how each person reacts differently yet finds their own truth in it, and we, as an audience, perceive that truth and are drawn by it. In other words, we need time to explore just how far we can go.

Now both these sections of work require time, and time, as we well know, is always at a premium in a rehearsal period. However, if at the start of rehearsals one whole day, or two half days, can be given over to this work so that it can be fully explored and the principles laid, then it can be taken forward in quite short stints and thus inform the work as you go. It will also become clear how and where the work is necessary. I am quite certain that, by creating a collective awareness and trust in this way, a considerable amount of time is saved overall and, not least, it will add to the creative input.

SPECIFIC WORK ON TEXT

The rest of the book, from Chapter Seven on, is about the action of the text – for it never stands still. As you work it is continually gathering depths and opening up meanings, and the more you can enter the text via means other than thinking through the surface logic of motive and emotion, the more it will surprise and the more connected you will feel. Language always makes its subliminal mark.

So what I have laid out is a collection of exercises which will take the language into another area of awareness: by putting together different actions and objectives with the text that is spoken, sometimes opposing ones, the work will open up different reactions in ourselves and further meanings will spring out. It can be an exciting process.

THE ISSUES

All the work, in effect, revolves round the meeting between actor and director, both of whom want to serve the play as well as possible. Actors are so often not given the time or the space to discover the language on their own terms and make it their own, and this can then get in the way of experiencing the excitement when the language is discovered at exactly the right moment – that is to say, when it reveals something specific in the character, and is in its way revelatory – and this excitement can be a turning point. At the same time, the director quite rightly has an overall view of the style of the writing and how it should be expressed, its speed and rhythm – all part of the style of the production – which the actor needs to take on board, for that also can inform.

Both are on a journey, for both are intent on finding ways to get their concept of the story across as potently as possible. The director wants to make the story both clear and vivid, using whatever visual means he/she deems necessary; the actor wants to connect with the world of the character, and to discover and live through the character's feelings, making them personal to him/herself. But I think both these journeys are so often done at the expense of investing in the words themselves as a creative force. Work is not done on the language for its own intrinsic value, its rhythms and its choice, and we impose a meaning, an intention, on it too early and so pin it down to make it reflect our own concepts, whereas surely the excitement of language is that it is always open to surprise – so are we missing the possibilities? As in life, words can erupt and open up questions as we speak, so in a text we have to listen to what the words are doing at a creative level. They are not simply thoughts or feelings written down; they are the spirit in action.

The rest of the work in the book is therefore about finding the action of the words, how one word leads to another, one thought to another – finding their movement and finding their spaces. It is also about finding the cost of the language, be it comedy or tragedy, and how we can connect with our inner imagination while communicating this to the listener. It is also about the need for language.

STYLE AND SPACE

But inevitably it is more complicated than this for there is still both the matter of style and the specific theatre space, and how they react on each other. The director will have a view of how the text needs to be defined, and that defining of text is in itself part of the style of the production, and thus is intrinsic to the political overview. I say this with a certain doubt in my mind for I think directors have become more interested in the visual aspects of a production than in the language, and therefore do not necessarily have a view of that language as being part of the creative life of the play – it tells a story but does not go deeper than that. This makes a further reason for collective work on text.

There was a time, of course, when directors had very strong feelings about how text should be spoken, and they directed the speaking in much the same way as they directed the movement on stage: this usually resulted in a rather stylised approach which was right for the time but is not appropriate any more. However, there is a balance to be found for if, as we must believe, style and meaning are interlocked, finding a collective view on that style is essential. As we have seen, a modern writer hears his/her writing in a very particular way – the rhythm and the phrasing convey its exact meaning and nuance – and our job has to be to look for that key and make it integral to the end product. With Shakespeare, or any classical text, for that matter, it is more complex, for these works are open to so many different choices – what period we set them in, our angle on the play's relevance for now – that we have to search for the right balance which serves that particular view of the play.

More and more classical work is being performed in studio spaces, and this is extremely valuable for it at once makes them more immediate and more accessible. Because the audience is involved in a different way, and perhaps more involved with the situations and the characters at a personal level, I think the mixture of personal and state politics is revealed more clearly, and this can open up so much that is often hidden – hidden by the size of movement and pitch of voice that is required for a large space. But this, of course, raises two questions: first, how do we achieve the size of the imagery of that heightened language within a confined space? And conversely, how do we achieve a sense of intimacy, that sense of speaking to each other appropriate for now, in a large theatre across a big stage space? How we deal with the space we are inhabiting has to be addressed for it inevitably changes an actor's approach and style, and his/her entry into character. The director, therefore, must take both these issues on board – style and space – for they are interactive.

Of course the actor must have the skill to 'do' what is asked for by the director, but that 'doing' must come from the perceived need of the text, which the actor has to hear. Often the director does not realise this and gives the actor voice directions, but this can never be satisfactory because, unless these directions are found in a creative way, the result can never be quite real. I am not asking that we 'feel' everything, but rather that we perceive the need of the moment which can come from outside, i.e. the space and the text, as well as from the inner imagination. So the actor is always having to juggle that secret personal response with the need to put it across to the audience. But, and this is important, it is the private voice which holds that resonance, that vibration, which grabs the audience and which we have to tap into.

This is why I believe it's crucial for a group to do initial work not only on voice but on sounding out text together, passing text round and taking time to listen. This is not to conform or sound like each other, but to find how you as an individual can respond to what excites you in that writing while keeping a collective response and rhythm going. For the rhythm is the motor always; there can be spaces within that rhythm, but if we drop it the play stops for that moment. And this work need not be done on the text of the play you are working on, but on other texts which may inform it in different ways. Most important, it will open out a group awareness and confidence.

THE WORK ITSELF

My focus is going to be mainly on Shakespeare because he takes us to so many places in his writing, both poetic and rough, and so gives us a great start into text work of all kinds, be it classical or modern, Webster or Beckett. Shakespeare gives us that kick-start we need, but the exercises work equally well for all writing. Of course, we have to take into consideration the verse form and metre, but because Shakespeare uses it in such a natural way, it simply serves to tune our ears to the rhythm in language – be it verse or prose.

I think we are not nearly as bold or imaginative as we could be when working on Shakespeare texts because we are afraid of

doing it 'wrong': so much has been written about the plays –
what they mean, the rhythms and forms of rhetoric, and how it
should be spoken – that we are inevitably wary, and then we
begin to lose our instinctive response to its sound and resonance, and what that can tell us. And let me reiterate here that
this has nothing to do with dialect or accent, for it is the
muscularity and variety within the language that informs. Plus,
quite rightly, we do not want to sound extravagant and over the
top, and therefore untruthful, but all this mitigates against us
fulfilling the sound of the language in a true way, and finding
that balance between the heightened and the naturalistic, the
violent and the gentle – all the qualities which give the text the
variety and texture and music which have excited audiences
through so many generations. For although we now tend to
enclose our feelings by expressing them in a minimal way, we
still have that pressure cooker inside us which can explode at
any moment. And language does still explode around us – it is
still as volatile as a cab drive in New York, or a football crowd
supporting Manchester United or Real Madrid.

So, how do we fulfil this extravagance in Shakespeare's
language, and allow it to be both volatile and truthful – and for
now? We can all feel when the speaking fulfils and satisfies, but
we do have to practise: we have to sound it out and to listen and
respond.

I do not want to go over the same ground as *Voice and the
Actor* and *The Actor and the Text*, which contain detailed analysis
of metre and rhythm and speech structures, but I have rewor-
ked some of those exercises in order to take them on further,
and a number of the texts which I refer to will be the same. But
what is quite different and new is that I have redefined all this
work as part of an ongoing rehearsal process: this clarifies all the
exercises on text and puts them specifically into a work
situation, which in turn opens them out in a way that will
impact on the discovery of character and of motive and of the
world of the play – discovering the 'other' in the language.

All this work has been developing over a number of years,
through my work with the Royal Shakespeare Company, but I
have been able to table it in this way as a direct result of time
spent with directors in New York. To watch directors, each with
different methods and approaches, put the work into practice on

the scenes they have chosen, has confirmed the value of the exercises for me, for in every case they were seen to be effective, and to work actively and not theoretically. They were also seen to open out ideas about the motives and objectives of the scenes themselves.

So to sum up: director, actors, designer and theatre voice teacher come together as a group to read and discuss the play, to unravel its meaning and significance, and to pool their ideas and get a common angle on it. If it is a classical play this will involve references to the definition of words, to historical contexts, and to academic research and points of view: all this is essential and must be embraced. But when the actor comes to speaking the text he/she must at some point be freed from the responsibility of all this, and be given time to explore the form and the sound of the text for its own sake so that other meanings and resonances can surface. This is not a luxury but a necessity, for it will inform character, plot and motive in unexpected ways – in ways that are organic to the speaker. I suppose most of the exercises have a lot to do with resistance in one form or another, for this allows the actor to feel the true need of the words and their cost, plus the need to reach through to someone else. This in itself is good for it takes the focus off him/herself and alerts us to what has to be done – the active. The actor has all these instincts inside, but needs the time and the space and the confidence to let them root.

The purpose is always to make us aware of alternative meanings, of ambivalences, and of resonances in sound that add depth to the work, and which we can only discern when we are hearing what those words are doing above and beyond their literal or pre-determined meaning. All the work can be used at different stages of rehearsal: as you get deeper into the work on character and motive, the more an exercise will refine and reveal. Even a simple task such as beating out the metre on a speech may possibly illuminate something for us. For best results the exercises should be layered through the rehearsal process, either with the whole group, or during work on specific scenes.

Surprisingly the exercises work equally for tragedy or comedy: simply by helping you find the spaces and the timing, the force and the precision, the image and the definition, they highlight what is there in the text so that the underlying textures of rhythm and sound and pacing are allowed to surface, be it sad or comic or ironic. Above all they tell us something of how the language erupts, its unexpectedness, for there is never a straight line to show how a character thinks and behaves. We are always on the move, and that in itself is exciting.

I have listed the exercises in groups but that does not mean that there is an order in which they should be done, for different times in rehearsal demand different work. The group work can be just as important and as useful at the end of a rehearsal period as at the beginning. I think it is good to jump to and fro, and to keep coming back to those beginnings of structure and subtext and metre etc., for they will always make you hear something fresh.

You will find that each group of exercises has a common theme: this I hope will make it easier to select the one most appropriate for the scene in rehearsal, but do not feel under any pressure to choose the 'right' exercise, for you cannot necessarily tell beforehand how useful it will be. If it helps, that is good, if not, it will no doubt define something and will lead you to another which suits better. However, I would say that those from Chapter Nine onwards, because they are involved in the subtleties of motive and situation, are possibly best done when you are a little way into rehearsal – you just have to experiment. Here is the list:

Chapter Five – The Voice Itself
sitting down in the voice

Chapter Six – Collective Work
story-telling
passing text round
jostling
being 'on' the word

Chapter Seven – The Subtext
the world of the play
the vocabulary of character
dialogue – interchange between characters
ladders of thought
the word itself

Chapter Eight – Structures
rhythm and metre
speech structures
vowel and consonant lengths
patterns of rhetoric
prose rhythms

Chapter Nine – Dialogue and Resistance
Dialogue:
  finding a shared shape and music
  repeating phrases
Obstacles:
  restraining the actor
  reaching across
  building barriers
  getting attention
  manipulation

Chapter Ten – Landscapes of the Mind
Imagination/memory:
  inner v. outer landscape
  spaces in your mind
  drawing a picture
  imaging
Haunting/loneliness:
  trying to make contact with someone
  running away – ghosts

Chapter Eleven – Alignments and Symbols
Politics:
  finding relationships
  conspiracy
  oneupmanship
  playing games
Concretising thought:
  making an object symbolise a thought
  building an altar or a sculpture to represent feelings/
    ideas
  finding the centre line – the search for justification

Chapter Twelve – Working the Space
exploring the resonance of the space in terms of the
  required volume and muscularity

All these exercises have evolved out of working with actors in rehearsal, on particular speeches or scenes, and they change according to the needs of the moment. They are to be viewed simply as a starting point to open up the possibilities, and they can be shifted around and improvised on to suit the work in hand. They will always change when the imagination takes over.

A word of comfort: the collective exercises on voice and text in the first chapters are more complicated to set out and explain than they are to do. And just to reiterate – if time can be set aside at the beginning of a rehearsal period to explore them so that their purpose is fully understood and heard, then different exercises, or parts of exercises, can be done quite briefly throughout rehearsal in order to keep feeding the work and keeping us open to the possibilities. It will then become a central part of our thinking and our approach – and of the words living inside.

5 The Voice Itself

We have to keep reminding ourselves that we, as actors, are continually in the process of telling a story, and the audience wants to hear that story. We still want to be told stories even in this age of Internet technology; it is surely something primitive within us which will never be blotted out, and the voice has the power to capture the interest of the audience. It is the voice that can draw us into the story, however offbeat or minimal the language being used.

Therefore, we have to practise ways of feeling at home with the voice, of hearing your own vibration, of what I call 'sitting down' in it, and this is partly to do with not being too ready, and of hearing fully what you are responding to, i.e. letting the beat come back to you so that it can be fully absorbed before you respond and take it on further or change its direction according to the need of the moment.

Now because the actor is always under pressure to be interesting, to keep the play alive, this is difficult to achieve. There is an overall speed which the director quite rightly needs to attain, but this must not be at the expense of the thought being fully realised, or the voice being rooted. So we have to practise feeling the voice rooted, however up to speed we are and whatever movement is required.

So, besides the work that is done by each actor individually on their own voice, it is important that some voice work is done within the group, for not only does it set up a group confidence, it also opens our ears in a very specific way to the questions and problems that everyone has with their voice, and makes us more aware of how to deal with them. It is also very good to realise that everyone has unanswered questions about their own voice, and things that they are not sure about. As you will see, quite a lot of the work can be done in pairs: this is important in that it sharpens our awareness of our own bodies and of our own reactions to the exercises.

These are the exercises that I would do with a company in rehearsal, but of course every voice teacher will have different ways of working – there is no one right way. As Gwynneth Thurburn used to say, 'There is only breath.' However, I thought it might be useful to set them down in full. In a rehearsal situation time is limited, but if every so often you go through one whole sequence in order to get the full benefit of the work, at other times you can choose a short sequence which seems useful for that particular moment in rehearsal. It is, for example, particularly useful to do those exercises which are about feeling the vibrations in the body, plus those sharpening the consonant muscularity before you begin rehearsals.

As you will see, each section has a number of variations. For instance, the initial preparation exercises on breathing and relaxation can either be done on the floor or in chairs. I have set out the one in chairs first as I think it helps to pinpoint very specifically all the parts of the body involved.

EXERCISES

Breathing and relaxation – in chairs (sequence one)
Stand up and spread round the room. Have a good stretch and a shake up.

Get into pairs and take one chair between you. One sit and one stand.

Those seated – take time to get comfortable on the chair with your seat fully grounded. Do not sit on the front part only as this will arch your back. Feel the weight spread over the whole of your seat.

Backs: Those standing – I want you to feel your partner's spine, so put one hand down their back slowly but firmly, making sure it is straight.

With the fingers of one hand, work down each knob of the spine, pressing firmly but gently on each one so that you feel each part of the spinal column.

Shoulders: Now put your hands firmly on your partner's shoulders, pinching down each shoulder. Put one hand firmly on the front of the right shoulder to support it, and with the heel of the other hand press that shoulder out so that you feel it widening.

Repeat this several times.

Now to the other shoulder and do the same.

Heads: Those sitting – drop your head forward, keeping your chin in. Feel the pull in your neck. Now pull your head up slowly, keeping your chin in.

Repeat this, focusing on the muscles in the back of the neck.

Now do it wrong once so that you turn your head up with the chin out – you will feel the difference.

Let your head drop to one side and stretch. Then to the other side and stretch. Pull up, moving your head in a circle very gently to feel it loosen – like ball-bearings on top of the spine.

Those standing – support your partner's chin very gently, and with the other hand holding the neck, very minimally move their head round so that it feels loose. Then with the hand on the back of the neck, gently pull the head up through the spine so that you stretch the back and feel the elasticity in the spine.

Repeat twice. All this must be done gently but firmly, and be particularly careful when supporting the chin as any pressure there will immediately make your partner protective of their head, and so tense up.

Now put one hand on each shoulder, and those sitting lift your shoulders about half an inch, then drop, then take a moment to let go.

Repeat this, taking your time. The important thing about this is that you notice the moment between dropping the shoulders and then taking a moment to let them settle that bit more. This is the feeling that you need to remember so that you can recapture it at any moment – any moment you feel tense. It is particularly useful just before you go on stage.

It is good to shake the shoulders up and down vigorously once or twice now – you will notice that you will not get the same sense of letting go as when you do it slowly and quietly, taking time to notice when they settle. Both partners will notice the difference.

This is really an important sequence – to experience fully that sense of the shoulders completely letting go, yet straight and in a good position.

Arms: Those standing – I want you to feel the weight of each arm. Go to one side and lift the upper arm gently. Hold a moment until you feel its full weight – it may take time. Then lift the arm from the wrist and shake gently – again to feel the weight. Lay the hand back on the lap.

Repeat with the other arm. Take time to feel the full weight of each arm.

Breathing: Those standing – put your hands on your partner's ribs where they are at their widest, thumb on the spine and hands round the side of the ribs. Hold quite firmly.

Those sitting – breathe in slowly through your nose, feeling your ribs widening against your partner's hands. (Breathing in through the nose stimulates the ribs.) Open your mouth wide and sigh out – keeping the throat open. Consciously empty right out and take a moment to feel the need to breathe. Breathe in – and then open and sigh out. Whenever you breathe out, either sighing or slowly to a count of 10 or 15, be sure that your throat is open and that you are not controlling it there in any way – there should be no scraping sound.

Repeat, only this time breathing out slowly to the count of 10. Repeat, humming out to the count of 10. Repeat, singing out on different vowels, e.g. OO, OH, AH, AY, EE, I.

Rest a moment, then when ready, repeat, increasing the outgoing breath to 15 counts.

You can extend this to 20 counts when you are ready.

Those standing – during these exercises focus on the movement of the ribs, but keep checking the shoulders and neck to see if there is tension. If there is tension, gently release it. Also, when your partner is singing out, gently tap both the chest and the back so that you both feel the vibrations in the body.

When all this is finished, change positions and repeat.
Remember:

- It is very important that each time you breathe out you take that moment to consciously sigh everything out and wait for a split second in order to feel the need for the next breath. This not only stimulates the intake of the next breath, but it earths you and stops you rushing.

- We are breathing out to the counts of 10, 15 and even 20, not in order to control the breath – for in the end, the thought will do that – but in order to stimulate the ribs so we open their capacity to the full.

What is important about this exercise is that we are stretching the ribs so that we can become aware of resonating space in the chest, for it is this space that gives the voice its body and its weight and its true vibration. It is this resonance that gives us confidence in our own sound.

Also remember that everyone has a different capacity, so do not worry if you do not seem to be taking in as much as the next person. What matters is that you feel the elasticity in your own ribs and that they respond to your need for breath – and that you get the maximum capacity out of them.

I do not think we use the rib breath consciously any more when we are acting, but it is there when we need it. Our concentration must be on the stomach breath and on rooting our voice down to the centre. Nevertheless, it is important that we can always feel our ribs flexible and open so that the chest resonance remains intact.

Breathing and relaxation – on the floor (sequence two)
Stand up and spread round the room. Have a good stretch and shake your body. Find a good space on the floor.

Backs: Partner One – lie on the floor. Crook your knees up with your feet about a foot apart and your knees straight. Decide whether you feel more comfortable with your legs crooked or flat – usually your back feels more comfortable when they are up. Feel your back spread fully across the floor, i.e. there should be no arch in the middle of the back. Take time to feel your weight spreading across the floor – do not hurry this. Feel your shoulders free and your arms and wrists free.

Partner Two – check your partner's back to feel it spread. Make sure your partner is comfortable and that their neck is even along the floor. If their neck is arched back, put a book under their head – not a thick one, but just so the head feels adjusted and comfortable. Now one at a time lift each arm, first from the elbow and then the wrist, taking time to feel its weight.

Shoulders: With one hand support one shoulder at the back, lifting it slightly, and with the other hand hold the top half of the arm and roll the shoulder joint round off the floor quite vigorously. Lay the shoulder out flat across the floor, feeling it wide and spread.

Repeat with the other shoulder. The aim is to get the top part of the back to spread across the floor and be free of tension.

Heads: Lift the head a couple of inches – turn gently to one side, and then to the other, then back to the middle, making sure the neck feels free. Always deal gently with the head as one feels very protective about it. Now pull the head gently but firmly so that you feel the spine lengthening. You will probably feel it stretch about an inch. Then lay the head back down on the floor.

Those on the floor will now feel their backs comfortably long and wide across the floor. Try to keep this feeling when doing all the exercises.

Ribs: Partner Two put your hands on your partner's ribs and those lying repeat the sequence of breathing exercises that we did in the chair, always taking time to breathe everything out before you take the next breath in, and also to feel the resonance in the chest and back.

When putting your hands on their ribs, take care to keep your fingers together, and press gently round the sides of the ribs, so that you will feel them widening as they breathe in.

When they hum out, test the vibration in the chest.

Stomachs: We have exercised the ribs and hopefully they should remain open and free. Now for the next step: put your hand on your partner's stomach below the waist so that you feel the movement of the stomach breath.

Those lying: breathe down, feeling that breath go as deep as possible. Breathe out gently through an open mouth. Repeat, but this time breathe out through a sustained 'F' sound, so that you feel the channel of breath coming through from the stomach being resisted by the lips. This will make you aware of the starting point of the breath and how that connects with the sound.

Repeat this – breathing out on 'V' – here you will feel vibration on the lips and in the chest. Repeat a couple of times so that you feel this vibration fully in your head – it should even make your ears tickle.

These exercises will help you to feel the stomach breath connect with the sound.

Now breathe down, then very gently sing out on 'OO' – any note – but again being conscious of that breath starting the sound. It should be a gentle sound and not a fully sung one. Repeat on different vowels.

The partner: keep checking on the shoulders and neck, then let them lie free for a moment so that they can focus on feeling the back being long and wide.

Those lying: when you are ready, roll over and, keeping your back as open and free as possible, stand up slowly. Stand for a moment to feel your back wide and long, as it was on the floor.

Change round and repeat.

Breathing and relaxation – working individually (sequence three)

We will begin with floor work. Find a space and lie down. Make sure you have plenty of room, plus if you need a book under your head, have one ready. Have a good stretch and get comfortable.

As before, crook your knees up and decide whether you feel more comfortable with them crooked up or flat. Whichever way, the important thing is to feel your back in touch with the floor all the way down, and not arched at any point. Take time to feel your back wide and long, and to feel your weight across the floor.

Now lift each shoulder one at a time – roll it round and lay it across the floor – feeling it widen as you lay it down.

Then your head – move it to one side then to the other, then back to the middle. Press it gently back into the floor, then release it and feel the difference. Repeat this. Take a moment to think of your head lengthening out of your back, your shoulders free and your back spread.

Now put the backs of your hands on your ribs at the side: I purposely say the backs of your hands because the wrists will be more relaxed that way. Press your hands firmly against your ribs, keeping your shoulders free. Breathe in slowly through your nose, then open your mouth and sigh out, keeping your throat open. Take a moment to sigh everything out and wait for that need to breathe. Repeat this. Keeping this format, breathe in and then breathe out slowly to the count of 10. Repeat, this time humming out for 10 – moving your lips round while you hum so that you feel the vibrations.

Breathe in, then sing out on 'OO' and subsequently on 'OH', 'AH', 'AY' and 'I', always feeling your throat open.

You can go through the same sequence making the outgoing breath longer, i.e. for 15 counts and then 20. This is simply to stimulate the ribs and get them working.

Centring the breath (sequence four)

To focus on the stomach breath, put one hand on your stomach below the waist so that you can feel how deep you can take your breath into the centre – for that centre is the starting point of the voice. Take the breath down, feel the muscles in the stomach allowing for that movement, and then sigh out.

Repeat, breathing out through 'F'. Repeat, breathing out on 'V', feeling its vibration. Repeat, breathing out on 'Z', then on a voiced 'TH'.

Each time feel the vibration in the front of the face and in the chest. Keep your head and shoulders free. Breathe down and sing out very gently on 'OO' – the important thing is to feel the breath starting the sound – it should be absolutely smooth with no glottal attack at any time. Repeat this sequence on any vowels you want – just get familiar with the sensation of the breath touching out the sound.

When this feels steady, take your time and roll over on to your side and stand up. Stand for a moment, feeling the length and breadth of the back as it was on the floor. Now roll your head very minimally round – hardly moving it but feeling it absolutely free. Imagine you have a string coming down from the ceiling and attached to the middle of your head. Imagine that it is pulling you up on to your toes, so that you can feel the back lengthening. Do this a couple of times, making sure that your neck is absolutely free and your chin neither lifted up nor pulled back. Now stand normally and bounce a couple of times on your knees, feeling them free. Put your hand on your stomach below the waist and breathe down then out through 'F'.

Repeat and out through 'V'.

Now, keeping your hand on your stomach, speak 'OO' three times. This is to be done on one breath but with a little space between each vowel. Just feel the breath touching the vowel out each time and starting the sound. Repeat on any of the following vowels – OH, OW, AH, AY, EE, I. This is the feeling you need to find each time – that the breath is starting the sound.

It is that feeling of rooting the voice that we have to practise and get familiar with, so that it becomes integral to how we use our voice.

Now we are going to practise this with movement, so that however much you move you can still at will connect with the breath.

Get into a circle and put an object down on the floor in the middle. Breathe down – feel the breath rooted then sing out on 'OO' three times, aiming the vowels at the object like three darts. Let the breath touch each vowel out one at a time.

Then run to somewhere else in the room, stop, focus on the object and sing out again on another three vowels. Do this several times, each time getting still and connecting with the breath before you sing the vowels.

You can do other things, e.g. jump a couple of times before you sing the vowels or get into a very tense position yet keep the vowels open and free. The important thing is to get familiar with the feeling of connecting with the breath and rooting the sound down however much you may be moving around. You can vary this by aiming the vowels at different points in the room, or even at a point out of the window.

Finding the vibration of the body (sequence five)

Each person sit down and take time to feel your body weight on the floor. Set up a hum together and rock on the floor, feeling your seat vibrating with the hum, then open the mouth and sing it out on 'AH'. Experiment with this vibration by verbalising 'V' and feeling the vibration on your lips.

Then hum again – this time lifting your seat off the floor and bouncing it several times – also to feel the vibration.

Now, settling quite comfortably, and with your hand on your lower stomach, breathe down into your stomach, checking the incoming breath with your hand. Sigh out through an open mouth – there should be no sound in the throat of the breath being tight in any way. It should be quite free. This time, as you breathe in, rock slightly back, and come forward as you breathe out.

Repeat this, but now with the palms of your hands in front of your mouth and listen to the breath as it comes out – you will be able to hear a warm vowel resonance. Repeat this and as you breathe out, touch it out with sound on 'AH' three times. Feel that sound coming from the centre.

This is an excellent way of checking that free passage of sound.

It is good to put this into practice on a few lines of text – something you are familiar with or have been working on – not to make sense of it but simply to feel the vibration of the words in your body. Speak it again, rolling round on your seats and bouncing on them. Then get on all fours and speak it into the floor – this is an excellent way of feeling the resonance in your chest.

Also in this position, sound out the voiced consonants 'V', 'Z', 'TH', 'gegege', 'dedede', 'bebebe', etc., always feeling the vibration bouncing off the floor.

Muscularity (sequence six)

Now stand up, and again sound out the voiced consonants as above, slightly overdoing them so that you feel the resonance coming to the front of the face.

Each time you do 'bebebe', feel the whole of your lips pressing together and exploding apart for each 'be' sound. You need to feel it very strong and firm.

We have got to engage with this muscularity all the time: this is what gives the words their spring and their cost.

It is this muscularity which will define them, yet without making them noticeable:

Now let us test out the vowel sounds, first those made with the rounding of the lips and the words in the same vowel sequence:

OO	00	OH	AW	o	OW
boot	cook	hope	fought	cot	mouth
cool	hood	gold	fall	fond	howl

Cup your hands round your mouth as you speak them to feel the sound in the front of the mouth. Now experiment with the vowel lengths: you will notice that the vowel is longer when followed by a voiced consonant, plus if there is more than one voiced consonant, it lengthens accordingly:

e.g.	feet	feel	field	fields	
	chase	chain	change	changed	etc.

How we hear these different lengths is vital because it changes the movement within the line, and it is this variety within the metre that makes the speaking infinitely varied.

Now the tongue vowels – those made with different placings of the tongue:

AH	u	ER	a	e	AY	i	EE	I
pass	hut	hurt	hat	wet	waste	hit	heat	height
harm	hull	bird	mad	well	shelve	fill	feel	strive

It is important that we recognise that everyone will hear these vowels differently according to their own particular dialect – but the point is we must make ourselves constantly alert to the muscularity in the language whatever the variants.

The text (sequence seven)

In the next section on story-telling, the main piece of text I want to look at is the speech of the Player King in *Hamlet*: it is the most wonderful piece of narrative, full of rich images and textures. It is Aeneas's Tale to Dido which Hamlet remembers the actor performing once: it makes an excellent piece to test out all the work that we have been doing on breathing and relaxation. Here is the first section which Hamlet himself starts off:

> The rugged Pyrrhus, he whose sable arms,
> Black as his purpose, did the night resemble
> When he lay couched in th'ominous horse,
> Hath now this dread and black complexion smeared
> With heraldy more dismal. Head to foot
> Now is he total gules, horridly tricked
> With blood of fathers, mothers, daughters, sons,
> Baked and impasted with the parching streets,
> That lend a tyrranous and a damned light

To their lord's murder: roasted in wrath and fire,
And thus o'ersized with coagulate gore,
With eyes like carbuncles, the hellish Pyrrhus
Old grandsire Priam seeks.

Hamlet, II.ii.

The speech is about the murder of King Priam by Pyrrhus during the fall of Troy: on first reading it may seem difficult, but if you read it through two or three times, getting your mouth round the words, the story will become quite clear. You may not be familiar with one or two heraldic allusions like 'gules', which is a heraldic red, and 'tricked' which means 'spotted': but apart from that the words are self-explanatory, i.e. 'impasted' meaning 'turned to paste'.

Progression (sequence eight)

Prop the book up on a table or shelf where it is easy to read. Shake your shoulders to feel free. Bounce down on your knees so that you feel your weight. Take a moment to feel your back long, neck free and shoulders settled.

Now put one hand on your stomach below the waist and fill down, then out through 'F' to feel that channel of breath. Breathe down again and this time speak the first three lines of the text down to 'th'ominous horse'. Take time to breathe down, then read the next line and a half down to 'dismal'.

Breathe down again and read two and a half lines to 'sons'. Breathe down and go to 'murder'. Breathe down and go to the end.

Repeat this so that you get familiar with the routine, then try it in three breaths so that you do the first four and a half lines to 'dismal' then to 'murder' and then to the end. Each time you go through it, it will get easier.

This is the structure of the exercise and it is good to do through once in this way so that you experience its progression. Before you do it sitting on the floor, it is good to come together in the group and experience together the muscularity of the consonants and their vibration. So get into a fairly close group and vibrate a few voiced consonants together, then repeat words like 'rugged', 'sable arms', 'ominous horse'. Go through the lines feeling out the muscular words – they can be slightly exaggerated in order to feel them forward in the mouth. Feel every consonant vibration, particularly those in the middle of words, e.g. 'eg' in 'rugged', 'b' in 'sable'.

Further resonance (sequence nine)

As in the sitting exercise we have just done, take time to feel your weight on the floor. Rock gently – letting your seat go – and with your hand on your lower stomach to focus the intake of breath, breathe down and then out through 'F'. Then breathe down and speak the text with the same phrasing we have just practised.

When this feels comfortable, repeat, rolling round on your seat and bouncing, feeling the vibration on the floor.

You can also do it on all fours, feeling the resonance in the chest and the consonants bouncing back from the floor. Or you can take one line and roll round on the floor, feeling the resonance through the body.

All the work so far can be done together as a group: this sometimes takes a little getting used to as you cannot hear your own voice on its own, i.e. by itself, but that in a way is an advantage because it makes you focus on how you are using your breath rather than on the end result of how your voice sounds.

All these exercises are useful in some way for getting the voice ready: ready for whatever space you may be working, and for whatever text you may be speaking. It is this connection between the movement of the language and how it helps to shape the thought that is vital.

Sitting down in the voice (sequence ten)

This seems all too simple, but the result can in its way be revelatory. Although the change in the voice may seem minimal, there is something about that sense of experiencing the voice centred which gives an authority to the sound – a sense of presence – however quietly you may be speaking.

Work in pairs. One sit on a chair, and the other sit on the floor just a few inches in front, but with your back to your partner.

Those on chairs, support your partner's back with your hands.

Those on the floor, feel your weight on the floor, then lean back against your partner. Do not push but simply feel them supporting your back.

Those on chairs, take time to feel their weight.

Those on the floor, put one hand on your stomach and breathe down. Feel it settle, then breathe out through 'F' so that you feel that channel of air, then fill down again and start to speak the text. As you speak, roll very minimally on your seat to keep that sense of weight and to feel the sound centred right down.

Those on chairs, do not let them push or lean too far – simply keep making them aware of their weight and their voice rooted.

Both partners, listen for the resonance.

When you feel comfortable with this, we need to take it on a step further by hearing the voices individually. This I know takes time but is worth doing as it tells us so much about how to centre the breath, plus it allows people to hear the difference in their voice, which in turn gives you the spur to achieve it.

So, the person sitting, choose a piece of text, preferably something that you know and to which you have a personal response – a sonnet is ideal. Speak it in this position, feeling your weight against your partner, centring the breath, and getting a real sense of sitting in the voice.

This takes a little time but you will feel a great sense of freedom.

I have taken this text from Hamlet to illustrate how you can work the breath, but of course there are countless pieces of text you can use, such as Prospero's speech from *The Tempest* in Act V, scene i, beginning:

Ye elves of hills, brooks, standing lakes and groves . . .

or a speech from *Titus Andronicus*, Act III, scene i, beginning:

If there were reason for these miseries . . .

or one of Berowne's speeches from *Love's Labour's Lost*, plus any of the texts we will be using in the next chapter. It is just important to practise.

I have set out the exercises very fully, but do not be daunted: as I have already said, choose a sequence that seems appropriate for the time. And take comfort – it takes much longer to read them through and digest them than it does to do them!

6 Collective Work

As you will have gathered, I believe that collective work on text is central to the rehearsal of a play, because it not only opens our ears to the possibilities but it allows us to be provoked by the language. It frees the actor from the responsibility of making the sense clear and opens out the humour and the roughness.

Because how we read a text and how we interpret it is seen as an individual function, which of course to a large extent it is, we do not see the value of this work. Many directors use a movement person and realise the value of bringing a company together through movement work, which not only makes the actor more expressive physically but helps to create a company feeling. I believe this collective work is just as important for text, for it makes us listen in a different way, it makes us bolder in tackling text and gives a spontaneity to the speaking.

The first two sections, story-telling and passing text around, are quite similar in that they are both about heightening our sensibility to language and our physical involvement in the uttering of it. They are about listening both to the text and to each other, and hearing how we each respond to the sound of language in different ways: and it is exciting to hear how we each find a different truth in its sound.

The second two sections, jostling and being what I like to call 'on' the word, help us release the action of the words, and not only the action but the aggression, for while we are speaking we are being assertive. We so often forget that when we are speaking we are always speaking against something, and be-cause we work so much on our own we forget that and the

speaking is passive. By speaking against something I mean that even if we are agreeing with what someone has said, we are in fact agreeing against the opposite, and once we have spoken we cannot take it back – it is as active as that.

The work is also about listening, and allowing for that moment of recognition of what has been said in order to fuel our own response which will then take us further on the journey. This last point may seem elementary, a basic premise for the actor, but in practical terms we all know how difficult it is not to prepare our reply before we have let the words from the previous speaker drop into our consciousness and inform that reply. This limits the possibilities for it does not allow for the switches of thought – or the surprise. And that moment of hearing and of recognition does not slow us up because it provides the spur to the next thought, which in turn gives another dynamic and a new speed, but because we are so afraid of letting the ball drop we have to keep testing this out for ourselves in order to really believe it. But we must remember that the audience also needs these moments of recognition, for these are the moments that keep their curiosity alive.

But perhaps the prime reason for this work on text is that it gives us the opportunity to play with language, to hear and feel what the sounds themselves do – how the texture and rhythm of the language not only add to the meaning but also evoke a response from both speaker and listener, and we must take that response seriously for it is part of the truth of the writing.

STORY-TELLING

I want to set down three pieces of text which I have found useful to work on specifically in terms of telling a story: you will, I am sure, find many others. I usually work on them in the following way:

(i)   First we all read it through together to get familiar with the story – clearing up any difficult points as we go.

(ii) Then we get into a circle and divide it up into phrases so that each person has a part of the story to tell. We then speak it through a couple of times so we become familiar with the order.

(iii) Then focusing on the story, we start to move round the room while speaking, first gently and then more vigorously.

(iv) We then run, and as each person speaks they jump on a chair or a table and make a gesture relating to the story.

(v) Lastly, we get into a circle, each person coming into the middle of the circle to tell their part of the story. In this way we come back to the simplicity of the story itself.

The aim, as you see, is to involve the body in the language, to find its extravagance and its physicality, and when that is explored fully to then bring the language right down by speaking it quietly, engaging each other with the story, yet keeping all the size and vividness which was discovered in the violence of the movement. With an eye on time as always, I want to say that the work does not have to be done all at once but can be done at intervals, and this in a way is better, for its value lies in opening our ears to the sensuousness of the language – i.e. how meaning and sound are interrelated – and how each person finds a confidence in their own voice by taking the time that is needed to respond to the thought. We need time to absorb this so that it can gradually feed into the rehearsal process.

And what better text to work on than the speech of the Player King, to awaken our ears to the innate power of language, to its cadence and music, to its textures and rhythms? It is the most wonderful piece of primitive story-telling. And by working on something so big and so expansive we will open ourselves up in a way that is normally not possible, so that in simply speaking that language we may experience a freedom in the sound – and also perhaps an elation. We want to discover the size of the images which tell this epic story, yet keep it truthful to ourselves and appropriate to the time. And of course we need to look no further than Shakespeare for our instructions as, two scenes later in Act III, scene ii when the actors are about to perform the play to the court, Hamlet/Shakespeare exhorts them with the following words:

Speak the speech, I pray you, as I pronounced it to you, trippingly on the tongue. But if you mouth it as many of our players do, I had as lief the town crier spoke my lines.

And further on:

> Be not too tame neither. But let your own discretion be your tutor. Suit the action to the word, the word to the action, with this special observance, that you o'erstep not the modesty of nature. For anything so o'erdone is from the purpose of playing, whose end, both at the first and now, was and is to hold, as 'twere, the mirror up to nature, to show virtue her own feature, scorn her own image, and the very age and body of the time his form and pressure. Now this o'erdone, or come tardy off, though it make the unskilful laugh, cannot but make the judicious grieve; the censure of the which one must in your allowance o'erweigh a whole theatre of others.

I think we are so familiar with this piece of text that we do not always read it carefully enough: for it says so much to us now not only about how we have to continually negotiate between style and content, all the things we have been talking about, but also warns us not to be seduced by cheap reactions, by people wanting to be entertained, for this belittles the gravity of the work. We must not make 'the unskilful laugh' or the 'judicious grieve'. So often this speech is cut or done in an exaggerated style which makes people laugh, and I believe this to be a betrayal of something very fundamental to this play – and to our perception of language. I remember Edward Bond once said: 'A child does not play for frivolous reasons: an actor does not act for frivolous reason.'

So to the story – Aeneas's Tale to Dido, Act II, scene ii. I am setting the first Player's speech out initially without the lines of dialogue between Hamlet and Polonius, because it is the story which is central to our purpose. However, we will look at those interjections afterwards because, as always with Shakespeare, it is those seemingly unimportant remarks which tell us so much about the societal realities of the time, and these hold particular significance in terms of perceptions of theatre and our belief in language – both for that time and for today.

FIRST PLAYER   'Anon he finds him,
              Striking too short at Greeks. His antique sword,
              Rebellious to his arm, lies where it falls,
              Repugnant to command. Unequal matched,
              Pyrrhus at Priam drives, in rage strikes wide,

But with the whiff and wind of his fell sword
Th'unnervèd father falls. Then senseless Ilium,
Seeming to feel this blow, with flaming top
Stoops to his base, and with a hideous crash
Takes prisoner Pyrrhus'ear. For lo! his sword,
Which was declining on the milky head
Of reverend Priam, seemed i'th'air to stick.
So as a painted tyrant Pyrrhus stood,
And like a neutral to his will and matter
Did nothing.
But as we often see, against some storm,
A silence in the heavens, the rack stand still,
The bold winds speechless, and the orb below
As hush as death; anon the dreadful thunder
Doth rend the region; so after Pyrrhus' pause,
A rousèd vengeance sets him new a-work,
And never did the Cyclops' hammers fall
On Mars's armour, forged for proof eterne,
With less remorse than Pyrrhus' bleeding sword
Now falls on Priam.
Out, out, thou strumpet Fortune! All you gods,
In general synod take away her power!
Break all the spokes and fellies from her wheel,
And bowl the round nave down the hill of heaven,
As low as to the fiends!'

EXERCISES

Now for the work. I am sure your instincts will tell you what to
do, but here is one way to proceed: First sitting down, preferably
on the floor, gently mutter the text through as a group several
times to get the gist of the story. Do not worry if you do not
understand every word literally. Look up what you must, but on
the whole it will become clear as you work it through together.
I want us to depend on our initial intuitive response to sound
and meaning rather than to a literal one.

When you are ready, get into a circle and divide the text up
into phrases: if this is done in a circle it makes it easier to
establish the order. As you divide it, keep the story as intact as
possible. It divides quite easily into either one line or one and a
half lines, though at the beginning of the piece it may have to
be two lines. How much text you get through will depend on

how many there are in the group, but let it take you as far as it can. You can always finish it off by speaking the end lines together as a group.

When it is divided up, proceed as follows: Take a good few minutes to get familiar with your own lines. You need to be sure of them. It is quite good to do this walking round the space. Then when it is time, all stand still and, wherever you are in the space, speak the lines in order.

When that becomes easy, do the same but now running round the space quite vigorously so the lines have to be quite big in order to reach everyone.

Repeat, but this time when it comes to your line, jump on a chair or a table, whatever is around, and make a gesture with your line as you speak it. The gesture will reflect your response to the story and this in turn will give the language size and space.

Then, when you are ready, get into a circle, quite an open one, and on your line spring into the middle and tell your section of the story. This can be with a gesture, and it can be as loud or as quiet as you want. The point about this progression is that by running and making a graphic gesture you will feel the size of the image, plus get a pleasure and a freedom out of releasing the language with the movement. Do it as many times as is helpful.

When it comes to telling the story in a circle then the central aim must be to tell it simply and truthfully, and this involves taking on board the line you were given and then passing your own line on to the next person, so that it expresses both your vision of the story without losing the unity and progression of the whole. It will then have a collective energy and a collective sensibility.

Now part of this collective response must be an awareness of what is happening in the language, its sounds and cadences, all of which serve the story – so let us go through it for these points:

- the first half-line needs to start low and slow to give time for our excitement to be stirred – and to get us ready for the story
- then those first six lines lift through, with their caesuras, their breaks, until we come to

- 'th'unnervèd father falls' – and that needs a moment's space for us to take in its tragic import
- on the way notice the onomatopoeic words – 'drives' and 'rage' set against 'whiff' and 'wind'
- it starts again with 'Then senseless Ilium . . .' Take time with 'Then' in order to arouse our curiosity
- know that Ilium is Troy – this gives Priam his status even though he is lacking his conscious sense
- 'and with a hideous crash' – the noise of Priam falling stops Pyrrhus in his tracks and we are suspended in time for a moment
- it then lifts through to 'Pyrrhus ear'
- and it goes on raising our curiosity and holding us in time from 'So as a painted tyrant Pyrrhus stood' until 'Did nothing'
- 'painted tyrant' is an amazing image, like someone in a painting, and it gives us that moment of hiatus, all for a moment is motionless – and Pyrrhus 'did nothing'
- and then the pitch lowers and we start again – 'But as we often see, against some storm . . .' and, taking its time, it relentlessly goes through to 'Now falls on Priam'
- notice the power of phrases like 'a roused vengeance sets him new a-work' and 'Mars's armour, forged for proof eterne . . .'
- 'forged' takes a long time to speak and is a powerful image plus 'proof eterne' is inexorable
- and then it flowers into rhetoric for the last five lines – 'Out, out, thou strumpet Fortune! . . .'
- how the rhythm and cadence emphasise the outrage contained in the ritualistic language

When you have explored this part of the story fully, we can then follow with the last part of the speech, which continues in spite of Polonius's comments:

But who, are woe! had seen the mobled Queen . . .
Run barefoot up and down, threatening the flames
With bisson rheum; a clout upon that head
Where late the diadem stood; and for a robe,
About her lank and all o'er-teemèd loins,

A blanket in the alarm of fear caught up –
Who this had seen, with tongue in venom steeped
'Gainst Fortune's state would treason have pronounced.
But if the gods themselves did see her then,
When she saw Pyrrhus make malicious sport
In mincing with his sword her husband's limbs,
The instant burst of clamour that she made,
Unless things mortal move them not at all,
Would have made milch the burning eyes of heaven
And passion in the gods.

I have always found it useful to work on this as a concerted piece of speaking, conducting it like a piece of music: what is useful about this is that we can hear together the very cadence in the language and how that in itself can move us emotionally.

So experiment with the sound as follows:

But who, are woe! had seen the mobled queen . . .

It starts on a low note with those extended first vowels – 'who' and 'woe' – we then get the rich image of 'mobled queen' which takes time to speak. It then lifts through to:

Run barefoot up and down, threatening the flames

The stress on 'run' gives the line a jagged quality which feeds the image of the demented movement of Queen Hecuba. 'Flames' has to lift through to the next line.

With bisson rheum; a clout upon that head
Where late the diadem stood; and for a robe,
About her lank and all o'erteemed loins,
A blanket in the alarm of fear caught up –

'Rheum' finishes off one thought and rests for a moment, then 'a clout upon that head'. This image isolates time for a moment and is strangely up in the air, and because it is so specific it is very moving – and the voice lifts it out accordingly. We then bring it back down for that dark and painful image – 'About her lank and all o'erteemed loins'. A woman who has born so many children – the pain of labour is in the language.

The story resumes on 'Who this had seen . . .' so the voice has to be based again, and then gradually lift through to 'would treason have pronounced.' That needs a moment for us to take it in.

> But if the gods themselves did see her then,
> When she saw Pyrrhus make malicious sport
> In mincing with his sword her husband's limbs,
> The instant burst of clamour that she made,
> Unless things mortal move them not at all,

The story then resumes, so the voice has to be based again, for this is the pith and climax of the story so we need to hold it back for a moment until we get to 'mincing with his sword'. Here the metre presses the action forward and lifts us relentlessly through to 'the instant burst of clamour'. Then there is that next moment of hiatus where time is still for a moment while we question the very ethos of the gods: 'Unless things mortal move them not at all . . .' And finally the firm restraint of the last lines which stress the gravity of the end:

> Would have made milch the burning eyes of heaven
> And passion in the gods.

Let us not forget that the image of the sword 'mincing her husband's limbs' is not outstanding in its cruelty; actions as cruel as this are being carried out every day somewhere in the world. It must therefore be fully realised.

I certainly would not be this didactic about approaching any other texts, but simply by pointing out the textures and rhythms, the cadences and suspensions within the lines, I wanted to make us aware of the power of the language and how that can be moving in itself. Of course, this is the way I hear it, and it may not be quite the way you want to hear it, but at least it will give us an awareness of that 'other' sound. And certainly, when I have worked this with a group, and I have done so many times, there comes a point when they feel moved by the actual speaking of it, for it brings together that sense of suspense in the story with the different weights and textures of the words, irrespective of dialect, and so strikes a common chord within us.

Now for those interruptions: the first one comes after the first piece of text which Hamlet speaks and then hands on to the First Player, saying, 'So proceed you.'

POLONIUS   Fore God, my lord, well spoken, with good accent and good discretion.

Ever the courtier, but nevertheless making judgement on the speaking, and not listening to the story itself.

The next one comes at the end of the second section – the main part of the story:

POLONIUS   This is too long
HAMLET   It shall to the barber's, with your beard.
               Prithee say on. He's for a jig or a tale of bawdry, or he sleeps.
               Say on. Come to Hecuba.
FIRST PLAYER   But who, ah woe! had seen the mobled Queen –
HAMLET   The mobled Queen?
POLONIUS   That's good. 'Mobled Queen' is good.
FIRST PLAYER   Run barefoot up and down

Hamlet, II.ii.

This time it is Hamlet who interrupts, but we feel it is because he needs to savour those words 'mobled queen' by speaking them aloud. Polonius then has to repeat them to show that he too appreciates them. So we get a whole picture of a man who cannot hear what is in the soul of the writing because he always has to be listening with his mind, judging and assessing, and thus reducing the value of the words. And we must ask ourselves, does this happen today? Do we spend so much time looking up the roots of the word, discussing the possible meanings, plus analysing the forms of the rhetoric, etc., that we cannot hear the worth of the word itself any more?

But Polonius's last comment is both perceptive and endearing, though I am not sure that was his intention, for when the First Player has spoken those final two lines:

Would have made milch the burning eyes of heaven
And passion in the gods.

Polonius says:

> Look whe'er he has not turned his colour, and has tears in's eyes.
> Prithee no more.

It is perceptive in that he sees what the speaking is doing to the Player, and it is ambivalent in that it may be that he does not approve of this show of emotion: but it is also endearing because we feel that for a moment he has been caught off-guard and he cannot quite deal with the situation. The central point for us is that the actual speaking of those lines, giving them their proper weight and time, can be a moving experience for the speaker. As Edward Bond said, 'Words must go through you'.

Now obviously we have to interpret all this sensibly and in context: this is an expansive and tragic piece of story-telling, and the speaking also needs to be expansive and extravagant, and it would not be appropriate within the context of a character. But what I want to say is that it is not to do with investing those words with an emotion that you feel they should have, rather it is being so 'on' the word that the word itself is the power within. And this can happen when we are being very quiet and simple – just the speaking of words, uttering them, can be a powerful act. This is equally so for modern text as for Shakespeare.

But I do stress that this awareness of the very nature of the language and how it is part of our own evolution is something we must have confidence in, and we must take this awareness into everything we do, for however minimal and naturalistic the text there is always that sound which takes us somewhere else – takes us into that other world.

There are many other stories which can be worked on in this way. One that I am particularly fond of is Shakespeare's 'Rape of Lucrece'. It is nowhere near as epic as the Player King, but the extremity of the feelings, though private, are just as extreme. It is a long poem so I have taken the section which tells of the actual rape: if this is too long for your purpose you can always work on a part of it. I do not want to be so specific about the speaking of it because I think the story will tell itself, but I simply want to alert us to various points in the verse. It is written in stanzas of seven lines each, the first five lines rhyming alternately and ending with a couplet, plus each line is made up of five iambic beats. Because it is a piece of narrative verse, the iambic beat does not have the same flexibility that it has in the dialogue of a play, and this regularity of metre points up the need to explore the different movements in each line. To find the syncopation within a line, like a piece of jazz, can be exciting, and this is how alive it can be. The verses I have set out are only a small part of the whole poem, and come quite near the beginning: the numbers beside each verse are solely for our own reference.

I would suggest that we would work on it in the same way as for the Player King, for although the writing is not so outgoing and overt, we still want to explore the measure of the feeling and the violence of the action, and I think this is found by being physically involved. We will notice how each verse takes us to a slightly different place, and we have to be given that split moment to recognise this: we are helped into this because so often the verse begins with a joining word such as 'now', 'but', 'then', 'this said', etc. I love the word 'now' – as soon as you have uttered it, 'now' is over! Plus you will notice how the final couplets either resolve that part of the story or are a reflection of the situation: whatever, they lend a slightly different angle on the story.

V. 1 Takes us straight into the room – it has an ominous darkness about it, the darkness of sin. It sets the scene.
V. 2 Lifts the story and keeps our curiosity because it is not until the fifth line that we have the verb, i.e. we come to the point. Antitheses – 'fair' and 'foul' – and that word 'deflower', which is almost antithetical in itself.
V. 3 Then the suppressed assertion of his will, and how he argues his purpose through in antithetical terms –

blackest sin – absolution
love's fire – fear's frost
eye of heaven – misty night
shame – sweet delight

V. 4 Taking up the story again – with the implicit antithesis of his guilt and her innocence: this is highlighted by the images of the dove and the night-owl, and the serpent, with its sting. The story is suspended for a moment while these images are laid.

V. 5 Now back to the reality of the story, with its dark picture of the enclosed chamber with no escape.

Vv. 6 to 12 These stanzas suspend time by describing how her beauty first blinds him, and then excites him: images of extreme purity set against ugliness and sin.

V. 13 Then with the volatile change of tone and rhythm on 'As the grim lion fawneth o'er his prey . . .' we are back into the action and the violence of his intentions with words like 'hunger', 'rage', 'lust', 'mutiny', 'uproar', etc.

V. 14 In this verse the violence of the images and the intransigence of the rhythm leads us inevitably to the action – 'gives the hot charge' – and then the release – 'bids them do their liking' – and the sense of anarchic freedom.

From 'The Rape of Lucrece'

1.   Now is he come unto the chamber door
That shuts him from the heaven of his thought,
Which with a yielding latch, and with no more,
Hath barr'd him from the blessed thing he sought.   340
So from himself impiety hath wrought
    That for his prey to pray he doth begin,
    As if the heavens should countenance his sin.

2.   But in the midst of his unfruitful prayer,
Having solicited th'eternal power,   345
That his foul thoughts might compass his fair fair,
And they would stand auspicious to the hour,
Even there he starts – quoth he 'I must deflower.
    The powers to whom I pray abhor this fact;
    How can they then assist me in the act?   350

3.   'Then Love and Fortune be my gods, my guide!
My will is back'd with resolution.
Thoughts are but dreams till their effects be tried;
The blackest sin is clear'd with absolution;
Against love's fire fear's frost hath dissolution.   355
    The eye of heaven is out, and misty night
    Covers the shame that follows sweet delight.'

4.   This said, his guilty hand pluck'd up the latch,
And with his knee the door he opens wide,
The dove sleeps fast that this night-owl will catch.   360
Thus treason works ere traitors be espied.
Who sees the lurking serpent steps aside;

> But she, sound sleeping, fearing no such thing,
> Lies at the mercy of his mortal sting.

5.   Into the chamber wickedly he stalks,   365
> And gazeth on her yet unstained bed.
> The curtains being close, about he walks,
> Rolling his greedy eyeballs in his head.
> By their high treason is his heart misled,
>   Which gives the watchword to his hand full soon   370
>   To draw the cloud that hides the silver moon.

6.   Look as the fair and fiery-pointed sun,
> Rushing from forth a cloud, bereaves our sight;
> Even so, the curtain drawn, his eyes begun
> To wink, being blinded with a greater light;   375
> Whether it is that she reflects so bright
>   That dazzleth them, or else some shame supposed;
>   But blind they are, and keep themselves enclosed.

7.   O, had they in that darksome prison died,
>   Then had they seen the period of their ill!   380
> Then Collatine again by Lucrece' side
> In his clear bed might have reposed still;
> But they must ope, this blessed league to kill;
>   And holy-thoughted Lucrece to their sight,
>   Must sell her joy, her life, her world's delight.   385

8.   Her lily hand her rosy cheek lies under,
> Coz'ning the pillow of a lawful kiss;
> Who, therefore angry, seems to part in sunder,
> Swelling on either side to want his bliss;
> Between whose hills her head entombed is;   390
>   Where, like a virtuous monument, she lies,
>   To be admir'd by lewd unhallow'd eyes.

9.   Without the bed her other fair hand was,
> On the green coverlet; whose perfect white
> Show'd like an April daisy on the grass,   395
> With pearly sweat, resembling dew of night.
> Her eyes, like marigolds, had sheath'd their light,
>   And canopied in darkness sweetly lay,
>   Till they might open to adorn the day.

10.   Her hair, like golden threads, play'd with her breath –   400
> O modest wantons! wanton modesty! –
> Showing life's triumph in the map of death,
> And death's dim look in life's mortality.
> Each in her sleep themselves so beautify
>   As if between them twain there were no strife,   405

But that life liv'd in death, and death in life.

11.   Her breasts, like ivory globes circled with blue,
A pair of maiden worlds unconquered,
Save of their lord no bearing yoke they knew,
And him by oath they truly honoured.   410
These worlds in Tarquin new ambition bred,
    Who like a foul usurper went about
    From this fair throne to heave the owner out.

12.   What could he see but mightily he noted?
What did he note but strongly he admired?   415
What he beheld, on that he firmly doted,
And in his will his wilful eye he tired.
With more than admiration he admired
    Her azure veins, her alabaster skin,
    Her coral lips, her snow-white dimpled chin.   420

13.   As the grim lion fawneth o'er his prey,
Sharp hunger by the conquest satisfied,
So o'er this sleeping soul doth Tarquin stay,
His rage of lust by gazing qualified;
Slack'd, not suppress'd; for standing by her side,   425
    His eye, which late this mutiny restrains,
    Unto a greater uproar tempts his veins.

14.   And they, like straggling slaves for pillage fighting,
Obdurate vassals fell exploits effecting,
In bloody death and ravishment delighting,   430
Nor children's tears nor mother's groans respecting,
Swell in their pride, the onset still expecting,
    Anon his beating heart, alarum striking,
    Gives the hot charge and bids them do their liking.

Now for a complete contrast in content, style and period: this section from Lorca's 'Lament for Ignacio Sanchez Mejias' is so alive and vivid and different, it makes a wonderful piece to work on together. The poem is in four parts:

Cogida and Death
The Spilling of the Blood
Body Present
Absent Soul

They are all very good to work on, but this second part, 'The Spilling of the Blood', is the one I like to use because it is at once so vivid and so simple. In it he tells the story of his friend Mejias'

death, and the images he uses to describe each stage of his
passing take us into so many places – places both of dream and
of reality.

The section begins with the line 'I do not want to see it!' This
line is repeated a number of times throughout the sequence,
each time taking us deeper into that world. It is an epic piece of
story-telling in a modern idiom:

'The Spilling of the Blood'

I do not want to see it!

Tell the moon to come
for I don't want to see the blood
of Ignacio on the sand.

I do not want to see it!
The wide-open moon,
horse of the quiet clouds,
and the grey bullring of dream,
with willows at the barriers.
I do not want to see it!
For my memory scorches.
Call for the jasmines
with their little whiteness!
I do not want to see it!

The cow of the old world
passed her sad tongue
over a muzzle of blood
spilt on the sand,
and the bulls of Guisando,
half death, and half stone,
bellowed like two centuries
weary of treading the earth.
No.
I don't want to see it!

Ignacio climbs up the terraces
with all his death on his shoulders.
He looked for daybreak,
but there was no daybreak.
He seeks his own sure profile,
and a dream misleads him.
He sought his handsome body

and was faced with his unsealed blood.
Don't tell me to see it!
I don't want to feel the jet
each time with less force;
that jet that illumines
the rows of seats, and pours
over the corduroy and leather
of the thirsty multitude.
Who shouts to me to look?
Don't tell me to see it!

His eyes did not close
when he saw the horns near,
but the terrible mothers
lifted their heads.
And across the ranches
went a breath of secret voices
calling the heavenly bulls,
herd-leaders of the pallid mist.

There was no Prince in Seville
who could compare to him,
nor any sword like his sword
nor any heart so earnest.
Like a river of lions
his marvellous strength,
like a marble torso
his fine-drawn caution.
The air of Andalusian Rome
gilded his head
where his smile was a nard
of wit and of skill.
What a great bullfighter in the ring!
What a splendid mountaineer in the mountains!
How soft with the wheat-ears!
How hard with the spurs!
How tender with the dew!
How dazzling in the feria!
How tremendous with the last
banderillas of darkness!

But now he sleeps endlessly.
Now mosses and grass
are opening with sure fingers

the flower of his skull.
And his blood goes singing now,
singing by marshes and meadows,
sliding on frozen horns,
wavering soulless through the mist
stumbling on its thousand hoofs
like a long, dark sad tongue
till it forms a pool of agony
by the starry Guadalquivir.
Oh white wall of Spain!
Oh stubborn blood of Ignacio!
Oh nightingale of his veins.
No.
I don't want to see it!
There is no chalice that could hold it,
no swallows that could drink it,
no frost of light to cool it,
nor any song, nor flood of lilies,
there is no glass to cover it with silver
No.
I don't want to see it.

Again I would work on it in the same progression as with the Player King, so that you start by making it physically active, with gestures which can be quite dramatic in order to find the size of the feelings, and then to speak it very quietly in a circle so that you bring it back to its simplicity and its terrible truth. It is quite long, so you may only want to work in detail on the last part, beginning, say, from 'There was no prince in Seville.' Speak two lines each, and the very end can be done together in ritual form. There is both size and tenderness in the images, and it occupies such a wide space in our imagination that it is wonderfully uplifting to work on.

PASSING TEXT ROUND

Louis MacNeice wrote: 'In any poet's poem, the shape is half the meaning.' This is true not only of poetry but of all writing which asks for our imaginative involvement, for there is something in the sound which moves differently and takes us into another place. The focus in this section, then, is on listening for the shaping of the phrases, on the texture of vowels and consonants, so that an awareness of form becomes part of the way we approach text.

One of my first impressions of Peter Brook was seeing him work an exercise at the beginning of rehearsal: the group got into a circle and, using the first four and a half lines of Hamlet's soliloquy 'To be or not to be . . .', they spoke one word each round the circle, and they continued with this for some time until it became like one person speaking. This would be repeated in subsequent rehearsals. And the more I worked with actors, the more this exercise came back to me for it spoke so much about the need to be in tune with each other and listening for each other, not by any means to sound similar, but rather to keep the rhythm of the play and the rhythm of that world intact: for if the rhythm of the play is fractured then the world of the play is disturbed.

Now of course by rhythm I mean how the interplay between sense stress and metre stress, plus the length and weight of vowels and consonants, make for the infinite variety of movement within a single line of iambic pentameters. The wonderful thing is that you cannot pin rhythm down, you cannot make rules, and a line will vary each time you speak it – but our sense of that underlying rhythm will keep it centred. I like to do this work in a circle and keeping still, so we can totally focus on where these rhythms take us, and how they reinforce the meaning.

There are many pieces of text that I am sure you will want to try out, and they will be informed by the play you are working on, but here are five pieces which I like to use – four in verse and one in prose. These first two pieces illustrate the extremes of weight within one line: the first, a speech of Berowne's from *Love's Labour's Lost*, though serious and philosophical in content, has the most wonderful feeling of buoyancy and lightness. I have worked it through in *The Actor and the Text* but I think it is worth looking at again for these very qualities. In a very complex plot during which the men have turned against their loves, the king asks Berowne to prove to him and to the two young lords, Dumaine and Longaville, that their love is lawful and right. Berowne has a long speech in which he argues his case through. Here is a section of it:

BEROWNE   But love, first learnèd in a lady's eyes,
               Lives not alone immurèd in the brain
               But with the motion of all elements
               Courses as swift as thought in every power,
               And gives to every power a double power,
               Above their functions and their offices.
               It adds a precious seeing to the eye:
               A lover's eyes will gaze an eagle blind.
               A lover's ear will hear the lowest sound,
               When the suspicious head of theft is stopped.
               Love's feeling is more soft and sensible
               Than are the tender horns of cockled snails.
               Love's tongue proves dainty Bacchus gross in taste.
               For valour, is not Love a Hercules,
               Still climbing trees in the Hesperides?
               Subtle as Sphinx; as sweet and musical
               As bright Apollo's lute, strung with his hair.
               And when Love speaks, the voice of all the gods
               Make heaven drowsy with the harmony.
               Never durst poet touch a pen to write
               Until his ink were tempered with Love's sighs.
               O, then his lines would ravish savage ears,
               And plant in tyrants mild humility.
               From women's eyes this doctrine I derive:
               They sparkle still the bright Promethean fire;
               They are the books, the arts, the academes,
               That show, contain, and nourish all the world;
               Else none at all in aught proves excellent.
               Then fools you were these women to forswear,
               Or, keeping what is sworn, you will prove fools.
               For wisdom's sake, a word that all men love,
               Or for love's sake, a word that loves all men,
               Or for men's sake, the authors of these women,
               Or women's sake, by whom we men are men –
               Let us once lose our oaths to find ourselves,
               Or else we lose ourselves to keep our oaths.
               It is religion to be thus forsworn,
               For charity itself fulfils the law,
               And who can sever love from charity?
                                        Love's Labour's Lost, IV.iii.

As you will hear, the verse is very regular, i.e. there are no sudden eruptions, but there is such an interplay of vowel and consonant lengths which vary the movement of the lines that you are never conscious of it being regular – so listen out and experiment with these. And because Berowne is working through his argument and playing with ideas and being persuasive rather than forceful, there are few places where the sense stress actively goes against the metre stress. There are, of course, a few lines where the stress is broken at the beginning:

Courses as swift as thought in every power . . .

Or:

Never durst poet touch a pen to write . . .

But they soon even out through the second half of the line and, as in the following line, are often helped out by the caesura in the middle:

Subtle as Sphinx;/as sweet and musical . . .

Plus there are many places where the stress evens out over two words:

Love's feeling . . .
Love's tongue . . .

The length of the voiced consonants at the beginning enables us to lengthen out those first words and thus spread the stress.

All these points highlight the different movements in the lines, the syncopation, and the way you can poise on an unstressed word to give it added weight without actually breaking the metre. All this is interspersed with the texture of images:

the tender horns of cockled snails
For valour, is not Love a Hercules

Or the onomatopoeia of the line, 'A lover's ear will hear the lowest sound' or the sudden violence of, 'O, then his lines would ravish savage ears'. And then the wonderful buoyancy of those four lines beginning, 'They sparkle still the bright Promethean fire' Then as he winds up his argument, the regularity of the rhythm takes over in the last six lines and lifts it through.

> Then fools you were these women to forswear

This is followed by the repetition of:

> Or for love's sake . . .
> Or for men's sake . . .
> Or women's sake . . .

And finally:

> Or else we lose ourselves to find our oaths

Leading to the final definitive summing up of the last three lines:

> It is religion to be thus forsworn,
> For charity itself fulfils the law,
> And who can sever love from charity?

Our clue to Berowne, I think, is in the lines:

> Never durst poet touch a pen to write
> Until his ink were tempered with Love's sighs

By this we know that Berowne is steeped in literary allusions, and that all his images are not merely flights of romantic fancy, but have precision and wit and are part of his whole literary perception and his world. They therefore need to be accurately defined.

Start at the beginning and take one line each: speak it through quietly to yourselves to get familiar with it, and then speak it round in the circle. If you do this several times, each time you will hear different spaces, different rhythms – a different music. Whatever part of the text is left can be worked together to find the shape of the argument.

This second text could not be more different in rhythm and weight: it is a speech of Titus from *Titus Andronicus*. Titus has just learned of his daughter Lavinia's rape, and that her tongue has been cut out and her hands cut off: it erupts out of the extremity of his grief. In an exercise one cannot possibly plumb the depths of its import, nor should one even attempt to do so, but if we speak it round line by line we can hear something of the depth of feeling in the very rhythm and weight of the language and how it stretches out to encompass his grief. The fact that he is still expressing this grief in words means that he is still fighting, and we can hear that action in his words. We know he is still fighting because he does go on to plot the death of Tamora's two sons and serve them up to her in a pie. But what I want you to feel is just how much these vowels and consonants are stretched out in order to plumb his grief, and just how primal that is – and how it is a part of the ritual wailing in all languages.

TITUS   If there were reason for these miseries,
        Then into limits could I bind my woes.
        When heaven doth weep, doth not the earth o'erflow?
        If the winds rage, doth not the sea wax mad,
        Threatening the welkin with his big-swollen face?
        And wilt thou have a reason for this coil?
        I am the sea. Hark how her sighs doth blow.
        She is the weeping welkin, I the earth.
        Then must my sea be moved with her sighs,
        Then must the earth with her continual tears
        Become a deluge overflowed and drowned,
        For why? my bowels cannot hide her woes,
        But like a drunkard must I vomit them.
        Then give me leave; for losers will have leave,
        To ease their stomachs with their bitter tongues.
                                    Titus Andronicus, III.i.

Work this round in lines, listening for the different texture and rhythm in each line. In those first lines you will hear how the length of the vowels, coupled with the voiced consonants, many of them continuant, give the lines a tangible length and weight:

If there were reason for these miseries
. . . bind my woes

And how this weight takes us into the depth of his grief:

woes – weep – rage – sea

Even the short vowels are extended – 'wax mad'.

As in the late plays, the sense often breaks in the middle of the line, giving a caesura: the rhythm has a steadiness to it, an inexorability, and though there is one line that actively breaks the metre with the first word, 'Threatening the welkin with his big swollen face', the rest has to be negotiated, for many of the lines start with a poise between the first two words. In the first line, 'if' suspends for a moment to make us ready for the thought, and the stress could lie equally on the second word, 'there'. This happens a number of times.

Then there are a number of stressed syllables which fall together – 'winds rage', 'sea wax mad', and then the regular rhythm of the final six lines which add the finality.

The next two speeches I have worked through before in my last book, but here I want to look at the specific phrasing and find what we get from that: I want to make us aware of the shape of the thoughts, their different lengths and textures, and just how much that tells us about the state of the character. The first is from *Measure for Measure*: Claudio has been sentenced to death by Duke Angelo for sleeping with his betrothed Juliet before they were married. Angelo has told Isabella, Claudio's sister, that if she consents to sleep with him he will spare her brother's life: Isabella refuses. In this speech Claudio is begging his sister to reconsider her decision:

CLAUDIO   Ay, but to die, and go we know not where,
                To lie in cold obstruction and to rot;
                This sensible warm motion to become
                A kneaded clod; and the delighted spirit
                To bathe in fiery floods, or to reside
                In thrilling region of thick-ribbed ice,
                To be imprisoned in the viewless winds
                And blown with restless violence about
                The pendent world; or to be worse than worst
                Of those that lawless and incertain thought
                Imagine howling, 'tis too horrible.

The weariest and most loathed worldly life
That age, ache, penury, and imprisonment
Can lay on nature is a paradise
To what we fear of death.

Measure for Measure, III.i.

First read it through together several times so that the sense is clear: then read it round, keeping that sense going, but this time from punctuation mark to punctuation mark. What is important about this is that because you are separating each part of the thought, you hear how the whole thought moves, how it is continually moving forward and propelling to the next idea, yet going to different areas within that one thought. Now every edition of Shakespeare is edited differently and so will have different punctuation but that does not matter, for it will still open up the possibilities and will still focus on the syntax of the thought.

As you work through it, listen for those two vowels in the first line: 'Ay, but to die' Listen too for the antithetical thoughts:

delighted spirit – fiery floods
restless violence – pendent world

There is such texture in the language. The thoughts get longer and wilder as he describes his feelings until we get to ' 'tis too horrible', and then the relative calm of the last four lines which tie the thoughts up in a more philosophical vein. His turmoil of mind is tangible in this movement of language.

When you have handed it round several times in this way, go back and do it once working it line by line. This way, it will become even clearer how the movement of each line shifts.

Second this speech of Cordelia from *King Lear*: Cordelia, now Queen of France, has come to find Lear who has been turned out by her sisters and is now wandering on the heath. A sighting of him has just been reported to her and she has brought her soldiers with her. What is so wonderful about the speech is its mixture of tenderness, authority and wisdom – you know she is in touch with the earth.

CORDELIA   Alack, 'tis he! Why, he was met even now
As mad as the vexed sea, singing aloud,

Crowned with rank fumiter and furrow-weeds,
With hardokes, hemlock, nettles, cuckoo-flowers,
Darnel, and all the idle weeds that grow
In our sustaining corn. [*To soldiers*] A century send
    forth:
Search every acre of the high-grown field
And bring him to our eye.   [*Exeunt soldiers*]
[*To Doctor*]   What can man's wisdome
In the restoring his bereavèd sense?
He that helps him, take all my outward worth.
                           King Lear, IV.iv.

Take the same progression as for Claudio's speech: in this way you will hear the rhythms of those first two lines, and the openness of those vowels, 'why', 'mad', 'sea', 'aloud'. Then you will hear how the rhythm becomes regular as she names the plants, plus the words 'sustaining corn', which have such strength.

Then her rhythm changes when she is giving orders to the soldiers, and then she comes back to the rooted philosophy of the last two and a half lines. There is also a weight to that word 'can' for it holds the meaning of two words, i.e. 'what can man do'. We learn so much simply by hearing those rhythms, they then become inseparable from the meaning.

JOSTLING

Now for something quite anarchic and different: these next two sections can be done collectively when you come together as a group, or during work on specific scenes, for they both renew our surprise in the language. When we speak in everyday life we are always on the edge of finding the word: we may know precisely what we want to say, but we do not know beforehand quite what words we will choose. We can be surprised by them, and they may take us in another direction. The actor, of course, has learned the words but somehow must still allow the words to surprise.

First, jostling: find a piece of text which you can all speak together. I have set out Lear's speech when he is addressing the storm as a start but it can be from any play you like or a passage from this book. Or it can be a speech from the play you are working on. The latter would in fact be better because it would inform the work more directly, and usually there is a speech from one of the central and more public scenes which would be suitable, providing the actor playing it does not mind.

All you do is come together in quite a close group, and as you speak the text, jostle one another. Although you know it is a kind of game which has been set up, you still feel a sense of irritation and annoyance at being pushed – a totally instinctive reaction. This quite unconsciously makes us feel that little bit aggressive and the language responds accordingly – the muscularity and energy of the language becomes apparent. But more than this, because we are moving quite vigorously, we cannot hold on to our voice in any way. It is being released from lower down and it stops being controlled and releases that innate but hidden strength, that primitive need to speak and not make our voice behave. And I think this is very interesting. But take care that you do not go on too long or get too rough. Here is the speech:

> LEAR   Blow, winds, and crack your cheeks! Rage! Blow!
> You cataracts and hurricanoes, spout
> Till you have drenched our steeples, drowned the cocks!
> You sulphurous and thought-executing fires,
> Vaunt-curriers of oak-cleaving thunderbolts,
> Singe my white head! And thou all-shaking thunder,
> Strike flat the thick rotundity o' the world,
> Crack Nature's moulds, all germens spill at once
> That makes ingrateful man!
>
> *King Lear*, III.ii.

Alternatives:

(i) Get each member of the group to do one of their own speeches from the play. Ask them to stand in the centre with the group in a fairly close circle round them. The group should then jostle or nudge them while they are speaking so that they are propelled round the ring. Often very good things spring out of this: even though you are holding on to the sense of what you are saying, because you are not in control of your body the language is erupting in a way that is not being controlled, and you react in surprising ways so that other insights open. I have heard very good things come out of this. Plus the voice acquires an added firmness and vigour, and we hear this and feel a strength from it.

(ii) You can in fact work through a scene in this way, and perhaps vary it by opening up the space a little and walking round in it, but still keeping that sense of knocking against something or someone.

BEING 'ON' THE WORD

Secondly, being 'on' the word: this exercise is to realise the value of each word, so that however unimportant the word seems – e.g. 'in', 'or', 'as' – it still has an active place in the speaking. It stops us from using words as clumps of sense and is often quite revelatory in what it opens up.

You will need someone to lead the exercise – the voice teacher hopefully – and you can work it on any text in this book, or perhaps a sonnet. The purpose is to speak it together, and first of course to make sense of it. Then speak it again, really being with each word and not pre-empting the next. This is very difficult to do for we inevitably want to present the sense of the whole phrase: so the leader has to listen very carefully and not let the group continue before they have fulfilled each word. They have to keep asking 'what?' Here is Sonnet 23:

As an unperfect actor on the stage
Who with his fear is put besides his part,
Or some fierce thing replete with too much rage,
Whose strength's abundance weakens his own heart;
So I, for fear of trust, forget to say
The perfect ceremony of love's rite,
And in mine own love's strength seem to decay,
O'ercharg'd with burden of mine own love's might.
O, let my books be then the eloquence
And dumb presagers of my speaking breast.
Who plead for love and look for recompense,
More than that tongue that more hath more express'd.
    O, learn to read what silent love hath writ!
    To hear with eyes belongs to love's fine wit.

By taking that moment to find the next word you will hear how the thought is cumulative and how words like 'as', 'so' and 'or' activate the next thought:

Who with his fear is put besides his part . . .
replete with too much rage

It is an incredibly charged piece of writing about not being able to speak your feelings, and very poignant, I think, so this exercise suits it rather well.

It is quite slow and painstaking at first, but as you get into a different mindset, i.e. a mindset which does not take any word for granted, it gets easier, and other meanings open up, and another dynamic of the thought. You do not want to take too long over this exercise at any one time, but it is worth doing at intervals on different pieces of text. It is particularly good for the actor to do this on a piece of their own text at different times during rehearsal: it keeps it fresh and alive.

7 The Subtext

The next two chapters, 'The Subtext' and 'Structures', are about discovering what is going on in the language, or I like to say under the language, and its relevance to the play and the characters in the play. In other words, we will be explaining the play's life, for words are living thoughts. They are about ways by which the actor can make this awareness an intrinsic part of their own personal discovery through the play.

I am starting with the work on subtext because I think we react to it quite instinctively and this immediately gives us a basic confidence. The work on structure is more concerned with rules, i.e. syntax and grammar and basic rhythm, which at first can seem daunting until we realise that these so-called rules evolved through the evolution of man's need to communicate and therefore make sound, different needs creating different sounds and rhythms. However, once we get our heads round these rules and start to trust them we realise that they are not something which we have to impose, but rather they provide the form, the structure and the covert meaning which we can instinctively respond to, and which then become a solid basis for the work – and a source of strength.

In this section, much of the work has to do with repeating the text in some way, and the reason for it is this: as we repeat words we isolate them from their grammatical and literal meaning, we take them out of context, and this means that other shades of meaning can surface. Just look at the most famous four and a half lines in the language, or in many other languages, for that matter:

To be or not to be – that is the question;
Whether 'tis nobler in the mind to suffer
The slings and arrows of outrageous fortune
Or to take arms against a sea of troubles
And by opposing end them.

Hamlet, III.i.

Speak those lines through, and as you do so repeat some of the words several times. You will hear how as they are repeated they take on other meanings, deeper meanings – 'be', 'question', 'shame', 'outrageous', 'troubles' – and every person will react differently and every person will have a different image as they speak. By repeating the words we will hear and question them afresh. Understanding Shakespeare can often be like doing a cryptic crossword – it can never be quite pinned down – and this is why it gives such a feeling of elation when we work on it for it always keeps the questions open.

Nothing written on a page is ever totally naturalistic, however ordinary it may seem on the surface, for there is always an intention behind it: it is always taking us to a place in our imagination, defining something beyond the literal, and this makes the words chosen very particular. There is then a fine line to be drawn between keeping the language true for the moment, that is to say sounding natural to our ears, yet somehow making the audience alert to the nature of that language and its full import, i.e. taking them unawares into that other world. The actor therefore needs to tune into this in a way that makes him/her aware of the language choices yet allowing them to alight on the listener without stress or emphasis.

We also need to take this on board: words tell us not just about the character, their feelings and motives, they frame for us the political context of the play, for how we communicate with each other on a personal level is conditioned by the societal realities of the world around us.

We need to look at the text from three different perspectives:

(i)   The world of the play.
(ii) The vocabulary of character.
(iii) Dialogue – that is to say, the interchange between characters.

I will be adding two more sections which set out exercises to heighten our awareness still further, and which can be used for either dialogue or solo work:

(iv)   Ladders of thought
(v)   The word itself

All the work is about making us aware of the precise choice of the word and what that tells us of the situation, the character and the underlying motive. There are a number of tactics that can be used which are all to do with repeating, echoing, questioning, challenging, and the procedure will vary according to the purpose. In each case I will lay out particular scenes or speeches and describe work which can be done on them, but they are intended purely as examples – for what is important is that the exercises will work on any speech or scene and will help to bring out the specific nature of that scene. This may seem strange, but because we are throwing up language in this way we are continually hearing the words afresh, and they can surprise and take on added layers of meaning, so that we will hear the comic intention equally with the serious, the heightened language with the ordinary – they alert us to what the words are doing.

I think the exercises have to be chosen on instinct, and this has to do with where you are in rehearsal, whether you need something rough to get the energy going, etc., but it is always useful to remember that when we are saying words that are special we are apt to be careful with them, so that just doing an exercise which makes them spring out can release another energy – and perhaps an added meaning.

THE WORLD OF THE PLAY

I opened this book by quoting from *Hamlet* and saying how the first line, 'Who's there?', takes us directly into the centre of that play. And in *The Actor and the Text* I have already written about the sexuality which is apparent in the opening dialogue between Theseus and Hippolyta in *A Midsummer Night's Dream*: words which are not directly sexual but in context take on a sexual nuance and could only take us into that midsummer's night world. When I ask a group to sit down and listen to those first three speeches in *A Midsummer Night's Dream* and repeat the words which have a sexual connotation, they are always surprised, not so much by the openly sexual words, but by how the implications become cumulative, reinforced by the sounds themselves, and words like 'moon', 'lingers', 'withering', 'steep', 'wooed thee with my sword', 'love', 'injuries', leap out and take on added meanings in context, and become more dangerously sexual. We must never forget the inclusivity of the English language, i.e. how the use of different sounds, vowels and consonants can add to and even manipulate our perception of the meaning.

It is, I believe, incredibly revealing to do this same work on the beginning of *King Lear*. The very first dialogue, the short interchange between Gloucester and Kent with Edmund in the middle, is very smooth and politic, and it is in prose. If we repeat words which seem to be evasive in their meaning, we soon gather that they are clearly anxious about Lear's decision to divide up the kingdom and what that portends – they are feeling each other out. But it is also interesting because it opens out the whole issue of bastardy and those born in wedlock, what is open and what is kept hidden, and who has rights and who has not. I think it disturbs us right at the start because it opens up the possibility of corruption and lack of honesty at the centre of Lear's court, it also makes us ready for the false convolutions of Goneril and Regan.

But now to Lear's big speech on which the whole play hinges: in it he expresses his wish to announce the dower he intends for each daughter, but first he wants to know from each of them how much they love him, so that he can allot the land accordingly. If we read it carefully we will notice just how much the words are about quantity:

LEAR   . . . Tell me, my daughters,
     Since now we will divest us both of rule,
     Interest of territory, cares of state,
     Which of you shall we say doth love us most,
     That we our largest bounty may extend
     Where nature doth with merit challenge. Goneril,
     Our eldest born, speak first.

GONERIL Sir, I love you more than word can wield the matter,
Dearer than eyesight, space, and liberty,
Beyond what can be valued rich or rare,
No less than life, with grace, health, beauty, honour,
As much as child e'er loved, or father found;
A love that makes breath poor and speech unable;
Beyond all manner of 'so much' I love you.

CORDELIA [Aside] What shall Cordelia speak? Love, and be silent.

LEAR Of all these bounds, even from this line to this
With shadowy forests and with champains riched,
With plenteous rivers and wide-skirted meads,
We make thee lady. To thine and Albany's issues
Be this perpetual. What says our second daughter,
Our dearest Regan, wife of Cornwall?

REGAN I am made of that self mettle as my sister
And prize me at her worth. In my true heart
I find she names my very deed of love;
Only she comes too short, that I profess
Myself an enemy to all other joys
Which the most precious square of sense possesses,
And find I am alone felicitate
In your dear highness' love.

CORDELIA [Aside]   Then poor Cordelia!
And yet not so, since I am sure my love's
More ponderous than my tongue.

LEAR To thee and thine hereditary ever
Remain this ample third of our fair kingdom,
No less in space, validity, and pleasure
Than that conferred on Goneril – Now, our joy,
Although our last and least, to whose young love
The vines of France and milk of Burgundy
Strive to be interested: what can you say to draw
A third more opulent than your sisters? Speak!

CORDELIA Nothing, my lord.
LEAR Nothing?
CORDELIA Nothing.
LEAR Nothing will come of nothing. Speak again.
CORDELIA Unhappy that I am, I cannot heave
My heart into my mouth. I love your majesty
According to my bond, no more or less.

             King Lear, I.i.

After the convoluted and clearly false protestations of the two elder sisters, the spareness of Cordelia's reply is shocking – she is wordless. But it is not simple, for it may be that she feels she cannot match her sisters' false effusiveness, it may be that she is so full of feeling that she cannot find the words to express herself adequately, or it may be that she is trying to shock him into sense. Whatever, that word, 'nothing', rings out like a bell, and it curiously gives a music to the whole first part of the scene where the language, though convoluted and extravagant, has neverthless been at the prosaic level of the business of ownership: the scene spins on that one word.

In order to hear what that language is telling us we need to hear it quite simply, without acting it in any way. And to do this the group should sit round in a circle with those playing Lear and the three sisters sitting in the middle: as the scene is read, we ask the rest of the group to repeat the words which have to do with quantity, either quantity of love or quantity of land. What of course then becomes apparent is that you cannot quantify love in this way. We then begin to hear the very essence of Lear's thinking – that he is equating love with possessions. We further perceive that there is something profoundly wrong in his value judgement – a lack of judgement so severe as to make us question his veracity. And that is why Cordelia's one word, 'nothing', is so strong, for we know, in the end, she is trying to shock him into sense. She goes on to give him her reasons, balanced and truthful:

CORDELIA   Good my lord,
      You have begot me, bred me, loved me.
      I return those duties back as are right fit,
      Obey you, love you, and most honour you.
      Why have my sisters husbands, if they say
      They love you all? Haply, when I shall wed,
      That lord whose hand must take my plight shall carry
      Half my love with him, half my care and duty.
      Sure I shall never marry like my sisters,
      To love my father all.
LEAR   But goes thy heart with this?
CORDELIA   Ay, my good lord.
LEAR   So young, and so untender?

| CORDELIA | So young, my lord, and true. |
| LEAR | Let it be so! Thy truth then be thy dower! |

King Lear, I.i.

At which point Lear breaks, cursing Cordelia by invoking Hecate and the barbarous Scythian, and in the end banishes her from his sight.

So the sound of the language goes from the fulsome sounds of the two sisters

more than word can wield the matter ...
Beyond what can be valued rich or rare ...
she names my very deed of love.

plus Lear's replies

shadowy forests ...
champains riched ...
wide-skirted meads.

to the simplicity of Cordelia's 'nothing' and 'So young, my lord, and true', and then to the barbaric language of Lear's curse. It is the most wonderful piece of writing, first in its heartless elegance, then in its violence and how it erupts, and ultimately in its simplicity from Cordelia. Later, in the dialogue between Lear and Kent, it takes on an added tension and we hear in Kent something of the cost that goes with loyalty to such a king, as he tries to make Lear see reason.

It is not the only time Shakespeare makes us understand what it is like to be wordless: the feeling is wonderfully expressed in these first eight lines of Sonnet 23:

As an unperfect actor on the stage
Who with his fear is put beside his part,
Or some fierce thing replete with too much rage,
Whose strength's abundance weakens his own heart;
So I, for fear of trust, forget to say
The perfect ceremony of love's rite,
And in mine own love's strength seem to decay,
O'ercharged with burden of mine own love's might.

I have looked at the *King Lear* scene at some length because it illustrates so clearly how the choice of vocabulary takes us immediately into the centre politics of a play, and therefore into its world. For a much shorter example, we can look at the beginning of *Antony and Cleopatra*. It opens with this speech of Philo, a friend of Antony:

PHILO   Nay, but this dotage of our general's
           O'erflows the measure. Those his goodly eyes,
           That o'er the files and musters of the war
           Have glowed like plated Mars, now bend, now turn
           The office and devotion of their view
           Upon a tawny front. His captain's heart
           Which in the scuffles of great fights hath burst
           The buckles on his breast, reneges all temper
           And is become the bellows and the fan
           To cool a gipsy's lust.
           [*Flourish. Enter Antony, Cleopatra, her ladies Charmin and
           Iras, the train, with eunuchs fanning her*]
                 Look where they come.
           Take but good note, and you shall see in him
           The triple pillar of the world transformed
           Into a strumpet's fool. Behold and see.
                          Antony and Cleopatra, I.i.

The very use of that word 'measure' at the beginning is the key, for at the centre of the play is the notion of extravagance – of feelings and actions beyond what is normal and which in the end destroy. Yet the actor playing Philo does not need to emphasise the extravagant words, for they are just part of his attempt, as a friend of Antony, to rationalise the situation and to define them for himself. Yet at once we are plunged into a world where the measure, the balance, is out of alignment.

We could look at every play in this way to find the centre, the hierarchy, we are being taken to. In *The Winter's Tale*, Archidamus and Camillo take us straight into the political world of the court of Bohemia, where no one quite trusts each other, and they are feeling each other out. In talking about their kings, Bohemia and Sicilia, their convoluted politeness is almost absurd.

Or the obvious example, the beginning of *Romeo and Juliet*: first the prologue which sets out the situation very clearly, and then the beginning of the quarrel between the servants, where we see how the hostility between the two houses has affected the whole society down to the servants. This scene is so often done with comic intent, but it is in fact about the loutish cruelty and violence and sexism which prevails in a society riddled with petty hostility.

All this said, I believe it is essential that at a point early in rehearsal we sit down and read the beginning of the play we are working on to focus the attention specifically on the language, its choice and form, for it provides the framework to our thinking. And I emphasise that this must not be done as an academic exercise. We should not be told what to notice, we must hear and discover for ourselves, for as we listen we will hear the resonances implicit in the words. We must listen with our minds open.

EXERCISES

1. Get the group to sit on the floor if possible. Sitting on the floor is informal, so we subconsciously let go of our minds and are more open to what we hear. If sitting on the floor proves difficult for anyone for whatever reason, then certainly they should sit on a chair, but it is good to be in a position where there is no sense of hierarchy. The director will then allot however many actors are needed to read the scene. (They need not necessarily be the ones cast for those parts.) As they read, the rest of the group should mutter words that they hear – either words that grab the attention or words that can be related to what seems central to that scene (the director will make the choice).

2. This is a starting point, but as you get further into rehearsal it is useful to keep reminding oneself of how the world is in the language: you can repeat the exercises on different parts of the play and, because the foundations are laid, this can be done quite briefly.

3. I think it is particularly useful at some point to go through a scene, or part of a scene, while jostling each other: the energy of the language erupts in a surprising way and often shifts the meaning. It releases its roughness and any inhibitions the actor may have about language disappear.

This work can be done on any play, classical or modern. The beginning of Webster's *The Duchess of Malfi*, for instance, opens with a scene between Delio and Antonio, both stewards of the duchess's household. Delio's first speech tells us of the corruption at the centre of the court, and when, near the end of the speech, he sees Bosola and the cardinal approaching, he says:

> Here comes Bosola,
> The only court-gall: yet I observe his railing
> Is not for simple love of piety:
> Indeed, he rails at those things which he wants;
> Would be as lecherous, covetous, or proud,
> Bloody, or envious, as any man,
> If he had means to be so.

After a short piece of dialogue the cardinal leaves, and Bosola, a gentleman of the horse to the duchess, has this wonderful outburst of spleen against the cardinal and his brother, the Duke of Calabria:

BOSOLA   He and his brother are like plum-trees that grow crooked over standing-pools; they are rich and o'erladen with fruit, but none but crows, pies, and caterpillars feed on them. Could I be one of their flattering panders, I would hang on their ears like a horseleech till I were full, and then drop off. I pray, leave me. Who would rely upon these miserable dependancies, in expectation to be advanced tomorrow? What creatures ever fed worse than hoping Tantalus? Nor any man ever died away more fearfully than he that hoped for a pardon. There are rewards for hawks and dogs when they have done us service; but for a soldier that hazards his limbs in a battle, nothing but a kind of geometry is his last supportation.

The Duchess of Malfi, I,i.

The language is dripping with corruption, and just to repeat those words to do with greed and opulence takes us to its very centre – the whole world of the play is there.

In a modern play the language may well be quite minimal, as at the beginning of Beckett's *Waiting for Godot*, but if we listen to that subtext it will tell us about the space needed for that minimal language to have its effect – and to land on the hearer. Or it can be very charged, as in Arthur Miller's *The Crucible*, where the words are of sin, and hidden powers, and witchcraft, words which not only take us, the listener, into that world, but in fact inform the very way the character thinks and reacts. This perhaps tells us how we can all be influenced by the very choice of words which are spoken.

The bottom line of the work is this: we hear the language without any preconceptions of what it ought to mean, and in this way we will enter the frame of the play and open out the excitement of the sound itself.

One more thing. As we repeat words we will start to notice the opposites, i.e. weight against lightness, heat against cold, and this is very important for the substance of Shakespeare's thought and argument is built on opposites. And this we must take on board for in everyday life we are always speaking against the opposite: however minimally or passively we may be expressing ourselves, we are always affirming ourselves against the opposite idea, and I think this is something the actor has always to keep in mind for it keeps the language active.

VOCABULARY OF CHARACTER

Here I want to look at individual speeches to discover just how much the choice of vocabulary tells us about the person, and for the actor how that choice is intrinsic to inhabiting the character. We will start by repeating words in much the same way as for the previous exercise. This is particularly useful for the actor because he/she will hear them at the same time as speaking them, or fractionally after, and because they are being repeated back they somehow reach a different part of one's consciousness. This is difficult to explain, but I think this exercise takes us into another area of hearing what the words are doing to us as we speak them, as well as the sense we are actually trying to convey. The actor therefore is responding to the text at a subconscious level as well as at the conscious level of conveying the specific thought – they are both subjective and objective at the same time. It is also sharpening the group awareness to the choice of language and therefore to the underlying situation and motive of the character.

I want first to look at two speeches on their own, i.e. speeches taken out of the context of the specific scene. The first is Laertes' advice to Ophelia before he embarks to return to France. It is long and wordy, but it tells us a lot for those very reasons.

LAERTES	For Hamlet, and the trifling of his favour,
	Hold it a fashion and a toy in blood,
	A violet in the youth of primy nature,
	Forward, not permanent, sweet, not lasting,
	The perfume and suppliance of a minute,
	No more.
OPHELIA	No more but so?
LAERTES	Think it no more.
	For nature crescent does not grow alone
	In thews and bulk, but as this temple waxes
	The inward service of the mind and soul
	Grows wide withal. Perhaps he loves you now,
	And now no soil or cautel doth besmirch
	The virtue of his will. But you must fear,
	His greatness weighed, his will is not his own.
	For he himself is subject to his birth.
	He may not, as unvalued persons do,
	Carve for himself. For on his choice depends
	The safety and the health of the whole state.
	And therefore must his choice be circumscribed
	Unto the voice and yielding of that body
	Whereof he is the head. Then, if he says he loves you,
	It fits your wisdom so far to believe it
	As he in his particular act and place
	May give his saying deed; which is no further
	Than the main voice of Denmark goes withal.
	Then weigh what loss your honour may sustain
	If with too credent ear you list his songs,
	Or lose your heart, or your chaste treasure open
	To his unmastered importunity.
	Fear it, Ophelia, fear it, my dear sister,
	And keep you in the rear of your affection,
	Out of the shot and danger of desire.
	The chariest maid is prodigal enough
	If she unmask her beauty to the moon.
	Virtue itself 'scapes not calumnious strokes.

The canker galls the infants of the spring
Too oft before their buttons be disclosed;
And in the morn and liquid dew of youth
Contagious blastments are most imminent.
Be wary then. Best safety lies in fear.
Youth to itself rebels, though none else near.

Hamlet, I.iii.

What is interesting about this speech is that it purports to be so dry and well thought out – it is 'courtier speak' – yet in the very images of nature that he uses, objective as they are, we hear his real concern for his sister and the way nature, or innocence, can be corrupted:

A violet in the youth of primy nature . . .
The canker galls the infants of the spring
Too oft before their buttons are disclosed

The words that we need to repeat, or rather mutter, in response are those to do with innocence or its opposite, with power and its opposite: as we speak these words we will perceive in Laertes not only his tenderness for his sister, but his awareness of the power of the state and how it can corrupt. Perhaps that is why he wants to get away. But what we also realise is that he can only communicate with her in a very formal and rather academic way, suppressing any desire to express intimate feelings, and from this we apprehend something of the male brain-washing to which Ophelia has been constantly exposed, and which ultimately breaks her.

The second speech is from *The Winter's Tale*. The two kings, Leontes of Sicilia and Polixenes of Bohemia, have been friends from boyhood. Polixenes has been visiting Leontes and is about to go home, but Leontes wants him to stay. Leontes has asked his wife, Hermione, to persuade Polixenes to stay a month longer. As the scene progresses, we realise that Leontes has done this to confirm his belief that Hermione is attracted to Polixenes and is being unfaithful to him: he is feeding his jealousy.

LEONTES	Is he won yet?
HERMIONE	He'll stay, my lord.
LEONTES	At my request he would not.

Hermione, my dearest, thou never spok'st
To better purpose.

HERMIONE   Never?

LEONTES   Never but once.

HERMIONE What? Have I twice said well? When was't before?
I prithee tell me. Cram's with praise, and make's
As fat as tame things. One good deed dying
    tongueless
Slaughters a thousand waiting upon that.
Our praises are our wages. You may ride's
With one soft kiss a thousand furlongs ere
With spur we heat an acre. But to the goal,
My last good deed was to entreat his stay.
What was my first? It has an elder sister,
Or I mistake you. O, would her name were Grace!
But once before I spoke to the purpose. When?
Nay, let me hav't; I long!

LEONTES   Why, that was when
Three crabbed months had soured themselves to
    death
Ere I could make thee open thy white hand
And clap thyself my love. Then didst thou utter
'I am yours for ever.'

HERMIONE   'Tis Grace indeed.

The Winter's Tale, I.ii.

I am concerned at the moment only with Hermione's main
speech. Now one can point out all the obvious sexual words in
that speech, but when you start to mutter them back, they
emerge in a different way: 'cram', 'fat as tame things', 'praises
are our wages', 'ride's', 'soft kiss', etc. As with the beginning of
A Midsummer Night's Dream, the effect is cumulative. Her
speech and language is so different to the language she later
uses when defending herself in the trial. Then, it is very direct
and challenging and strong: here, it is hot language, and we
realise that there is something deeply sexual at the centre of this
world in which she is immersed. Somewhere it is sick, and we
understand why Polixenes wants to get away. But in playing her,
the actor must find the need for those words.

I have just cited these two speeches with the aim of alerting
us to choice in language and how it takes us under the surface
of the character. The matter of both these speeches, Laertes and

Hermione, could be put quite succinctly and clearly in other, less evocative words, but we would be missing the flesh and the bone that is present in them.

There is so much we could look at – Edmund's first soliloquy in *King Lear*, for example, and his obsession with the word 'bastard' and 'base', and just how his awareness of these two words has informed his behaviour. But it is equally useful to work on something less emotionally charged, such as a speech from one of the histories like Burgundy's in *Henry V*, Act V, scene ii is a wonderfully politic speech about the futility of war and the imbalance that it leaves behind – beauty v. chaos, desolation v. plenty.

One could also look at a speech bringing news, such as the scene at the beginning of *Macbeth* when the Captain is reporting the battle to Duncan, and he speaks of the bravery of Macbeth. It is so vivid and full, and by the end it is almost hallucinatory, as his wounds start to grip and in the end overcome him. This speech is so often done quickly to stir up excitement and get the play moving, but I think there is so much to come out of the fact that these are probably the last words he will say. They are difficult to find, and his need to fulfil them is all he has left in his life.

It is always good to start with the simple exercise of repeating words, but as you get further into rehearsal there are a number of ways to take the work on – ways which will take us deeper into the language and into the discovery of hidden motives and feelings.

EXERCISES

This work on individual speeches can be done with either the whole group, or in the context of the scene being rehearsed. It can, as I have said, be done at different stages of rehearsal and on different parts of the play, and each time both the listeners and the speaker will hear new things.

1. The actor stands, or sits, in the middle of the group, and the rest mutter the words that either take their interest, or the words which seem central to the character.
2. The actor in the middle speaks the text with the rest of the group questioning him/her as they speak – either

questioning the precise word or the whole thought. This forces the speaker to be very specific in order to clarify the text. It also very slightly disconcerts the speaker and knocks him/her a little off course so the familiar rhythm is interrupted, and the words are found with a fresh energy.

3. As a variation, the group can argue with the speaker. This makes the speaker more aggressive, but it also helps to assert his/her own belief and so define the thinking, the argument, that bit more clearly.

4. Also interesting is to have one actor speaking the text, with another actor standing behind and, quite quietly, speaking as much of the text as you can into their ear. You may not be able to get all the words in, but the aim is to repeat as much of the speech as is possible.

All these exercises help to identify the language, which both defines and feeds the thought, and which in turn feeds the emotion.

INTERCHANGE BETWEEN CHARACTERS

Now to dialogue. This work I think is best done a little way into rehearsal when the basic motives are clear. What it does is make us aware of how each character is changed by what another character has spoken, and how their very choice of words affects how he/she replies. For what has been said is always kicking us into our next thought, making us think on the moment and, as in real life, we may know what we want to say beforehand but what comes out is different. It has been changed as a direct response to what has been said to us.

To clarify this I want first to look at some dialogue in the same scene of *The Winter's Tale*, but a little further on. It takes place between Leontes and Camillo, a favoured lord of the court, after Leontes has watched Polixenes and Hermione walk off together talking, Hermione presumably believing she is doing what Leontes wants. We have already witnessed a little of Leontes' jealousy, but now we see it in its full force.

LEONTES   Camillo, this great sir will stay here longer.
CAMILLO   You had much ado to make his anchor hold;
             When you cast it out, it still came home.

LEONTES	Didst note it?
CAMILLO	He would not stay at your petitions; made
	His business more material.
LEONTES	Didst perceive it?
	[*Aside*] They're here with me already, whisp'ring, rounding,
	'Sicilia is a so-forth.' 'Tis far gone
	When I shall gust it last. How came't, Camillo,
	That he did stay?
CAMILLO	At the good queen's entreaty.
LEONTES	'At the Queen's' be't. 'Good' should be pertinent;
	But so it is, it is not. Was this taken
	By any understanding pate but thine?
	For thy conceit is soaking, will draw in
	More than the common blocks. Not noted, is't?
	But of the finer natures, by some severals
	Of head-piece extraordinary? Lower messes
	Perchance are to this business purblind? Say.
CAMILLO	Business, my lord? I think most understand
	Bohemia stays here longer.
LEONTES	Ha?
CAMILLO	Stays here longer.
LEONTES	Ay, but why?
CAMILLO	To satisfy your Highness and th'entreaties
	Of our most gracious mistress.
LEONTES	Satisfy
	Th'entreaties of your mistress? Satisfy;
	Let that suffice. I have trusted thee, Camillo,
	With all the nearest things to my heart, as well
	My chamber-councils, wherein, priest-like, thou
	Hast cleansed my bosom, I from thee departed
	Thy penitent reformed. But we have been
	Deceived in thy integrity, deceived
	In that which seems so.
CAMILLO	Be it forbid, my lord!
LEONTES	To bide upon't, thou art not honest; or,
	If thou inclin'st that way, thou art a coward,
	Which hoxes honesty behind, restraining
	From course required; or else thou must be counted
	A servant grafted in my serious trust
	And therein negligent; or else a fool
	That seest a game played home, the rich stake drawn,
	And tak'st it all for jest.

CAMILLO   My gracious lord,
I may be negligent, foolish, and fearful:
In every one of these no man is free,
But that his negligence, his folly, fear,
Among the infinite doings of the world,
Sometimes puts forth. In your affairs, my lord,
If ever I were wilful-negligent,
It was my folly; if industriously
I played the fool, it was my negligence,
Not weighing well the end; if ever fearful
To do a thing where I the issue doubted,
Whereof the execution did cry out
Against the non-performance, 'twas a fear
Which oft infects the wisest. These, my lord,
Are such allowed infirmities that honesty
Is never free of. But, beseech your Grace,
Be plainer with me; let me know my trespass
By its own visage. If I deny it,
'Tis none of mine.

LEONTES   Ha' not you seen, Camillo –
But that's past doubt, you have, or your eye-glass
Is thicker than a cuckold's horn – or heard –
For to a vision so apparent rumour
Cannot be mute – or thought – for cogitation
Resides not in that man that does not think –
My wife is slippery? If thou wilt confess –
Or else be impudently negative,
To have nor eyes nor ears nor thought – then say
My wife's a hobby-horse, deserves a name
As rank as any flax-wench that puts to
Before her troth-plight. Say't and justify't.

CAMILLO   I would not be a stander-by to hear
My sovereign mistress clouded so, without
My present vengeance taken. 'Shrew my heart
You never spoke what did become you less
Than this, which to reiterate were sin
As deep as that, though true.

LEONTES   Is whispering nothing?
Is leaning cheek to cheek? Is meeting noses?
Kissing with inside lip? Stopping the career
Of laughter with a sigh? – a note infallible
Of breaking honesty. Horsing foot on foot?
Skulking in corners? Wishing clocks more swift;

> Hours, minutes; noon, midnight? And all eyes
> Blind with the pin and web but theirs, theirs only,
> That would unseen be wicked? Is this nothing?
> Why, then the world and all that's in't is nothing,
> The covering sky is nothing, Bohemia nothing,
> My wife is nothing, nor nothing have these nothings,
> If this be nothing.

CAMILLO   Good my lord, be cur'd
> Of this diseas'd opinion, and betimes;
> For 'tis most dangerous.

LEONTES   Say it be, 'tis true.

CAMILLO   No, no, my lord.

LEONTES   It is; you lie, you lie.

The Winter's Tale, I.ii.

The language in this scene is rich with subversive meanings. Both men are feeling each other out. Leontes can contain his jealousy no longer and is quite open with Camillo about his certainty of Hermione's infidelity. Camillo does not at first believe that Leontes can even think this of his wife, but when he realises Leontes is serious he tries to dissuade him from this thinking in the most politic and respectful terms possible. The language is tortuous, as is the form, twisting and turning: the way Leontes grabs on to that word 'satisfy' with its sexual innuendos unintended by Camillo, the way Camillo twists and turns in his argument, well thought out because he needs to answer every accusation of Leontes' in order to save his skin. Leontes' frustration at Camillo's disbelief and his speech beginning 'Is whispering nothing?' – full of questions, and also full of unvoiced consonants – gathers momentum and becomes wilder and wilder to end with those last three lines which show his total dislocation:

> Why, then the covering sky is nothing, Bohemia nothing,
> My wife is nothing, nor nothing have these nothings,
> If this be nothing.

Camillo answers:

> Good my lord, be cur'd
> Of this diseas'd opinion, and betimes;
> For 'tis most dangerous.

So what we need to uncover from this is just how much this language infects and affects both of them. The vocabulary is rich with corruption, sin and disease, and therefore conversely with honesty and trust. Words relating to these concepts would yield much: 'slippery', 'flax-wench', 'hobby-horse', 'inside lip', 'skulking', 'wicked'. When spoken next to their opposites, these words become more vile.

In order to get at the complexity of the thoughts I would do an exercise whereby the character listening would question aloud what is being said to him. So the actor playing Camillo would, as Leontes speaks, be questioning Leontes' motives – Why is he saying that? What does he mean? What is he implying? – until the horror of the implication finally lands. At the same time Leontes would be questioning Camillo's honesty and the validity of his argument. In this way we clarify both Camillo's dilemma in dealing with Leontes' madness, and with Leontes' need to justify his position. A variation on this would be to argue with the other character under one's breath – this would make the thinking more aggressive. In both cases the character speaking is aware of the need to make their words impinge on the other.

Both these ways are useful in that they help to clarify the through line of the argument and give us options about motives and objectives which help to firm up character relationships within that situation. In this particular text the movement of the thoughts is extremely complex, tortuous even, for each thought is made up of several different parts which have to be held together within the one whole. This is technically difficult, and these exercises help us to deal with that tortuousness, honouring each part of the thought while clarifyiing the whole.

An interesting exercise on the speech of Leontes beginning 'Is whispering nothing?' would be to get the actor to speak it with two people on each side of him, slightly behind, whispering the words in his ear as he speaks them. The actor then gets a kind of schizophrenic reaction to the words, as though they were coming from different sides of his brain, so that the whispering of that word 'nothing', with all its repetitions, is quite disturbing. We will also become conscious of the predominance of unvoiced consonants giving the whole speech a shifty and covert undercurrent.

And now I want to look at something totally different: the very first dialogue between Romeo and Juliet. They have not spoken together before, and it is in the form of a sonnet:

ROMEO   If I profane with my unworthiest hand
         This holy shrine, the gentle sin is this.
         My lips, two blushing pilgrims, ready stand
         To smooth that rough touch with a tender kiss.
JULIET   Good pilgrim, you do wrong your hand too much,
         Which mannerly devotion shows in this.
         For saints have hands that pilgrims' hands do touch,
         And palm to palm is holy palmer's kiss.
ROMEO   Have not saints lips, and holy palmers too?
JULIET   Ay, pilgrim, lips that they must use in prayer.
ROMEO   O, then, dear saint, let lips do what hands do!
         They pray: grant thou, lest faith turn to despair.
JULIET   Saints do not move, though grant for prayers' sake.
ROMEO   Then move not while my prayer's effect I take.
         [He kisses her]
         Thus from my lips, by thine my sin is purged.
JULIET   Then have my lips the sin that they have took.
ROMEO   Sin from my lips? O trespass sweetly urged!
         Give me my sin again.
JULIET   You kiss by th'book.

Romeo and Juliet, I.v.

Because it is written in sonnet form and is so overtly poetic, this speech can easily become over-romantic, even sentimental, and so not really get at the depth of commitment which is there. We need to apprehend that depth because it is what makes this love story a tragedy. If we were doing the exercise of repeating words back, the first word we would notice is the third one, 'profane', for it immediately tells us that the person speaking is at a level of commitment which is religious, and is therefore committing to something very profound – although he does go on to call it a 'gentle sin'!

We need to take a moment out and think about what religion meant at that time: Shakespeare was writing at a time when there was intense conflict between the Protestant and Catholic factions in England. To be on the wrong side could, and often did, mean death. So that word 'profane' has a seriousness and

145

gravity implicit in it which it does not have today in the Western world. Therefore, it is a word that Romeo cannot speak lightly, he has to find the word with all the meaning that surrounds it – and he is finding it while he is saying 'if'. It is that split moment on 'if' that gives true weight to the thought, and allows this to register with the listener.

If we remember that Romeo has up to this moment been flirting with an idea of love in the form of Rosaline, we will hear in the very choice of this word that he has suddenly found a depth in his feelings that is new and very sudden – the word erupts. The religious metaphor is carried right through to the end, and although both Romeo and Juliet play with the ideas and enjoy them throughout this first exchange, it is that metaphor which pins them down. Their belief in sin is an absolute and a concrete one, something which we do not register today in the same way – and that is where their love is.

If you get the two actors to sit down on the floor, either facing each other or back to back, and speak the words through, each repeating the words the other has said relating to sin or its opposite, it can be very moving and makes us aware of the true gravity of their feelings.

The third piece I want to look at is from that first scene of *King Lear* which we looked at earlier, but it comes right at the end. It comes after Lear and all his knights have left, leaving only Goneril and Regan: they are discussing what has just happened and how they will deal with Lear. Cordelia, who is now betrothed to the King of France, leaves them with the following words:

CORDELIA   Time shall unfold what plighted cunning hides;
Who covers faults, at last with shame derides.
Well may you prosper!

And Goneril and Regan, left alone, have this interchange – in prose:

GONERIL   Sister, it is not little I have to say of what most nearly
appertains to us both. I think our father will hence
tonight.
REGAN   That's most certain, and with you; next month with us.

GONERIL   You see how full of changes his age is. The observation
           we have made of it hath not been little. He always
           loved our sister most; and with what poor judgement
           he hath now cast her off appears too grossly.

REGAN   'Tis the infirmity of his age. Yet he hath ever but
           slenderly known himself.

GONERIL   The best and soundest of his time hath been but rash.
           Then must we look from his age to receive not alone
           the imperfections of long-ingraffed condition, but
           therewithal the unruly waywardness that infirm and
           choleric years bring with them.

REGAN   Such inconstant starts as we are like to have from him
           as this of Kent's banishment.

GONERIL   There is further compliment of leave-taking between
           France and him. Pray you, let us hit together. If our
           father carry authority with such disposition as he
           bears, this last surrender of his will but offend us.

REGAN   We shall further think of it.

GONERIL   We must do something, and i'th'heat.

King Lear, I.i.

This is a wonderful exchange to look at: first of all it is so spare, and in that spareness you understand they are feeling each other out. They seem almost at a distance from each other, as if both are travelling away – on their way to their own castles. I like to do an exercise with this that we shall look at in more detail again later. It involves each actor looking out of the window and drawing something which they can see outside as they are speaking. What comes out of this is that they are each in their own world, a world where they have to manipulate in order to survive, yet they are still tied inseparably to each other because of their mutual predicament and interests. It is so interesting to listen to this because we, as listeners, are not being given just the facts – we are also being taken somewhere else in the minds of those two characters.

So here is a summary of the exercises which can be done on any piece of dialogue. They can be done with up to four characters – I think with any more it would not be useful. Whatever the text you are working on, they will help to reveal the essence of the thinking, and will consequently open out options regarding objectives and motives and hidden agendas.

EXERCISES

1. I like to do an exercise where the actors sit on the floor back to back, slightly leaning against each other. This way they are not seeing each other in the normal way and being conscious of the need to put something across; rather they are feeling each other's vibrations, and this emphasises the sense of listening, not just to the logic of the words, but to the underlying implications. As they go through the text, the other actors repeat the words which either surprise them or which are in some way loaded in terms of their own character's reaction. I find this a very useful exercise in that it makes the actor really listen to what has to be responded to, and aware in a more profound way. The exercise can be done equally well with three or even four actors.

2. The next stage is that you go through the scene, but as the other actor is talking you comment on what they are saying, or even argue with it, or you question how you are going to deal with it. This way you are actively participating in what they are saying, which I think takes you deeper into the situation and thus gives your reply an extra dynamic and an added resonance, for it puts you in touch with your own world at the same time as forming the reply.

3. As a variation, you can listen to what the other character is saying, but before you reply with the actual text, you first speak your thoughts aloud, so that you clarify your intentions before you actually reply. All these exercises can be done standing, or walking round, or with your backs turned away, or simply in the rehearsal positions.

What is good about this work is that you are always speaking against something, and this galvanises your own thinking and so enlivens the word. But perhaps the most important thing to notice is how the words feed the thought: there seems to be a two-way action, for we have to search for the word we want, but once found it sends us on the next part of our journey. It seems we have to keep asking what comes first, the thought or the word? And there is no clear answer. But looking back, for instance, on the text of *The Winter's Tale*, it is quite clear that the words Leontes chooses to use feed his jealousy; they take him on a train that he cannot get off. Camillo realises this but is helpless to stop the train. Or in the *Romeo and Juliet* sonnet – the religious metaphor they use actively takes them deeper into the love they are expressing.

Other scenes which provide interesting examples:

- The dialogue between Troilus and Cressida, Act III, scene ii, when they declare their love. It is interesting to notice the very different male and female imagery by which they communicate.
- The dialogue between Isabella and Angelo, Act II, scene iv. The language is of soiling and putrification and sin – and of course inevitably the opposite is there, for this soiled language is set against purity and virtue.
- The dialogue between Brutus and Portia in *Julius Caesar*, Act II, scene i. The vocabulary here is about honour and strength versus illness and weakness – for that is the dilemma. It is both inspiring and shocking to hear how strong Portia is, the woman who will give herself a voluntary wound in the thigh as proof of her constancy.

LADDERS OF THOUGHT

We will be looking at speech structures in the next chapter to discover how the initial premise develops throughout a speech, and how one thought leads to another, but first I want to look at something quite simple which is to do with how the words themselves build into the meaning and add to it, so that the effect is cumulative: this gives a sense of dynamic to the way the thought develops. And this sense of dynamic has to come through the actor's voice, i.e. he/she has to know how to lift the ideas through, how to alight on the new idea so that it drops into the ear of the listener.

As an example, we will take that speech of Leontes, beginning 'Is whispering nothing?', and as we repeat the words back we will become conscious of their effect and how the words grow in potency until they overwhelm Leontes: 'whispering', 'leaning', 'kissing', 'inside lip', 'horsing', 'skulking', 'wishing', 'swift', 'nothing', 'nothing', 'nothing', etc. We see how the words themselves are a positive force in that growth – a ladder which leads us to the top, or the ultimate nadir – 'nothing'.

Or we could take a few lines from *Richard II*. The speech when he gives up the crown to Bolingbroke is his moment of realisation of what it means. We make a judgement on Richard by reacting to the speech as sentimental and self-pitying, but I think he is genuine at that moment. This, of course, does not excuse what he has done as king, but it deals with his own realisation and shock of what has happened and must be played for that reality.

> I'll give my jewels for a set of beads,
> My gorgeous palace for a hermitage,
> My gay apparel for an almsman's gown,
> My figured goblets for a dish of wood,
> My sceptre for a palmer's walking-staff,
> My subjects for a pair of carved saints,
> And my large kingdom for a little grave,
> A little, little grave, an obscure grave –
> Or I'll be buried in the king's highway,
> Some way of common trade where subject's feet
> May hourly trample on their sovereign's head,
> For on my heart they tread now whilst I live,
> And buried once, why not upon my head?
>
> *Richard II*, III.iii.

The ladder in this case is both going up and coming down:

> jewels – beads
> palace – hermitage
> apparel – almsman's gown
> goblets – dish of wood
> sceptre – walking-staff
> subjects – carved saints
> kingdom – grave
> heart – head

This is interesting because there is a two-way movement in his mind, i.e. the more he feeds his self-pity, the more striking become the antitheses. He is feeding his own downfall, his abjectness, by the very progression and extravagance of the images.

EXERCISES

These exercises can be set up with the group, or as work on a scene involving specific actors:

1. For work with one actor on a single speech: Get a piece of paper and a pencil, and as you work through the speech put a mark on the paper as each new idea or concept is mentioned. This way you will quite palpably see how the thought is developing.
2. It works in exactly the same way for a scene between two or three characters. You will need some paper and a pencil set on a chair or a table in the middle between you, and as you speak through the scene, each character has to make a mark on the paper on each word which develops the thought in some way and leads it through.
3. As a variation, the group can be involved in this by getting them to repeat the specific words as they hear them. Sometimes you do not spot the word until it is too late, but it does not matter for it is all the time keeping you alert to the ideas.

This exercise can be done quite lightly on any speech. For instance, Macbeth's soliloquy:

If it were done when 'tis done, then 'twere well
It were done quickly. If the assassination
Could trammel up the consequence, and catch
With his surcease success – that but this blow
Might be the be-all and the end-all, here –
But here upon this bank and shoal of time –
We'd jump the life to come.

Macbeth, I.vii.

The word 'it' leads to the word 'assassination', leads to the word 'consequence', leads to 'success', leads to 'end-all', etc. He cannot say the word 'assassination' at the beginning; he has to lead up to it. Gradually the idea takes hold and his ambition grows with the words and, as with Leontes, the images become wilder and further out of orbit.

Now I emphasise this exercise should be done lightly because it is not about meaning but simply about tuning our ears to the way the thoughts lift through. It can be done with equal effect on a romantic scene, e.g. this dialogue between Lorenzo and Jessica at the end of *The Merchant of Venice* as they await the return of Portia:

LORENZO   The moon shines bright. In such a night as this,
When the sweet wind did gently kiss the trees,
And they did make no noise – in such a night,
Troilus methinks mounted the Troyan walls,
And sighed his soul toward the Grecian tents
Where Cressid lay that night.

JESSICA   In such a night
Did Thisbe fearfully o'ertrip the dew,
And saw the lion's shadow ere himself,
And ran dismayed away.

LORENZO   In such a night
Stood Dido with a willow in her hand
Upon the wild sea banks, and waft her love
To come again to Carthage.

JESSICA   In such a night
Medea gathered the enchanted herbs
That did renew old Aeson.

LORENZO   In such a night
Did Jessica steal from the wealthy Jew,
And with an unthrift love did run from Venice
As far as Belmont

JESSICA   In such a night
Did young Lorenzo swear he loved her well,
Stealing her soul with many vows of faith,
And ne'er a true one.

LORENZO   In such a night
Did pretty Jessica, like a little shrew,
Slander her love, and he forgave it her.

JESSICA   I would outnight you, did nobody come;
But hark, I hear the footing of a man.

The Merchant of Venice, V.i.

There is nothing complicated in the thought; it is simply how they alight on each new idea that takes them further down the path. There is such a gentle game being played from 'The moon shines bright. In such a night' through 'Troilus methinks mounted the Troyan walls' to 'Did Thisbe fearfully o'ertrip the dew' to Dido and Carthage through to Medea and Aeson and finally to Belmont and culminating with Jessica's witty 'I would outnight you'. As you listen to it you will hear many more things, but quite simply it tells us how the words are like doors always opening to another idea.

THE WORD ITSELF

This section is about finding the depth of the word: it is a very simple exercise. I want to refer back to the beginning of the chapter when I asked you to speak the lines of *Hamlet*, repeating words as you went through.

EXERCISE

This can be done on any speech or piece of dialogue, on your own or in rehearsal. It should be done quite lightly and briefly.

Take any speech, and as you work through it repeat words that instinctively grab your attention, and repeat them several times – probably not more than one word per line. Each time it will make you hear and imagine that word afresh, for it will take it away from its place within the sentence and it will be informed by your own experience of that word. Just try it on a sonnet:

If the dull substance of my flesh were thought,
Injurious distance should not stop my way;
For then, despite of space, I would be brought
From limits far remote, where thou dost stay.
No matter then, although my foot did stand
Upon the farthest earth removed from thee;
For nimble thought can jump both sea and land
As soon as think the place where he would be.
But ah! thought kills me that I am not thought
To leap large lengths of miles when thou art gone,
But that, so much of earth and water wrought,
I must attend time's leisure with my moan,
   Receiving nought by elements so slow
   But heavy tears, badges of either's woe.

Sonnet 44.

This is a wonderfully metaphysical idea about thought and distance, time and space, and the desire to be with someone, and how the flesh holds you back. If you went through repeating different words, the whole thought would open out in a surprising way. It is a very simple exercise but its effect is palpable.

To sum up: all this work is about making us sensitive to what the words can mean, and how they can reach the subconscious understanding. It is never about stress: if you get meaning across through stress you cut out the options. Once you are told to stress a word, you lose its balance with the other words. It is always a matter of balance and poise and feeling the underlying energy. There is a code there somewhere.

But I must stress that the work is not only about uncovering the options but about keeping the work fresh. The further you get into rehearsal the more choices you have to make and therefore fix the intention of the text, but to come back to this work will keep it fresh.

8 Structures

I want to look at this whole question of structure from a purely practical point of view, and to look at its relevance to the actor inhabiting the text. How does the rhythm, the form, the shaping of thought help us into character?

It is useful to remember that all the rhythms and forms of speech evolved naturally as humans became increasingly articulate and started to make sounds into words. And as time went on there was a natural progression into forms of ritualistic language, and certain rhythms and combinations of sounds took on a significance of their own, directly connected with the need to express some kind of spiritual affirmation. I believe we are still left with the residue of this, for we are unaccountably moved by words spoken in a particular pattern, by how the sound of a voice can lift and inspire beyond the meaning, and how we can be manipulated by words well spoken. This is so in any language.

What I am saying, then, is that these forms, these sounds, these rhythms, were part of our evolution and existed before they were analysed by the mind, before they were given a name and quantified. They were part of a verbal society. But perhaps the more we started to write things down, to commit words to paper, the less in touch we became with this primal sound. Reading is a left-side brain activity which to a certain extent minimalises the imagination while we are in the process of doing it, and it is only when we take a moment off from that activity that we start to imagine.

Now to be practical: I will first focus on Shakespeare, because of its very specific form and because it opens our ears to language in such a total way, but we will be looking at what that tells us about other writing, particularly the plays of today.

To do this I want first to look at what I will call the different energies in the writing, each one contributing to the infinite variety of movement within the lines.

These energies are to do with the following:

(i)   Rhythm and metre.
(ii)   The energy of the line.
(iii) The caesura.
(iv)   Speech structures.
       Whole thought structures.
       Movement of individual thoughts.
(v)   Vowel and consonant lengths, plus the vowel itself.

Then we will look briefly at the following:

(i)   How a speech is shaped.
(ii)   The soliloquy – its movement and purpose.
(iii) Rhetorical devices used, e.g. assonance, alliteration, antithesis, rhyming, etc.
(iv)   The rhythms of prose.

I have written about these issues in detail in *The Actor and the Text* – setting out the rules, as it were – but here I want to take it further and look at how we can work on all these issues as a group, and how we can awaken our instinctive response to the sound so that it can inform the whole play. It is not about laying out the rules, for I know you are well aware of these, but rather about practical ways of hearing what is in the rhythms and spaces of the text – and its energy.

I think the valuable thing about doing this work in a group is that the focus is not entirely on you and whether you are doing it right. You hear other people: sometimes what you hear satisfies you and sometimes it does not, and that is a learning process in itself.

First, I will lay out the exercises which can be done on the text for each of the work sections. Then, to illustrate the exercises, I have selected four speeches – from *A Midsummer Night's Dream*, *Romeo and Juliet*, *Hamlet* and *Coriolanus*. They are short speeches and from different periods of Shakespeare's writing, but each illustrates very clearly the different energies we want to establish, and I will point out these as we go. I find it quite difficult to select texts because every piece you look at is so different and throws up so many things – rhythm, sound, complexity of thought – that you want to use them all, but the three I have chosen are particularly good. The important thing is that the work can be done on any text.

Shakespeare wrote in the rhythm of everyday speech. He could manipulate it and heighten it, but the basic rhythm was there, and that rhythm has not altered. I am sure that is why we still want to speak his work today.

THE IAMBIC PENTAMETER

Just to be quite clear: the iambic pentameter is a five-beat line, made up of one unstressed syllable followed by one stressed syllable:

te-tum, te-tum, te-tum, te-tum, te-tum
'Now entertain conjecture of a time'

Sometimes it has an extra unstressed syllable at the end – this we call a feminine ending. 'To be, or not to be – that is the question' has eleven syllables, and therefore a feminine ending.

When I am talking about the rhythm I am talking about an underlying beat which is the pulse of the writing, i.e. the five metrical beats. How you dispose of the weight of that pulse, its length and stress, will vary according to the sense and formation of the language. It's like singing blues or reggae, where you can dwell on one note for almost the length of the line, but you make up for it by the end of the rhythmic line. This, to an extent, is the same in Shakespeare – there is an infinite variety of movement to one iambic line which will vary according to the very shade of meaning you want to convey. And this is made possible by the different lengths and weight of the sounds themselves and how you choose to space them within the timing of the whole line.

To do these exercises you will need to choose a speech to work on: it can be from the play you are rehearsing, and this will help you to discover its particular and distinctive quality, or you can choose something else. First let us look at the iambic beat itself.

EXERCISES

Get everyone to sit round and speak the text together. As you read, very gently tap out the strong beats. This way you will hear when the metre stress goes against the sense stress, i.e. when the word that should be stressed is off the beat.

When metre and sense collide in this way, you will notice what it does to the rhythm of the thought – how it disturbs it. Also, you will notice the length of the syllables and whether they fit in easily. This of course is determined by the vowel and consonant lengths – both of which contribute to the texture of thought and meaning.

Sometimes the disruption of sense stress and metre stress can have quite a violent, even brutal, effect, and this tells us something of the state of mind of the character.

Also, you will notice how the varying length of the syllables gives an infinite variety to the movement of the lines. This gives the speaker room to play with the rhythm and the spaces in the line, to syncopate it, if you like, and so shift the stress and thereby the meaning.

This needs to be done two or three times so that you can notice what is happening in the rhythm of each line.

LINE ENERGY

Shakespeare wrote in both verse and prose; much has been written about the significance of this, and this you will know about. What we must acknowledge in the speaking is that the verse form is there for a reason and it has to be honoured. If we try to disguise it and make it sound like prose, we take away some of its power – and its pleasure.

All I want to do here is to get us away from regarding the marking of the line endings in terms of a rule, i.e. lifting the end of each line, but rather to make us aware of the organic drive of the verse, and that, by being aware of that line ending, we feel how the rhythm drives us to the next line and energises it.

There is one more thing, and it is important: research has been done to prove that we, as listeners, can only take in about six or seven seconds' worth of speech at any one time without a split moment's break. This roughly amounts to eight or nine words, and we need that break in order to take in the information which is being passed to us. So when we are looking at line endings or caesuras, it is useful to keep this in mind. They are not some kind of literary device invented by writers and poets, rather they are essential to our understanding. In everyday speech these spaces are there in order to accommodate the basic needs of the listener – in other words they are part of the evolutionary process.

EXERCISES

1. Having chosen a speech, get each person to sit in a circle and read one line. As you listen, you will hear whether the thought comes to a stop at the end of the line, or if it continues on to the next line. If the thought continues, hear how that moment of passing the line on to the next person gives us that suspension, and how it energises the next line. It also gives the listener a moment to allow the thought to drop in. Experiment with this. You will hear how that sense of the underlying beat drives the thought forward, and how organic it is to the writing. Do the speech several times so that people will have different lines to speak – this is important, for each person will speak a line differently, and this makes us aware of the variations possible.
2. Still speaking one line each, take an object – apple, ball, pencil – and as you pass the line on, pass the object also. Pass it as you speak the last word: this can be done standing or sitting.
3. As a variation, stand in the circle, speak your line directly to someone on the other side of the circle and cross to them as you speak.

FINDING THE CAESURA

The caesura is a break in the line, a split moment of poise. It is so often built into the middle of a line so that the listener is made ready for the end. That suspension holds our interest, and gives the end of the line another energy and points it up. As an example, take the first four lines of the prologue to *Romeo and Juliet*:

> Two households/both alike in dignity
> In fair Verona,/where we lay our scene,
> From ancient grudge/break to new mutiny.
> Where civil blood/makes civil hands unclean

To have that moment on 'households' allows the listener time to imagine a household – not just a house, but a house full of kitchens, clothes closets, people, etc. Likewise, we need a moment on Verona so we can place where we are in our mind.

To have that moment on 'grudge' gives 'new mutiny' an added impact, plus, of course, there are two stressed words together making it quite violent. Then the poise on 'blood' points up 'hands' – making us realise how complex is the mix of personal and political enmity.

EXERCISES

Go round the circle but instead of speaking a whole line each, the actor saying the beginning of the line must break it at a point that seems right. The next person will then take it on and finish the line.

It will be guesswork and you will not always break it at the right place, but after you have done it you will know whether it sounded right or not.

Do this several times so that you become aware of the possible choices.

You will find that the caesura is not there in every line, and this makes the line movement even more interesting. As a prologue, the *Romeo and Juliet* excerpt has a lot of information to impart, and for this reason the caesura is important. But having had eight lines with caesuras, the movement changes:

> The fearful passage of their death-mark'd love
> And the continuance of their parents' rage,
> Which,/but their children's end,/nought could remove,
> Is now the two hour's traffic of our stage

This is a matter of choice, and how we as individuals hear it, but to me the first two lines have no break, the third has two breaks and the fourth again is unbroken.

The first line of the last couplet has no caesura but the last line has a very important one, and can be just a little extended – for it is both selling us the play and rounding off the prologue:

The which if you with patient ears attend,
What here shall miss our toil shall strive to mend.

All this tells us of the negotiations and choices that can be made with the rhythm of a line.

SPEECH STRUCTURES

To me what is interesting in a speech is that you have two energies going on at the same time. One is the energy of the whole thought, i.e. the sentence, and how it is reasoned through. The other is that of the different parts of that thought, i.e. the phrases, which go to make up the whole. These individual thoughts or phrases are often in the form of an image which serves to define the whole and give it colour and depth. We hear how the character is breathing.

In the early plays, the syntax of the thought is often quite simple, and though it may be carried over several lines, it will, more often than not, naturally come to a stop at the end of a line – as in the speech of Berowne from *Love's Labour's Lost* which we looked at earlier. However, in the later plays, the thoughts are not only very convoluted, as we have seen in the extracts from *The Winter's Tale*, but also they often come to an end in the middle of a line, and this forces us to find a way of keeping the energy of the whole line intact, while giving each individual thought its own precise length and clarity.

So what we have to look at is the structure of whole thoughts, and for our purposes we will take a whole thought to mean a sentence ending either at a full stop, a colon, a semi-colon, a question mark or an exclamation mark: this tells us how the ideas and thoughts are being developed and clarified. And then we need to look at how the whole thought is broken up into its parts.

Before I lay out the exercises, I want to look at this speech of Egeus, from the beginning of *A Midsummer Night's Dream*, because it illustrates so clearly what I mean by the two energies. Egeus is asking the duke for the right to force his daughter to marry Demetrius, rather than Lysander whom she wants to marry. It speaks for itself:

EGEUS   Full of vexation come I, with complaint
         Against my child, my daughter Hermia./
         Stand forth, Demetrius!/My noble lord,
         This man hath my consent to marry her./
         Stand forth, Lysander!/– And my gracious Duke,
         This man hath bewitched the bosom of my child./
         Thou, thou, Lysander, thou hast given her rhymes,
         And interchang'd love-tokens with my child;
         Thou hast by moonlight at her window sung
         With feigning voice, verses of feigning love,
         And stolen the impression of her fantasy
         With bracelets of thy hair, rings, gauds, conceits,
         Knacks, trifles, nosegays, sweetmeats – messengers
         Of strong prevailment in unhardened youth –
         With cunning hast thou filched my daughter's heart,
         Turned her obedience which is due to me
         To stubborn harshness./And, my gracious Duke,
         Be it so she will not here before your grace
         Consent to marry with Demetrius,
         I beg the ancient privilege of Athens:/
         As she is mine, I may dispose of her;
         Which shall be either to this gentleman
         Or to her death, according to our law
         Immediately provided in this case.

                    A Midsummer Night's Dream, I.i.

Egeus first lays out his argument to the duke, and he does this over the first six lines. He then asks each of the young men to stand forth, presenting Demetrius as the man he wants his daughter to marry. He then addresses Lysander and accuses him of bewitching Hermia. That one word 'bewitched' is surely the pivotal word for it both justifies his anger and feeds his fears; it also puts us in a society where this belief is possible. He then continues to address Lysander, and as he does so gets increasingly involved with his feelings. The sentences become longer but, conversely, more broken up, as he becomes less in control of his thoughts. Realising that this is not helping his case, he pulls back and addresses the duke directly and with a certain dignity. He then sums up the situation and ends by seeking permission to have the right to dispose of Hermia as he wishes if she does not obey – even to her death. In essence, then, it is in three parts: first he lays out the premise, then he attempts to argue it through, and finally he sums up the options.

Now to look at how those three parts are broken up: the first part is fairly smooth, as Egeus attempts to make his position clear. He also needs to give due respect to Theseus. But when he starts to speak directly to Lysander, the word 'bewitched' is like an alarm bell which sets off his fears and takes over his reasoning: from then on it is very broken up. He uses words connected with witchcraft – 'gauds', 'conceits', 'cunning', 'filched' – all of which feed his state of mind. He then realises he may have gone too far and pulls himself back with 'And, my gracious Duke,' and ends on a calmer note in a much smoother and more controlled rhythm.

This is a straightforward speech and illustrates the points very clearly: it has a lightness of sound which belies the seriousness of the charge, but when we do find its different movements suddenly those last four lines take on a weight and gravity which shock us. How then do we find this movement of thought actively within ourselves, our bodies, particularly with a text which may be more difficult to unravel?

EXERCISES

1. With the speech you have chosen, go round the circle and speak one whole thought each, i.e. to a full-stop, colon, semi-colon, etc. You will then hear the matter, the reasoning, of each thought – its length and texture, and how it leads on to, and feeds, the next thought. Repeat this if necessary so that the meaning of the whole is clear.

2. To take this further, you need to move it in the space. Start by speaking it all together. Find your own space in the room. Speak one whole thought in one place, then immediately move to another part of the space and speak the next whole thought, and so on. What this does is make us aware of how each thought comes from a different part of one's

awareness, and has a different energy and rhythm and texture. This is a particularly useful exercise when working on a speech individually and we will be coming back to it later in more detail. Because you have moved to a different space for each thought, it makes you find the different quality of that thought, and how it has a different energy. It somehow makes you find it afresh.

3. To look at the phrases within the thought, get in a circle and speak round in turn, but this time speak the text only to each punctuation mark. You will hear how each part of the thought has a distinctive character – either an image or shade of thought – which is constantly shifting the direction of the whole.

4. Now to get the thoughts moving, spread round the room and, speaking through the text together, walk briskly round the space, changing directions on every punctuation mark. This tells us so much about how the thoughts are continually shifting and changing direction, plus it gets the blood moving so that we experience how we are being energised by the words.

5. As a variation, put two chairs in the centre of the circle quite close together. Get one person to sit and speak the speech, but as they do so they must move from one chair to the other on each punctuation mark. Do not speak while you are moving and make sure you are sitting before you speak; it needs to be done quite quickly so the whole thought is kept in the air. Not only do we hear the shift of the thoughts, but also we become aware of the effort involved in finding the words – they do not necessarily come easily. Plus it tells us much about the state of mind of the character, calm or agitated, in the present or reflective, and where the imagination is leading him/her.

The challenge is to be able to encompass imaginatively all these changes, yet keep the speed and reasoning of the whole thought intact; for in real life we think fast.

VOWEL AND CONSONANT LENGTHS

The combination of different lengths of vowels plus the combination of consonants, both voiced and unvoiced, gives the writing its particular texture, and that texture conveys so much about the underlying feeling and motive at a subliminal level. It also affects the rhythm and how it is disposed.

To open our ears, listen to these next two pieces of text, the first from *Henry V*:

Now entertain conjecture of a time
When creeping murmur and the poring dark
Fills the wide vessel of the universe.

Henry V, IV (prologue)

The first long vowel enables us to dwell on the word 'Now' and so give it its importance without disturbing the metrical stress which should go on 'entertain'; but the point is that that first word has a length which opens the text out and makes us ready for what is to follow. Also, throughout the piece the vowels are quite long – 'time', 'creeping', 'poring dark', 'wide', etc.

There is a fairly even distribution of voiced and unvoiced consonants, but there are a number of continuant consonants – 'time', 'murmur', 'poring' – which give it length, plus 'fills', which takes time to get the tongue round. It is not weighty, but it has a feeling of openness in its sound which gives it a resonance.

The following lines from *Macbeth* could not sound more different: the vowels are almost without exception short, the consonants mostly unvoiced, and the thoughts are rounded off with that word 'jump'. We hear a mind jumping about and clutching at ideas; it gathers weight as he goes on.

If it were done when 'tis done, then 'twere well
It were done quickly. If the assassination
Could trammel up the consequence, and catch,
With his surcease success – that but this blow
Might be the be-all and the end-all, here –
But here, upon this bank and shoal of time –
We'd jump the life to come.

Macbeth, I.vii.

It is obvious, I know, but both passages have the same underlying metrical beat yet the sound and weight of the

165

language could not be more different. And we have to keep our ears open to all these changes, for that is what grabs the listener's ear and makes it exciting to listen to.

When we are speaking, our emphasis is on getting the thought through and making it clear. We constantly shorten the consonants – they may be sharp and clear yet still clipped – and so we do not allow them their due time. To an extent we have lost the sense of their vibration, and so the texture of the language is not fully explored – and used. It is worthwhile, therefore, at different times during rehearsal, to focus on this.

The same goes for the vowel sounds. We are not aware enough of the effect of vowels and how they inform the emotional heart of the language. It is my contention that we made open sounds before we made closed ones, and it was only when we started to make closed, i.e. consonant-type, sounds that speech started to be formed as we began to impart information. I therefore think that it is the vowel sounds which take us into our feelings, and this is why I want to end this section by looking at what I call the vowel itself.

To focus on the possibilities of these sounds, and how they can stretch out, will add to our awareness of what the language can actively do to the listener. And working the language physically in this way ties it in with the need to get the words across.

EXERCISES

Every actor is familiar with articulation exercises, and these are always useful to get the voice warmed up. However, with regards to work on the text itself, it is the vibration and length that we need to tune into.

1. With the text you have selected, work through it together, consciously being very deliberate with the consonant sounds, making sure that the compound ones are fully verbalised and extending the voiced consonants so that you feel the full vibration of each one. All the time take note of their length and muscularity and feel the resonance forward in the mouth.
2. The jostling exercise is also good to do, because it not only releases the energy of the body, but it releases a certain

aggression which gives force to the consonants. Remember this feeling.

3. For the vowels, much the same applies. Go through the text noticing their length, and how a combination of voiced consonants may extend them.

4. Get in a circle, link arms quite firmly, and pull against each other as hard as you can while speaking the text. If you are reading it may prove difficult but do as much of it as you can – you will hear how the vowel sounds stretch out.

5. To focus on the vowel itself, work through a speech but instead of verbalising the whole speech, only verbalise the vowel sounds. It is quite difficult to do to begin with – you need plenty of breath and there should be no glottal stops. Each vowel must start smooth. What this does is give a remarkable insight into the weight and length of the vowels, and to the rhythm of the lines. The important thing is to focus on the meaning of the text as you do it, for then you will hear how the vowels can change length because of the underlying reason. For this reason it is particularly good to do it on a text that you are familiar with. It surprises us because it seems that the vowels hold the sense of the whole speech.

If you do the last exercise with the speech of Ophelia, which we will be looking at, it will open you out to so much: it is full of long, open vowels, and the final line and a half, with the long 'ee' sounds, tells us she is breaking in two. It is incredibly moving to hear. Vowels connect with something quite deep down inside, and we need to be in touch with their sound.

There is one other exercise which I am particularly fond of which came out of a workshop I attended on the Rudolf Steiner Approaches to Language; it needs to be done as part of the preparation voice exercises, but it does make us aware of the space of a vowel sound. It is about the shape of a vowel, and though perhaps a little off the wall, it is strangely exhilarating. You feel the vowels through the whole of your body. You will need a piano or a musical instrument to start you off.

Start by singing – 'mememe mememe mememe mah' – on each note up the scale. Make every 'm' sound very firm and muscular – make it bounce off the lips.

Do this several times so that you feel the vibration of the 'm' sounds, then do it running round the room as follows.

Run while you are singing the 'mememe' sounds, then as you sing the vowel sound 'ah', stand quite still and make a shape with your arms to fill that sound. The shape should come from your connection with the sound.

When you have done this a couple of times, repeat, but change the vowel sound. This way you can go through all the long vowels – OO, OH, AW, AH, ER, AY, EE, I, OW. You will notice how each vowel makes you find a different shape with your arms.

TEXTS

And now for the texts, and what we can glean from them with regards to the issues that we have just been through.

First Juliet, just after the nurse tells her that Romeo has killed Tybalt. Romeo is her husband and Tybalt her cousin, so she is totally split in allegiance. She does not yet know the circumstances of the brawl so instinctively she blames Romeo:

JULIET   O serpent heart, hid with a flowering face!
              Did ever dragon keep so fair a cave?
              Beautiful tyrant! fiend angelical!
              Dove-feathered raven! Wolvish-ravening lamb!
              Despisèd substance of divinest show!
              Just opposite to what thou justly seemest –
              A damnèd saint, an honourable villain!
              O nature, what hadst thou to do in hell
              When thou didst bower the spirit of a fiend
              In mortal paradise of such sweet flesh?
              Was ever book containing such vile matter
              So fairly bound? O, that deceit should dwell
              In such a gorgeous palace!
                                Romeo and Juliet, III.ii.

Metre: this is is fairly regular: it breaks on the third line on the word 'beautiful', which makes that line jagged and so points up the violence in the words. Many of the lines have very marked caesuras to point up the antithetical thoughts:

serpent heart – flowering face
beautiful tyrant – fiend angelical

However, to vary that movement you have fairly unbroken lines
like:

Did ever dragon keep so fair a cave . . .
When thou didst bower the spirit of a fiend

So the rhythm of the line is forever changing.

Thought structure: there is little progression here in that it is
simply expressing her anguish and disbelief at the news: it is an
outburst and does not lead to any decisive thought or action.
However, in the very juxtaposition of images there is wit and a
sense of absurdity – 'wolvish-ravening lamb!' Where does she
find all those images? That is why it is necessary to move on the
individual thoughts, i.e. the punctuation marks, to be aware of
the different places in her mind, her imagination. As she thinks
it through you will recognise her deep distress. As you move you
can even make a gesture on some of those images – or you can
crouch or stretch, according to how the image affects you.

Vowel and consonant lengths: these vary according to which
part of the antithesis they are expressing, but on the whole the
vowels are open and the consonants voiced and explosive,
reinforcing her anger and frustration. If you go through a few of
those lines first verbalising only the vowels, and then focusing on
the consonants, you will feel how those sounds affect the rhythm,
and how that rhythm bears out the feeling and extends it. When
you come to speak it normally, that texture, that relish that Juliet
feels in expressing her feelings, will still live in the words.

Now for *Ophelia*, and I think the sound of this is very special.
It comes just after her encounter with Hamlet where, in his
seeming madness, he berates her as a woman. It is possibly the
centre scene for Ophelia, for it is the turning point to her
subsequent madness:

OPHELIA   O, what a noble mind is here o'erthrown!
            The courtier's, soldier's, scholar's, eye, tongue, sword,
            Th'expectancy and rose of the fair state,

The glass of fashion and the mould of form,
Th'observed of all observers, quite, quite down!
And I, of ladies most deject and wretched,
That sucked the honey of his music vows,
Now see that noble and most sovereign reason
Like sweet bells jangled, out of time and harsh,
That unmatched form and feature of blown youth
Blasted with ecstasy. O, woe is me
T'have seen what I have seen, see what I see!

Hamlet, III.i.

Metre: the lines are very regular metrically. The first 'O' can be long but in fact it does not necessarily break the rhythm, plus 'what' can have the meaning almost of a question i.e. to what extent is he noble? The metre itself does not break cleanly until the penultimate line, 'Blasted with ecstasy,' although the end of the line before, i.e. 'blown youth', prepares us for it. The word 'blasted' and what it does to the line is seismic, for it is like she has been split down the middle by lightning.

Line energy: the lines are quite contained. There are only two that actively run on, and they are near the end as the thoughts become more disturbed.

Thought structure: the speech is quite straightforward. The first line tells us the subject, the premise, how all his qualities have come to nothing, and how she believes Hamlet to be mad. Through the next four lines she argues that premise through. She then begins to sum the facts up in terms of herself and what it means to her, and to end she rounds it off with a rhyming couplet – something which finalises her thoughts and, just by placing it all in context, somehow comforts her. But within those whole thought structures there is the movement of the individual thoughts, through which you hear the accumulation of her own distress, and which finally lead her to the phrase 'Blasted with ecstasy', which of course means madness. The very charge of that word 'blasted' tells us something of how she can identify with that thought.

Vowels and consonants: the consonants are fairly smooth for the first half, then when you get words like 'deject and wretched', or 'sucked' or 'jangled', it starts to get harsh and out of tune, and this leads us to 'blasted' and then the last line and a half which in its sound is the antithesis of all that has gone before. It is the openness of the vowels here that is so revealing – how those vowels are coming from the dark of her soul. If you speak it through verbalising only the vowel sounds, you will hear both the infinite variety of movement in the lines, plus the power of the vowels themselves, but of course it is the last line and a half that tells us so much:

O, woe is me
T'have seen what I have seen, see what I see!

It is a cry with no help in sight; perhaps the beginning of her own madness.

And finally Brutus from *Coriolanus*. This speech begins the dialogue between Brutus and Sicinius, two tribunes of the people, as they discuss Coriolanus and how he is ingratiating himself to the people in order to win their vote. But both know that in reality Coriolanus despises them. Here Brutus is describing the reaction of the crowd, knowing full well that if Coriolanus does get the people's vote their own positions are at risk. But they also despise the people and the language is packed with resultant irony:

BRUTUS   All tongues speak of him and the blearèd sights
Are spectacled to see him. Your prattling nurse
Into a rapture lets her baby cry
While she chats him. The kitchen malkin pins
Her richest lockram 'bout her reechy neck,
Clambering the walls to eye him. Stalls, bulks,
                        windows,
Are smothered up, leads filled, and ridges horsed
With variable complexions, all agreeing
In earnestness to see him. Seld-shown flamens
Do press among the popular throngs and puff
To win a vulgar station. Our veiled dames
Commit the war of white and damask in
Their nicely gauded cheeks to th'wanton spoil
Of Phoebus' burning kisses. Such a pother
As if that whatsoever god who leads him

Were slyly crept into his human powers
And gave him graceful posture.

Coriolanus, II.i.

The particular value for us in this speech is both in the texture of the language, i.e. the way the fullness of the vowels and consonants are continually knocking against the metrical stress, and also in the way the thoughts run on and break in the middle of the line.

Metre: this breaks on the very first line. The length of the word 'all' spreads over on to 'tongues', and though the metre stress is on 'tongues', the fact that 'all' takes so long to say gives it weight and spreads it over the metre stress. The rest of the line is quite syncopated to make up for the long first half. The first half of the speech is very full, and if you beat it out it is quite difficult to fit in all the sounds, particularly the multiple consonant sounds – mostly voiced. You have to negotiate with lines like the following, the first of which breaks the iambic pattern, and also has six strong beats instead of five, plus the second line is very full:

Pins her richest lockram 'bout her reechy neck
Clambering the walls to eye him. Stalls, bulks, windows

Line energy: in every case the lines run on and the sentences come to an end mid-line: but if we try moving at the end of each thought, we will hear how the energy of one thought inevitably feeds the next, so the line keeps its drive. Most of the lines have caesuras, though possibly the last three lines are unbroken.

Thought structure: the sentences are quite long and unbroken. The first one sets out his theme very clearly, and with no break. Each thought feeds the next with increasing irritation and builds throughout until you get to the final thought beginning 'Such a pother . . .'

Vowel and consonant lengths: it is a useful speech in which to explore the different lengths in the sounds and how they relate to each other. Some vowels are short but are lengthened and stretched by the consonant combinations, e.g. 'all tongues', 'stalls, bulks, windows', 'leads filled and ridges horsed', 'variable complexions', 'seld-shown flamens' (priests), 'th'wanton spoil'.

Brutus's frustration and anger is audibly apparent, but there is irony in the fact that the language is exaggerated and he is patently enjoying expressing both his disgust at Coriolanus's duplicity, and at the people who are taken in by him. He enjoys painting the images, capped by the final one.

> Such a pother
> As if whatsoever god who leads him
> Were slyly crept into his human powers
> And gave him graceful posture.

The absurdity of the word 'pother' at this point, both in meaning and in sound, expresses everything. The lines also have an ironic elegance as if trying to capture something of Coriolanus's overweening conceit.

To sum up this first section: I have gone into a certain amount of detail on all these points of rhythm and metre to be absolutely clear about the connection between sound and rhythm and how they interact with each other, and most important, the amount of freedom thay give us.

HOW A SPEECH IS SHAPED

We have already looked at this in some detail by examining the thought structures, both the length of the whole thoughts and how they may be broken up into parts. We have also seen how one thought kicks into the next. All this is clearly part of the shaping of a speech. But in almost every case a speech, long or short, has a specific overall form, and I just want to lay that form out as practically as possible.

A speech is itself an action, for it takes on board the issue or issues which are to be considered. It then questions them, argues them through in order to resolve them in some way, and then passes that resolve, or that question, on to the next speaker. It is therefore usually in three sections: three is the magic number. If it is a long speech it will, as it argues the points through, find analogies. It may go back in time, i.e. it may draw on past experience and link it to the present, or it may draw on a philosophical viewpoint, all of which will add weight and depth to the final argument. If it is a short speech, and very much part of an ongoing dialogue, it takes what is being said on board, develops it, and throws it back But what is important for us is that we are aware of this shape, this form, for it is intrinsic to the drive of the thought and the story it is telling. And words change us as we speak them. The form is as follows:

(i) First the premise is laid out.

(ii) This is then elaborated on and reasoned through. This involves opening out the initial issue in diverse ways: it may be with thoughts from the past, it may be with philosophical questions, it may be with images, or it may simply be a weighing up of facts.

(iii) It then pulls all these thoughts or questions together, and comes to some sort of conclusion. This may lead to action, or it may be that it leaves everything in the air. Whatever, it is a summing up in some way in order to pass the thought or the question on.

(iv) From this we see that a speech is usually built in three parts, but also within each part, as different analogies and thoughts evolve, you will often find that one sentence is built in threes. In some way this satisfies the ear.

For the actor all these points mean that you have to keep the through drive of the thought, while allowing each different part of that thought to have its own character and vision. Added to which there is always a resistance somewhere, for you are always speaking in response to someone else's idea, and this is what gives the initial impetus. However, this is not so in a soliloquy.

THE SOLILOQUY

There is something very interesting and enigmatic about a soliloquy: there are so many choices, for though the form is the same, i.e. the laying out of the premise, the development of the argument leading to some sort of conclusion, it is nevertheless the thoughts of a single character. And for the actor I think it begs two questions:

1. Has the character made up his/her mind about the resultant resolution before they start to speak, but in order to clarify their position and possibly justify themselves, they need to speak their thoughts through aloud?
2. Or does the character start with the initial thought or idea, not knowing what the end will be, so that it is the words themselves that feed the progression of the thought, and thus lead to a resolution?

What comes first, then: the thought or the word? I think it can happen either way. But what is important to realise is that in everyday life thoughts occur very quickly, and that a soliloquy therefore needs to give the impression of being as fast as thought. It is always active and always questioning and always going to different parts of the mind. Also, I think it is true to say that sometimes we make up our mind in our stomach as it were, unconsciously, before we consciously put the idea into words. This too can inform the reasoning behind a soliloquy.

I want to look at three soliloquies which are fed in different ways. If we look back at the Ophelia speech, for instance, we see how she lays out her premise:

O, what a noble mind is here o'erthrown!

She then elaborates on this by listing all Hamlet's attributes which have now been taken over by his madness. She finally comes back to herself and, in the final line and a half, she voices her own desolation. It in fact does not lead to any outside action; rather her action is to retreat into herself, and this is made final by the rhyme.

Let us look now at Macbeth's soliloquy, Act I. scene vii, beginning:

If it 'twere done when 'tis done, then 'twere well
It were done quickly. If the assassination
Could trammel up the consequence, and catch
With his surcease success – that but this blow
Might be the be-all and the end-all, here –
But here, upon this bank and shoal of time –
We'd jump the life to come.

Macbeth, I.vii.

175

He is contemplating the murder of Duncan and he opens with this whole metaphysical idea of time, i.e. when is an action done, which is fascinating in itself. As he contemplates the effects of the deed we are led to the subsequent image of 'this bank and shoal of time', and we are immediately taken into an area of unreality. He begins quite sanely but then as he contemplates the action, the whole idea of evil versus goodness, his images get wilder and wilder until he recognises that his ambition may lead him to disaster, and so gives up. We know that by the end a conclusion has been reached and that he has renounced the idea of murder, for when Lady Macbeth enters and asks him why he has left the chamber where Duncan is, he replies, 'We will proceed no further in this business.' He starts with an 'if', so at once we know the deed is not yet fixed in his mind, but it is the speaking of the words and the choice of the images that lead him to the final decision.

But if we look at Brutus's soliloquy in *Julius Caesar*, Act II, scene i, when contemplating the murder of Caesar, we are on quite a different tack. His first words, 'It must be by his death . . .' suggest that he has already made up his mind that Caesar must be killed, and the subsequent speech is about arguing the case through in order to justify that action with his conscience. He ends with:

And therefore think him as a serpent's egg,
Which, hatched, would, as his kind, grow mischievous,
And kill him in the shell.

This then has quite a different movement: the end is there in the beginning. He is not open to intervention, as Macbeth is.

But of course how we deliver a soliloquy is dependent on the particular style and convention of the production. It can be that the actor is required to address the audience directly, so that it is like recounting to them all that is in the character's mind and opening out the questions to them. Certainly this convention can be considered suitable for the character of Iago in *Othello*, and the same also applies to Aaron's speech in *Titus Andronicus*, Act II, scene i, when he is exulting over the fact that his mistress Tamora has now become Empress of Rome. It is the most extravagant and dazzling speech. These soliloquies have a public flavour, and we enjoy the humour and the irony.

But when we make them public we must be rigorous about the seriousness of what we are saying, for however much the audience may enjoy the Machiavellian dealings of those characters' minds, they must not be allowed to forget the evil that is there. It is too easy to cheapen the content. But, as always, it is a matter of choice and what is appropriate. Because of the age we live in, accustomed to television and a much more subtle way of speaking, this alters how we listen and how we interpret. For me soliloquies are about the private workings of the mind which we need somehow to overhear – they take us inside the character and force us to think and to question.

PATTERNS OF RHETORIC

Much has been written about the building of rhetoric and how it forms an organic part of the structure of Shakespeare's plays, the hierarchy into which everything fitted: this hierarchy was part of Elizabethan thought, and I think some knowledge of it is of great value to the actor, because it is a focusing point. Here are a few starting points which may help as a reference:

- God created the universe out of nothing.
- There was a hierarchy into which everything fitted – God, angels, stones.
- Man has both soul and body – passion and reason.
- Man is a microcosm of the universe: thus if man neglects order within himself, it will result in outward political disorder.
- There is a frame of order – the great chain of being. The plays frequently act out the opposite – the reality of disorder.
- Humours shaped man's temperament:
      earth – cold and dry – melancholy
      water – cold and moist – phlegmatic
      air – hot and moist – sanguine
      fire – hot and dry – choleric
- There was a belief in the influence of the stars.

Today, we tend to separate mind from matter, soul from body. It was Descartes who said that the mind is a purely thinking substance, and the body a soulless mechanism.

Opening out to this whole way of viewing the world is perhaps particularly important for us now. So much of the thinking of the central characters is informed by these metaphysical concepts, and we as actors need to know that the imagery in the plays is not fanciful and 'poetic' but is integral to the characters' objectives and tells us where they are in their mind, in their world, and in their person. But I also think we now tend to narrow our perspectives and put emotions at the centre of the work, i.e. how does the character 'feel', whereas the bottom line surely must be 'how best to survive'. And to survive we have to think. It does not lessen the importance of our feelings, rather it adds to them. But what is exciting for the audience is to hear how the mind of the character is working, how he/she ticks, for this is what gives it life, and I think we do not trust this enough. We centre too much on the characters themselves, and not on the world they are operating in.

All I want to do here is alert us to the patterns which are there in the writing, and which can help the actor find the centre of the speech and so help build a framework to the thought.

ANTITHESIS

With all this in mind, it is very clear how important antithetical thought is, because it makes us aware of the opposite, and therefore of the whole. An extreme example of this is the speech of Juliet which we have already looked at: the extremity of the images tells us of the extremity of her feelings, and how these very extremities heighten our awareness. But more complex for us is how these antitheses work when a speech is being reasoned through, i.e. when it is the ideas which are antithetical. The most obvious example to take is Hamlet's soliloquy when he poses the central question, central to us all – 'To be, or not to be – that is the question . . .' – which he then argues through so that the whole speech is a set of antithetical thoughts, which in the end come down on the side of staying alive. Or later in the long scene between Hamlet and Gertrude, Act III, scene iv, when he tries to make her face up to his father's death, and wants her to keep apart from Claudius, he tries to persuade her with the following lines:

QUEEN	O Hamlet, thou hast cleft my heart in twain.
HAMLET	O, throw away the worser part of it,
	And live the purer with the other half.
	Good night. But go not to my uncle's bed.
	Assume a virtue, if you have it not . . .

EXERCISES

When you are working through a speech or a piece of dialogue which contains antitheses, the following exercise is very helpful:

1. You need a piece of paper and a pencil. As you speak the text through, each time you come to a fresh antithetical word or idea, put a tick on the paper.
2. If you are working a dialogue between two or three characters, put the paper and pen on a table or chair between you and divide the paper into columns. On each antithesis, put a tick in your column.

What is good about this is that not only does it point up the opposites and make you think of them actively, but it also adds an excitement to the act of thinking. To have a good thought is always exciting: it also makes you think on your feet, for so often, because of the complexity of the thoughts, you are not aware of the antithesis until it has passed.

ALLITERATION AND ASSONANCE

This is quite simple: as you go through the text for the vowel and consonant textures, you will become aware of the repetition of certain vowels or certain consonants. However, it is important to remember that they are there to make us notice something – perhaps to point up a comic thought or to add poignancy to a sad one. Whatever, it is part of that subtext which needs to be heard.

RHYME

This again has a purpose: in the early comedies it is used extensively with the obvious intention of the enjoyment of wit and language. It obviously has to be used with discretion for it loses its point if it becomes too obvious, and we need to enjoy the surprise when the right rhyme is landed on. For just as children enjoy nursery rhymes because of the unexpectedness of the rhyme, so we enjoy the ingenuity and delight of language which is rhymed.

But there are times when a rhyme points up something quite different: for instance, the couplet at the end of Ophelia's soliloquy, with its combination of long open 'ee' sounds, reinforces her anguish. Or the rhyme at the end of Hamlet's speech, Act III, scene iv. After the long scene with Gertrude, and having killed Polonius, as he pulls the body of Polonius out of the room he says:

> Mother, good night. Indeed, this counsellor
> Is now most still, most secret, and most grave,
> Who was in life a foolish prating knave.

A terrible humour is in that rhyme.

So many soliloquies end with a rhyme, and by their very finality they underscore the state of the character. Here is an example from *Richard III*, after he has successfully wooed Anne in the presence of her husband's corse. He has a long soliloquy, at the end of which he says:

> RICHARD   Shine out, fair sun, till I have bought a glass
>   That I may see my shadow as I pass.
>   *Richard III*, I.ii.

And another from *Measure for Measure*. Isabella has begged Angelo to spare her brother's life, and he has responded by asking her to sleep with him:

> ISABELLA   Then, Isabel, live chaste, and brother die.
>   More than our brother is our chastity.
>   I'll tell him yet of Angelo's request,
>   And fit his mind to death, for his soul's rest.
>   *Measure for Measure*, II.iv.

Both serve to round off a section of the story: one is packed with bitter irony and the second with a bitter fatalism.

WORD PLAY

We have to keep our ears open for the play on words, for in Shakespeare it is so much part of the layers of awareness in a character. When Leontes, in the first scene of *The Winter's Tale*, tells his son 'Go play, boy, play: thy mother plays, and I play too,' the layers of meaning that the word 'play' has is not only ironic, they also tell us of Leontes' multiplicity towards his wife, his child, and himself. These word games are obviously there for a purpose, often to point up a certain absurdity in the situation. There are countless instances of this kind of play on words – puns, if you like – and I have listed a few of them in *The Actor and the Text*; the important thing is that we listen out for them and use them for their wit and for their irony.

EXERCISE

A useful exercise with a group would be to look at the following Sonnet 138.

One person in the group reads it through. The rest of the group sits round and listens without looking at the text. Mutter the puns and the word play as they occur.

When my love swears that she is made of truth
I do believe her, though I know she lies,
That she might think me some untutored youth,
Unlearned in the world's false subtleties.
Thus vainly thinking that she thinks me young,
Although she knows my days are past the best,
Simply I credit her false-speaking tongue;
On both sides thus is simple truth suppress'd.
But wherefore says she not she is unjust?
And wherefore say not I that I am old?
O, love's best habit is in seeming trust,
And age in love loves not to have years told.
Therefore I lie with her, and she with me,
And in our faults by lies we flattered be.

Sonnet 138

It teems with word play and it is all about truth – truth in love – and about uttering that truth. Notice 'swears', 'truth', 'believe', 'know', 'think', 'lies', and 'subtleties', which could mean 'subtle ties'. Then on to 'vainly', 'credit', 'simple truth', 'habit', 'seeming trust', capped by the final pun on 'lie' in the last couplet.

Each play on a word uncovers another layer in their love, which seems to be built up of both truth and lies: but somehow, because it is articulated, we get a sense of the completeness of their relationship.

PROSE

It never ceases to surprise me how certain rhythms evoke certain responses in the listener, and these responses do not seem to change with time. If you read through the following speech of Thersites in *Troilus and Cressida*, taking note of the punctuation, and letting the turns of phrases take you on, there is very definitely a rhythm there that makes you laugh: yet at first reading you probably will not understand it completely for it is by no means one of the easiest speeches of Shakespeare. It is in fact quite complicated in its analogies and sentence structure, but we hear its comedy in its rhythms. Thersites has just been involved in a dialogue with Achilles and Patroclus, during which he accuses Patroclus of being Achilles' male whore: left alone, he dismisses them with contempt, and he then turns his spleen on Agamemnon.

THERSITES   With too much blood and too little brain, these two may run mad: but if with too much brain and too little blood they do, I'll be a curer of madmen. Here's Agamemnon, an honest fellow enough, and one that loves quails, but he has not so much brain as ear-wax; and the goodly transformation of Jupiter there, his brother, the bull, the primitive statue and oblique memorial of cuckolds, a thrifty shoeing-horn in a chain, hanging at his brother's leg – to what form but that he is, should wit larded with malice, and malice forced with wit, turn him to? To an ass were nothing: he is both ass and ox. To an ox were nothing; he is both ox and ass. To be a dog, a mule, a cat, a fitchew, a toad, a lizard, an owl, a puttock, or a herring without a roe, I would not care; but to be Menelaus I would conspire against destiny. Ask me not what I would be, if I were not Thersites; for I care not to be the louse of a lazar so I were not Menelaus Heyday! Spirits and fires!

[*Enter Hector, Troilus, Agamemnon etc.*]

Troilus and Cressida, V.i.

There is something in that rhythm which delights us, yet we do not quite know why. But oddly, when you are working on it, the rhythm of prose is often more difficult to hear and to define than the rhythm of verse. Because verse has a very specific metre which we can hang on to, we can hear when it breaks – it is there underpinning the phrasing and structure of the text. But prose does not have this formal rhythm, and because it appears to be like everyday talk, we speak it naturalistically. We break it up and stress it for its sense, but in so doing we lose what it is telling us beyond the surface meaning, i.e. the underlying intention – its humour or its pathos. And that humour, that pathos, comes from the different lengths of phrases and how they are juxtaposed, and this has to be listened for. In *The Actor and the Text* I have gone into some detail on these points on a number of Shakespeare texts, laying them out on the page in phrases so that the form can be clearly seen as you read it, so I will not repeat that. But what I would say is that in working as a group on any prose play, be it classical or modern, it is vital that some time is given over to listening to the phrasing and the rhythm, and what these are telling us about the meaning and style of the whole work.

The exercises I would suggest are the same as those we did to find the structure of the thought phrases, but with this difference: we need to speak the text defining the words very clearly but without interpreting them in any way. We need to make sense of them but they should be spoken quite flat and without intonation, but being 'on' the word. In this way you will hear the precise rhythm and length of the phrase itself – and also how it differs from the one before and the one after.

EXERCISES

1. Take any speech and work it round the circle, each person speaking to a punctuation mark.

2. With one person only speaking, repeat the chair exercise – move from chair to chair on each punctuation mark. This will allow us to hear what the varying lengths of phrases tell us of the underlying mood/intention.
3. With everyone reading together, move round the space, changing direction on every punctuation mark.
4. Finally, either standing or sitting, read it through together. Do this very simply, and without expression, but marking the rhythms of the thoughts: it is a little like the pointing of a psalm.

It is crucial that we hear what the rhythms are telling us before we lay our own interpretation on the text, for this can inform our acting choices and so help us to enter that other character, and the world the writer has given us.

Let us now look at some texts: it is quite revealing, and also exciting, to read through some prose texts, even if you are not familiar with them, just to focus on the rhythms and hear their differences, and what those differences tell us. We will begin with three pieces of Shakespeare, two from *Henry V* and one from *Hamlet*, then we will look at Ford, and then some modern writing. The first is the hostess from *Henry V*, describing the death of Falstaff:

BARDOLPH   Would I were with him, wheresome'er he is, either in heaven or in hell!

HOSTESS   Nay, sure, he's not in hell: he's in Arthur's bosom, if ever man went to Arthur's bosom. 'A made a finer end, and went away an it had been any christom child; 'a parted ev'n just between twelve and one, ev'n at the turning o'th' tide; for after I saw him fumble with the sheets, and play with flowers, and smile upon his fingers' ends, I knew there was but one way; for his nose was as sharp as a pen, and 'a babbled of green fields. 'How now, Sir John?' quoth I, 'What, man, be o' good cheer!' So 'a cried out, 'God, God, God!' three or four times. Now I, to comfort him, bid him 'a should not think of God; – I hop'd there was no need to trouble himself with any such thoughts yet. So 'a bade me lay more clothes on his feet; I put my hand into the bed, and felt them, and

> they were as cold as any stone; then I felt to his
> knees, and so upward, and upward, and all was as
> cold as any stone.'
>
> *Henry V*, II.iii.

The way these thoughts are phrased tells us everything. It tells us how her mind is working and how she remembers each moment with absolute clarity – 'for his nose was as sharp as a pen'. It is wonderfully precise. And this is what makes it so poignant, for at those moments of great emotional stress we strangely remember the details, perhaps because we cannot deal with the bigger reality. And this clarity has to be weighed against the emotion, for if the actor over-invests that speech with feeling it actually loses its power.

And another speech from *Henry V* – the speech of the boy who serves Nym and Pistol and Bardolph. It is particularly useful for the actor playing the boy to do this exercise in order to find the humour which underlies his very well-reasoned argument: each point is laid very clearly, then commented on, which then leads to the pay-off, and this is done so subtly in the phrasing and the way it is served up. The actor playing the boy will be young and, while understanding its humour and how it works, will need the confidence to take the time needed for that humour to drop in to the awareness of the audience. Those spaces are crucial.

BOY As young as I am, I have observed these three swashers. I am
boy to them all three, but all they three, though they would
serve me, could not be man to me; for indeed three such
antics do not amount to a man. For Bardolph, he is
white-livered and red-faced; by the means whereof 'a faces it
out, but fights not. For Pistol, he hath a killing tongue and a
quiet sword; by the means whereof 'a breaks words, and
keeps whole weapons. For Nym, he hath heard that men of
few words are the best men; and therefore he scorns to say
his prayers, lest 'a should be thought a coward; but his few
bad words are matched with as few good deeds, for 'a never
broke any man's head but his own, and that was against a
post, when he was drunk. They will steal anything, and call it
purchase. Bardolph stole a lute-case, bore it twelve leagues,
and sold it for three half-pence. Nym and Bardolph are sworn

brothers in filching, and in Calais they stole a fire-shovel – I
knew by that piece of service the men would carry coals.
They would have me as familiar with men's pockets as their
gloves or their handkerchers; which makes much against my
manhood, if I should take from another's pocket to put into
mine own; for it is plain pocketing up of wrongs. I must leave
them, and seek some better service. Their villainy goes much
against my weak stomach, and therefore I must cast it up.

Henry V, III.ii.

And now Hamlet's speech on the arrival of Rosencrantz and
Guildenstern in Elsinore. They have been sent for by Claudius
and Gertrude to find out what is ailing Hamlet, for he seems to
be mad. They finally admit that they have been sent for and in
this speech Hamlet takes stock of his position, and possibly his
danger. For a moment Hamlet sees himself in relation to the
universe – he is in his own world. He speaks the following:

HAMLET   I will tell you why. So shall my anticipation prevent
your discovery, and your secrecy to the King and
Queen moult no feather. I have of late – but wherefore
I know not – lost all my mirth, forgone all customs of
exercises. And indeed it goes so heavily with my
disposition that this goodly frame the earth seems to
me a sterile promontory. This most excellent canopy,
the air, look you, this brave o'erhanging firmament,
this majestical roof fretted with golden fire – why, it
appeareth nothing to me but a foul and pestilent
congregation of vapours. What a piece of work is a
man, how noble in reason, how infinite in faculties, in
form and moving how express and admirable, in action
how like an angel, in apprehension how like a god: the
beauty of the world, the paragon of animals! And yet to
me what is this quintessence of dust? Man delights not
me – nor woman neither, though by your smiling you
seem to say so.

Hamlet, II.ii.

Just in that very rhythm we hear the stillness of his thoughts
intermixed with the disgust he feels both with his situation, and
with Rosencrantz and Guildenstern for what he sees as their
betrayal.

And now this piece of Jacobean text from *'Tis Pity She's a Whore* by John Ford. Vasques is the servant of Soranzo, a nobleman: Soranzo's wife, Isabella, has just had a baby out of wedlock, but she has successfully concealed it from everyone, even her husband, until now. Soranzo has just found out, and has sworn vengeance. Vasques, left alone, contemplates the situation:

VASQUES Ah, sirra, here's work for the nonce. I had a suspicion of a bad matter in my head a pretty whiles ago: but after my madam's scurvy looks here at home, her waspish perverseness and loud fault-finding, then I remembered the proverb, that where hens crow and cocks hold their peace there are sorry houses. S'foot, if the lower parts of a she-tailor's cunning can cover such a swelling in the stomach, I'll never blame a false stitch in a shoe whiles I live again. Up and up so quick? And so quickly too? 'Twere a fine policy to learn by whom; this must be known; and I have thought on't . . .

'Tis Pity She's a Whore, IV.iii.

If, in trying to make the sense clear, you try to clarify the meaning by laying stress on individual words, you lose the pattern of the whole thought, and this curiously makes it more difficult to understand. This very much pertains to Jacobean text, the sense of which is so often difficult to find initially: the secret is always to get inside the syntax of the thought structures, and then the whole shape of the speech adds up and suddenly becomes quite clear. There is not the subtlety of thought and subtext that there is in Shakespeare.

Now for some modern text to practise on the ear. This is very different because there are so many different influences at work – country, accent, changing fashions, etc. Writing has diversified so much: the Irish poeticism of O'Casey, the spareness of Beckett, the naturalism of Williams, the compression of Barker. It would be impossible to look at them all in detail, nor perhaps is it necessary, for once we are alert to listening for the different rhythms, we will discover all the different variations as we work on them. My only purpose in laying out these three texts is to alert us to their different rhythms and the world they take us into. So here are three pieces of modern, twentieth-century texts at random: Shaw's *Mrs Warren's Profession*, written in 1893, Arnold Wesker's *Roots*, written in 1959, and *Blasted* by Sarah Kane, written in 1998.

The passage from *Mrs Warren's Profession* comes near the end of the play when she is giving advice to her daughter Vivie, which Vivie then turns on its head and finally refuses. In the end she walks away from her mother. This of course is not 'modern speak', but Shaw's energy and drive is always good to hear. How he lays out an argument and builds it through, then starts again on a different tack and builds that through, until it comes to a final summing up, always to provoke an answer.

Mrs Warren: I mean that youre throwing away all your chances for nothing. You think that people are what they pretend to be: that the way you were taught at school and college to think things right and proper is the way things really are. But its not: its all only a pretence, to keep the cowardly slavish common run of people quiet. Do you want to find out, like other women, at forty, when youve thrown yourself away and lost your chances; or wont you take it in good time now from your own mother, that loves you and swears to you that its truth: gospel truth? [urgently] Vivie: the big people, the clever people, the managing people, all know it. They do as I do, and think what I think. I know plenty of them. I know them to speak to, to introduce you to, to make friends of for you. I dont mean anything wrong: thats what you dont understand: your head is full of ignorant ideas about me. What do the people that taught you know about life or about people like me? When did they ever meet me, or speak to me, or let anyone tell them about me? The fools! Would they ever have done anything for you if I hadnt paid them? Havent I told you that I want you to be respectable? Havent I brought you up to be respectable? And how can you keep it up without any money and my influence and Lizzie's friends? Cant you see that youre cutting your own throat

as well as breaking my heart in turning your back
on me?

Mrs Warren's Profession, Act IV.

This piece from *Roots* takes us into a very different world, a rural
community in the late 50s, and it is about the struggle that the
central character, Beatie, has to find her own roots.

Beatie: I am not talking about family roots – I mean – the – I
mean – Look! Ever since it begun the world's bin growin'
hasn't it? Things hev happened, things hev bin
discovered, people have bin thinking and improving and
inventing but what do we know about it all?

Jimmy: What is she on about?

Beatie: What do you mean, what am I on about? I'm talking!
Listen to me! I'm tellin' you that the world's bin growing
for two thousand years and we haven't noticed it. I'm
telling you that we don't know what we are or where we
come from. I'm telling you something's cut us off from
the beginning. I'm telling you we've got no roots. Blimey
Joe! We've all got large allotments, we all grow things
around us so we should know about roots. You know
how to keep your flowers alive don't you mother?
Jimmy – you know how to keep the roots of your vegies
strong and healthy. It's not only the corn that need
strong roots, you know, it's us too. But what've we got?
Go on, tell me, what've we got? We don't know where
we push up from and we don't bother neither.

Roots, Act III

In the introduction to the Penguin edition of the play, Bernard
Levin, the well-known theatre critic of the time, wrote something very interesting:

Mr Wesker's ear (it is a characteristic shared by many of the
post-war school of British playwrights – John Osborne, Peter Shaffer,
Robert Bolt) is extraordinarily acute, enabling him to record the
speech of his people with immense conviction. But Mr Wesker does
more. He is able to transmute his art into a kind of poetry.

This third piece is from *Blasted* by Sarah Kane: the scene is an
expensive hotel room in Leeds, but it could be anywhere. Cate

and Ian have spent the night there. Cate has gone into the bathroom to have a bath. There is a knock at the door and a soldier enters with a gun. The following is part of the scene that ensues:

The Soldier turns Ian over with one hand.
He holds the revolver to Ian's head with the other.
He pulls down Ian's trousers, undoes his own and rapes him –
eyes closed and smelling Ian's hair.
The Soldier is crying his heart out.
Ian's face registers pain but he is silent.
When the Soldier has finished he pulls up his trousers and pushes the
revolver up Ian's anus.

Soldier: Bastard pulled the trigger on Col.
What's it like?
Ian: *(Tries to answer. He can't.)*
Soldier: *(Withdraws the gun and sits next to Ian.)*
You never fucked by a man before?
Ian: *(Doesn't answer.)*
Soldier: Didn't think so. It's nothing. Saw thousands of people packing into trucks like pigs trying to leave town. Women threw their babies on board hoping someone would look after them. Crushing each other to death. Insides of people's heads came out of their eyes. Saw a child most of his face blown off, young girl I fucked hand up inside her trying to claw my liquid out, starving man eating his dead wife's leg. Gun was born here and won't die. Can't get tragic about your arse. Don't think your Welsh arse is different to any other arse I fucked. Sure you haven't got any more food, I'm fucking starving.

Blasted, scene iii.

It is an apocalyptic scene: the spareness and rhythm of the language shocks us into some understanding of the reality of war.

SUMMING UP

All the work that I have set out in this chapter can be done either as group work focusing on the play in rehearsal, or as work on specific scenes in order to open out the text in a practical way. In the next chapters, we will be focusing on exercises which can be done on specific scenes as you rehearse them, which will open up their particular objectives and motives by finding different ways into the pulse of the language.

But I want to add a postscript. I want to set out four speeches, three in iambic pentameter: one is from *Coriolanus*, one is from *The Tempest*, and the third from Jonson's *Volpone*. The fourth is from *The Family Reunion* by T.S. Eliot. I want to do this so that we keep alive to the different rhythms and spaces in the language which make it continually exciting to listen to. The first three are all in iambic pentameter, yet they are so completely different in sound, cadence and movement within the lines, that it points up for us just how pliant the iambic pentameter is, and the infinite changes of texture and mood it can create. And then to look at *The Family Reunion*, a piece of modern poetic writing which does not have the same metrical code but in its phrasing and line spacing we hear its very particular rhythm, and where it takes us. So much modern writing, which does not seem heightened when you read it first, has a specific spacing and form which we have to be alert to because it is basic to our understanding of the underlying intention.

The first is from *Coriolanus*. Aufidius and his lieutenant are talking about Coriolanus, and how he draws people to him. The lieutenant, concerned about Aufidius's position, warns him of the danger:

LIEUTENANT   I do not know what witchcraft's in him, but
                  Your soldiers use him as the grace 'fore meat,
                  Their talk at table and their thanks at end,
                  And you are darkened in this action, sir.

They then talk through the politics of the situation, and finally Aufidius draws to this conclusion:

AUFIDIUS   All places yield to him ere he sits down,
               And the nobility of Rome are his.
               The senators and patricians love him too.
               The tribunes are no soldiers, and their people
               Will be as rash in the repeal as hasty
               To expel him thence. I think he'll be to Rome

As is the osprey to the fish, who takes it
By sovereignty of nature. First he was
A noble servant to them, but he could not
Carry his honours even. Whether 'twas pride,
Which out of daily fortune ever taints
The happy man: whether defect of judgement,
To fail in the disposing of those chances
Which he was lord of: or whether nature,
Not to be other than one thing, not moving
From th'casque to th'cushion, but commanding peace
Even with the same austerity and garb
As he controlled the war; but one of these –
As he hath spices of them all – not all,
For I dare so far free him – made him feared,
So hated, and so banished. But he has a merit
To choke it in the utterance. So our virtues
Lie in the interpretation of the time;
And power, unto itself most commendable,
Hath not a tomb so evident as a chair
T'extol what it hath done.
One fire drives out one fire; one nail one nail;
Rights by rights falter, strengths by strengths do fail.
Come, let's away. When, Caius, Rome is thine,
Thou'rt poorest of all; then shortly art thou mine.

Coriolanus, IV.vii.

And *The Tempest*, as Prospero divests himself of his power:

PROSPERO   Ye elves of hills, brooks, standing lakes, and groves
                And ye that on the sands with printless foot
                Do chase the ebbing Neptune, and do fly him
                When he comes back; you demi-puppets that,
                By moonshine do the green, sour ringlets make,
                Whereof the ewe not bites; and you whose pastime
                Is to make midnight mushrumps, that rejoice
                To hear the solemn curfew, by whose aid –
                Weak masters though ye be – I have be-dimmed
                The noontide sun, called forth the mutinous winds,
                And 'twixt the green sea and the azured vault
                Set roaring war; to the dread rattling thunder
                Have I given fire, and rifted Jove's stout oak
                With his own bolt; the strong-based promontory
                Have I made shake, and by the spurs plucked up

The pine and cedar; graves at my command
Have waked their sleepers, oped, and let 'em forth
By my so potent art. But this rough magic
I here abjure, and when I have required
Some heavenly music – which even now I do –
To work mine end upon their senses that
This airy charm is for, I'll break my staff,
Bury it certain fathoms in the earth,
And deeper than did ever plummet sound
I'll drown my book.

The Tempest, V.i.

And the third, *Volpone*, lying in a large bed, laying out his plans
to entice gold and riches from those who visit him: this he will
do by making each one in turn believe he is dying and will leave
his wealth to them. He first talks to Mosca:

VOLPONE   Hold thee, Mosca.
[*Gives him money*]
Take, of my hand; thou strik'st on truth in all,
And they are envious term thee parasite.
Call forth my dwarf, my eunuch, and my fool,
And let 'em make me sport.

[*Exit Mosca*]

                    What should I do
But cocker up my genius and live free
To all delights my fortune calls me to?
I have no wife, nor parent, child, ally,
To give my substance to; but whom I make.
Must be my heir, and this makes men observe me.
This draws me clients, daily, to my house,
Women and men of every sex and age,
That bring me presents, send me plate, coin, jewels,
With hope that when I die (which they expect
Each greedy minute) it shall then return
Tenfold upon them; whilst some, covetous
Above the rest, seek to engross me, whole,
And counter-work the one unto the other,
Contend in gifts, as they would seem in love.
All which I suffer, playing with their hopes,
And am content to coin 'em into profit,
And look upon their kindness, and take more,

> And look on that; still beating them in hand,
> Letting the cherry knock against their lips,
> And draw it by their mouths, and back again. How now!
>
> *Volpone*, I.i.

In the first speech, Aufidius is arguing something through; at first he is cold and reasonable, but as his thoughts, his argument, build through, he becomes more impassioned, until he reaches his conclusion. The thoughts are quite complex and so run on from line to line, frequently finishing in the middle of a line. He builds his argument in threes:

> Whether 'twas pride . . .
> whether defect of judgement . . .
> or whether nature . . .
> but one of these . . .

Thus he leads to his conclusion, beating out those strong last four lines: they are rhetorical and inspire both him and his lieutenant.

Prospero's speech has an incantational quality: it is very musical, its beat is strong, and it lifts the cadence through until you come to 'I'll break my staff . . .' The sounds themselves are rich and musical, with assonance and alliteration, and its images are always surprising.

Volpone's speech is very direct, and is all to do with business and transactions. It has a sharpness and lucidity about it which is very appealing, and a wonderful movement within the lines. It takes us imaginatively into his particular world.

And now for Eliot. As the name of the play implies, there has been a family reunion – Harry, Lord Monchonsey, with his mother and aunts and various relatives. Harry is haunted by the need to escape in order to find himself, and is trying to explain this sense of being haunted to Mary, a distant cousin:

> **Harry:** That apprehension deeper than all sense,
> Deeper than the sense of smell, but like a smell
> In that it is indescribable, a sweet and bitter smell
> From another world. I know it, I know it!
> More potent than ever before, a vapour dissolving
> All other worlds, and me into it. O Mary!

Don't look at me like that! Stop! Try to stop it!
I am going. Oh why, now? Come out!
Come out! Where are you? Let me see you,
Since I know you are there, I know you are spying on me.
Why do you play with me, why do you let me go,
Only to surround me? – When I remember them
They leave me alone; when I forget them
Only for an instant of inattention
They are round again, the sleepless hunters
That will not let me sleep. At the moment before sleep
I always see their claws distended
Quietly, as if they had never stirred.
It was only a moment, it was only one moment
That I stood in sunlight, and thought I might stay there.

The Family Reunion, I.ii.

If you go through that piece line by line, feeling the suspension at the end of each line, you feel the sense of the 'other', the sense of trying to unravel something which you cannot understand, and in its way it is very powerful.

To illustrate the general structure of speeches, their shaping and rhetoric, I have focused on Shakespeare because the form is so palpable in his writing. Also, when I have talked about modern text, I have dwelt on the minimalism of the writing: this I have done in order to make us aware that even when the language is spare it still contains richness and power. But of course there is just as much expansive writing in modern work, i.e. the second half of the twentieth century, from Osborne down to the present day, and there is the same skill in shaping and rhetoric as there ever was, and it has to be worked on in the same way.

9 Dialogue and Resistance

The first part of this chapter is about the interaction of dialogue: how the end of one speech can kick-start the next and give it another dynamic. We will then look at how some kind of resistance or obstacle can give a different energy to a scene.

DIALOGUE

I suppose the more a scene is explored, and the more the motives and objectives are taken on board, the more we load the words with meaning and lose their freshness. None of this can be helped, but it does mean that at intervals during the rehearsal process, the actor has to take time off to do exercises on the interaction of the dialogue itself, for the patterns need to be broken; we need to let the words erupt. And to do this there are very simple exercises which can be worked on a scene, similar to the one suggested for subtext but with a different focus. That focus has to be on the word or the phrase that provokes the character's response. In other words, each character speaks the specific word or phrase which sets off his/her reply – the hinge if you like.

EXERCISES

1. This exercise is more suitable when the dialogue consists of short speeches. Each character must repeat the last word that has been spoken to them before continuing with their own line.

2. As a variation, when the speeches are longer, and particularly when there is a complex argument involved, repeat
   the last half of the line or phrase that has been spoken
   before you reply.
3. A further variation is that you repeat the word in the last
   speech that triggers your reply.

You have to experiment with the exercises in order to find the
variation which is most useful, but in each case, because you are
verbalising the word or words yourself, you will experience the
precise word or phrase that sparks you off and that you are
responding to. This may seem very simple, but it is extraordinary what effect it has, and how it can surprise. For one thing
it alerts you to the way thoughts turn, and makes you hear how
quickly a character is thinking. This often releases a humour or
wit just in the turn of the phrase that we had not noticed before.
Also, because you have spoken the word or phrase yourself, it
gives that moment to allow for the thought to drop in before you
reply: in other words, you are not too ready and so you have to
think on the moment. It makes you realise how quickly we
think in order to survive. And this moment does not hold you
up; rather it gives you the impetus, the dynamic, to take your
thought forward more quickly. And, very important, it gives the
audience that split second to prepare for what is to come, thus
raising their curiosity and their interest. It is an exercise that
always surprises.

It is also helpful in discovering how relationships develop
within a scene, for without copying the others' rhythm, you are
in fact finding the shared dynamic, whether it be of two people
getting closer, or of people arguing out their differences, and
this shared dynamic lifts us through. The characters either
become closer because of this shared rhythm, or in the end the
rhythm splinters and they draw apart. And what I mean by
'lifting the text through' is that we are taking the dialogue/the
story on further, and in so doing we unconsciously give another
energy to the voice. We may, however subliminally, slightly
alter the note – lift it or let it drop – and so add to the dynamic
of the whole.

Let us look first at two dualogues, of very different kinds,
where the characters are drawn closer together. The first is from

Richard III, and is between Richard and Lady Anne: Lady Anne is following the corse of her husband, Edward IV, to his burying ground. Richard enters and commands the bearers to put down the corse, at which Anne turns and curses him. With terrible irony, Richard (Duke of Gloucester) then proceeds to woo Lady Anne in the presence of her husband's corse. Here is a sample of their dialogue from the middle of the scene:

RICHARD	I did not kill your husband.
ANNE	Why, then he is alive.
RICHARD	Nay, he is dead, and slain by Edward's hands.
ANNE	In thy foul heart thou liest! Queen Margaret saw
	Thy murderous falchion smoking in his blood;
	The which thou once didst bend against her breast,
	But that thy brothers beat against the point.
RICHARD	I was provokèd by her slanderous tongue
	That laid their guilt upon my guiltless shoulders.
ANNE	Thou wast provokèd by thy bloody mind
	That never dream'st on aught but butcheries
	Didst thou not kill this King?
RICHARD	I grant ye – yea.
ANNE	Dost grant me, hedgehog? Then God grant me too
	Thou mayst be damned for that wicked deed!
	O, he was gentle, mild, and virtuous!
RICHARD	The better for the King of Heaven that hath him.
ANNE	He is in heaven, where thou shalt never come.
RICHARD	Let him thank me that holp to send him hither
	For he was fitter for that place than earth.
ANNE	And thou unfit for any place, but hell.
RICHARD	Yes, but one place else, if you will hear me name it.
ANNE	Some dungeon.
RICHARD	Your bedchamber
ANNE	Ill rest betide the chamber where thou liest!
RICHARD	So will it, madam, till I lie with you.
ANNE	I hope so.
RICHARD	I know so . . .

Richard III, I.ii.

It would be interesting to read this in two ways: first by repeating only the last word of the previous speech so we hear that moment where the thought drops in, for this tells us of the speed of thought; and then by repeating the words that most provoke your reply, so we get the progression of the argument, how it accelerates emotionally. For instance:

> I did not kill – Why, then he is alive
> Her slanderous tongue – thy bloody mind
> Fitter . . . earth – unfit . . . hell
> Dungeon – bedchamber

It is packed with these turns of thought. Later, almost at the end of the scene, when Richard has finally convinced Anne of both his remorse for his deed and his genuine love for her, there is this amazing piece of dialogue ending in eleven three-beat lines. It is as unreal as the situation:

ANNE	Arise, dissembler; though I wish thy death I will not be thy executioner.
RICHARD	Then bid me kill myself, and I will do it.
ANNE	I have already.
RICHARD	That was in thy rage. Speak it again, and even with thy word This hand, which for thy love did kill thy love, Shall for thy love kill a far truer love; To both their deaths shalt thou be accessory.
ANNE	I would I knew thy heart.
RICHARD	'Tis figured in my tongue.
ANNE	I fear me both are false.
RICHARD	Then never man was true.
ANNE	Well, well, put up your sword.
RICHARD	Say then my peace is made.
ANNE	That shalt thou know hereafter.
RICHARD	But shall I live in hope?
ANNE	All men, I hope, live so.
RICHARD	Vouchsafe to wear this ring
ANNE	To take is not to give. [*She puts on the ring*]
RICHARD	Look how my ring encompasseth thy finger.

He then asks her to let him take King Edward's remains so that he may be solemnly interred, but of course he plans to do no such thing. These lines become even more twisted:

heart – tongue
false – true
But shall I live in hope?
All men, I hope, live so.

There is something quite extraordinary about this piece for it becomes like a spell, which draws Anne in, and it is that rhythm that draws them together. However, that rhythm can very easily take the scene over and make it seem too easy: but simply by doing this exercise we hear the underlying motive, and at what cost both to Richard, who has to think hard on his feet to persuade her, and to Anne, who is being pulled by her conflicting feelings.

On a very different note, the wooing scene from *The Taming of the Shrew*, Act II, scene i: it starts with Petruchio's soliloquy as he waits for Katherina. This is a great soliloquy to look at because it has such a light easy rhythm to it: the mix of lines with and without caesuras give great scope for syncopation within them, plus the whole speech is made up of antithetical ideas.

PETRUCHIO   I'll attend her here,
                    And woo her with some spirit when she comes.
                    Say that she rail, why then I'll tell her plain
                    She sings as sweetly as a nightingale.
                    Say that she frown, I'll say she looks as clear
                    As morning roses newly washed with dew.
                    Say she be mute and will not speak a word,
                    Then I'll commend her volubility,
                    And say she uttereth piercing eloquence.
                    If she do bid me pack, I'll give her thanks,
                    As though she bid me stay by her a week.
                    If she deny to wed, I'll crave the day
                    When I shall ask the banns, and when be married.
                    But here she comes, and now, Petruchio, speak.
                                        [*Enter Katherina*]

This sets up the scene that follows. Here is a part of that scene:

PETRUCHIO   Hearing thy mildness praised in every town,
                 Thy virtues spoke of, and thy beauty sounded,

	Yet not so deeply as to thee belongs,
	Myself am moved to woo thee for my wife.
KATHERINA	Moved, in good time! Let him that moved you hither
	Remove you hence. I knew you at the first
	You were a movable.
PETRUCHIO	Why, what's a movable?
KATHERINA	A joint-stool.
PETRUCHIO	Thou hast hit it. Come, sit on me.
KATHERINA	Asses are made to bear, and so are you.
PETRUCHIO	Women are made to bear, and so are you.
KATHERINA	No such jade as you, if me you mean.
PETRUCHIO	Alas, good Kate, I will not burden thee!
	For knowing thee to be but young and light –
KATHERINA	Too light for such a swain as you to catch,
	And yet as heavy as my weight should be
PETRUCHIO	Should be? Should – buzz!
KATHERINA	Well ta'en, and like a buzzard.
PETRUCHIO	O slow-winged turtle, shall a buzzard take thee?
KATHERINA	Ay, for a turtle, as he takes a buzzard.
PETRUCHIO	Come, come, you wasp, i'faith you are too angry.
KATHERINA	If I be waspish, best beware my sting.
PETRUCHIO	My remedy is then to pluck it out.
KATHERINA	Ay, if the fool could find it where it lies.
PETRUCHIO	Who knows not where a wasp does wear his sting?
	In his tail.
KATHERINA	In his tongue.
PETRUCHIO	Whose tongue?
KATHERINA	Yours, if you talk of tales, and so farewell.
	[*She turns to go*]
PETRUCHIO	What, with my tongue in your tail? Nay, come again.

The Taming of the Shrew, II.i.

And so it goes on.

You will notice the endless play on words: 'tale' and 'tail', for instance, or 'buzz', which can mean the noise made by bees, or it could be the scandal which, Petruchio implies, may surround Kate. But why I wanted to look at this scene is because, rather like the passage from *Richard III*, it has a very pronounced rhythm which can in a way hijack the scene. There is a rhythm to it, of course, and one which here provokes laughter, and this we must not miss out on; but within that rhythm we need those moments to make us aware that they are both on the line. They are both having to think quickly and it must not sound easy for either of them, particularly Katherina, for then her interior story is lost. And if, by repeating the words that jab, we up the stakes in this way, it will ultimately be funnier. And it is those moments where we hold on the rhythm that reinforce the underlying beat, and that is what helps us to reinvent and keep the text alive.

I think every piece of dialogue benefits from this work at different times during a rehearsal period, but particularly at the end, when you are loaded with motive and subtextual intention, it is important to cast everything aside and just listen to the words that are feeding you.

And one more piece, because it is politically hot. It is from *Richard II*: the Lords Northumberland, Willoughby and Ross are rebelling against Richard's rule, and plan to defect to Bolingbroke. Northumberland is the leader of the conspiracy, but what is interesting is that the outcome is not straightforward, for they each have to feel each other out in order to see where their loyalties and alignments are. It is a dangerous time and they have to be careful.

NORTHUMBERLAND	Well, lords, the Duke of Lancaster is dead.
ROSS	And living too; for now his son is Duke.
WILLOUGHBY	Barely in title, not in revenues.
NORTHUMBERLAND	Richly in both if justice had her right.
ROSS	My heart is great, but it must break with silence
	Ere't be disburdened with a liberal tongue.
NORTHUMBERLAND	Nay, speak thy mind; and let him ne'er speak more
	That speaks thy words again to do thee harm.
WILLOUGHBY	Tends that thou would'st speak to the Duke of Hereford?
	If it be so, out with it boldly, man!
	Quick is mine ear to hear of good towards him.
ROSS	No good at all that I can do for him,
	Unless you call it good to pity him,
	Bereft and gilded of his patrimony.

NORTHUMBERLAND   Now, afore God, 'tis shame such wrongs are
                  borne
                  In him, a royal prince, and many more
                  Of noble blood in this declining land.
                  The King is not himself, but basely led
                  By flatterers; and what they will inform
                  Merely in hate 'gainst any of us all,
                  That will the King severely prosecute
                  'Gainst us, our lives, our children, and our
                  heirs.

ROSS   The commons hath he pilled with grievous
                  taxes,
                  And quite lost their hearts. The nobles hath
                  he fined
                  For ancient quarrels, and quite lost their
                  hearts.

WILLOUGHBY   And daily new exactions are devised,
                  As blanks, benevolences, and I know not
                  what.
                  But what o' God's name doth become of
                  this?

NORTHUMBERLAND   Wars hath not wasted it; for warred he hath
                  not,
                  But basely yielded upon compromise
                  That which his noble ancestors achieved
                  with blows,
                  More hath he spent in peace than they in
                  wars.

ROSS   The Earl of Wiltshire hath the realm in farm.
WILLOUGHBY   The King's grown bankrupt like a broken
                  man.

NORTHUMBERLAND   Reproach and dissolution hangeth over him.
ROSS   He hath not money for these Irish wars –
                  His burdenous taxation notwithstanding –
                  But by the robbing of the banished Duke.

NORTHUMBERLAND   His noble kinsman! – most degenerate King!
                  But, lords, we hear this fearful tempest sing
                  Yet seek no shelter to avoid the storm.
                  We see the wind sit sore upon our sails
                  And yet we strike not, but securely perish.

ROSS   We see the very wrack that we must suffer,
                  And unavoided is the danger now
                  For suffering so the causes of our wrack.

NORTHUMBERLAND Not so. Even through the hollow eyes of
          death
          I see life peering; but I dare not say
          How near the tidings of our comfort is.

WILLOUGHBY Nay, let us share thy thoughts, as thou dost
          ours.

ROSS Be confident to speak, Northumberland.
          We three are but thyself; and speaking so
          Thy words are but as thoughts. Therefore be
          bold.

NORTHUMBERLAND Then thus: I have from le Port Blanc,
          A bay in Brittaine, received intelligence
          That Harry, Duke of Hereford, Rainold Lord
          Cobham,
          The son of Richard Earl of Arundel
          That late broke from the Duke of Exeter,
          His brother, Archbishop late of Canterbury,
          Sir Thomas Erpingham, Sir John Ramston,
          Sir John Norbery, Sir Robert Waterton, and
          Francis Coint,
          All these well-furnished by the Duke of
          Brittaine
          With eight tall ships, three thousand men of
          war,
          Are making hither with all due expedience,
          And shortly mean to touch our northern
          shore.
          Perhaps they had ere this, but that they stay
          The first departing of the King for Ireland.
          If then we shall shake off our slavish yoke,
          Imp out our drooping country's broken
          wing,
          Redeem from broking pawn the blemished
          crown,
          Wipe off the dust that hides our sceptre's
          gilt,
          And make high majesty look like itself,
          Away with me in post to Ravenspurgh.
          But if you faint, as fearing to do so,
          Stay, and be secret; and myself will go.

ROSS To horse, to horse! Urge doubts to them that
          fear.

WILLOUGHBY   Hold out my horse, and I will first be there.
                              [*Exeunt*]
                              Richard II, II.i.

Northumberland's rhythm and rhetoric is incredibly persuasive, and the language is emotive. If you were rehearsing this you would of course explore in detail the motives and reasoning behind it all: how Northumberland gets Ross and Willoughby on his side, first by allaying their fears, and then by opening up the possibilities. Once this has been investigated and you are familiar with the scene, then if you did the exercise on repeating the final word of the previous speech, you would find that it would highlight how their reasoning is being sparked off, and also just to what degree Northumberland is manipulating them.

    dead – And living too
    Duke – Barely in title
    revenues – Richly in both

Also we hear so clearly how the language lifts through, and how, as they unite in purpose, they begin to share each other's rhythm. From the moment when Ross, replying to Northumberland, says,

    The commons hath he pilled with grievous taxes,

their rhythm becomes as one. And once Northumberland takes over with his long speech, we hear his triumph in the underlying steadiness of the beat.

There are, of course, so many scenes one could enumerate, but two immediately come to mind for me: one is the central scene between Hamlet and Ophelia, Act III, scene i, where repeating the last words of the previous speech would add an extraordinary depth to the replies:

    I never gave you aught.
        My honoured lord, you know right well you did . . .
    Are you honest?
        My lord?
    Are you fair?

What means your lordship? . . .
I did love you once.
Indeed, my lord, you made me believe so.
I loved you not.
I was the more deceived.
Get thee to a nunnery.

And so on. But it is the time those words take to drop in which makes them so shocking.

Also a good scene to draw on is the scene between Brutus and Cassius in *Julius Caesar*, Act IV, scene iii, when Brutus and Cassius have a heated argument, each accusing the other of betrayal in one form or another. It comes at a crucial point in the play, the night before the battle with Octavius Caesar and Mark Antony. It is very bitter and full of rancour, for as fast as one makes an accusation, so the other takes it up, argues it through and then proceeds to hit back with a further accusation. Here are some extracts:

wronged me – wronged yourself
itching palm – I an itching palm
Contaminate our fingers with base bribes
Brutus, bait me not
You love me not
I do not like your faults
A friendly eye could never see such faults
A flatterer's would not.

And so it continues. What is important in this scene is that the feelings are already there underneath, and that it is the words that sting and provoke the action and the reaction. So by repeating the words that sting, you would feel their hurt in your body – for just as, in our own lives, we have a physical reaction to words that hurt in some way, so it is worth exploring this response in terms of character.

And of course these exercises work particularly well for modern text, where the writing is not only often very spare (Pinter and Beckett, for instance), but also takes us into a kind of constructed world where the reality is not one we are in touch with normally, e.g. Timberlake Wertenbaker's *Our Country's Good*, or Caryl Churchill's *Top Girls*, or David Rudkin's *Sons of Light*.

I just want to lay out a piece of dialogue from David Mamet's *American Buffalo*. There is poetry in the spareness, plus an ear for the music of common dialogue:

The scene: Don's Resale Shop. Morning. Don and Bob are sitting:

Don: So?
Pause.
So what, Bob?
Pause.

Bob: I'm sorry, Donny.
Pause.

Don: All right.

Bob: I'm sorry, Donny.
Pause.

Don: Yeah.

Bob: Maybe he's still in there.

Don: If you think that, Bob, how come you're here?

Bob: I came in.
Pause.

Don: You don't come in, Bob. You don't come in until you do a thing.

Bob: He didn't come out.

Don: What do I care, Bob, if he came out or not? You're s'posed to watch the guy, you watch him. Am I wrong?

Bob: I just went to the back.

Don: Why?
Pause.
Why did you do that?

Bob: 'Cause he wasn't coming out the front.

Don: Well, Bob, I'm sorry, but this isn't good enough. If you want to do business . . . if we got a business deal, it isn't good enough. I want you to remember this.

Bob: I do.

Don: Yeah, now . . . but later, what?
Pause.
Just one thing, Bob. Action counts.
Pause.
Action talks and bullshit walks.

American Buffalo, I.

What a great piece of dialogue to come at the beginning of a play: our curiosity is at a peak. But what I think is interesting is how to keep that almost downbeat dialogue active, so that the motive, the feeling that informs it, is continually charged. It can be very easy to be seduced by the rhythm, and that is where I think these exercises can help, for they make the actor aware of the precise word that has to be responded to, and how that word provokes.

RESISTANCE

The work I am now going to look at is about resistance in one form or another: and how, when you put some sort of obstacle in the way of an actor, it releases the energy both of mind and body. For when the actor has to deal with an obstacle, part of his/her mind is thinking how to get round that obstacle, and this releases an unconscious response to the words, i.e. he/she is not thinking so hard about what they mean. The words are released in a different way, for the very effort involved in getting physically free of the obstacle gives the language a resistance, a force and a definition. We hear the need for the words – and their cost.

The importance of this work is that it allows us time to grasp the size of the language, and to feel that pressure cooker inside us. If the work is on classical and heightened text, it allows us to experience the length and size of the language without feeling false in any way – and this is because we are having to struggle to get the words out. For modern text I think it is almost the opposite in that it allows us to hear the size of the feelings inside, and the very fact that you are speaking those words when you are being physically taxed in some way will give them a significance, however much you underplay them. They are there for a purpose, however casual and off-beat the language.

Because this work is very active and physical and about what the language does to you when you speak it, I will not be giving specific examples about subtext and rhythm in the same way: the important thing is what the work makes you understand as you speak the words, and that will be different in every case. But I will list a few scenes as reference points.

What is good about the exercises is that they are games, and we all know they are games, but there is something in all of us that likes to win. There is a sense of combat about the work which we enjoy, and this feeds into the words and gives them a degree of relish. And we must never forget that while we are speaking, we are still affirming existence.

EXERCISES

There are five core exercises which I will set down, and these exercises can be improvised on in any way that you feel would activate the scene. By this I mean I will set down the basic principles, but each exercise is open to interpretation in relation to the scene, or scenes, you are working on, so that they can be played around with in any way that is useful. The exercises are seemingly straightforward, yet they do effect an amazing differ-ence – an extravagance coupled with the need for truth. They are as follows:

  (i)   Restraining the actor.
 (ii)   Reaching across.
(iii)   Building barriers.
 (iv)   Getting attention.
  (v)   Manipulation.

Restraining the actor

This is of course just what it implies: it is about holding the actor, or actors, back from the person they want to contact, either physically or emotionally. If the scene involves one character wanting to make contact with another character who does not want to be reached, then approach the exercise like this:

Each actor should stand on opposite sides of the room, and the actor speaking must try to get across to the other but is physically restrained by others in rehearsal. This works wonder-fully when one character wants to make the other character understand something about which they feel very deeply; that they almost want to get inside them to do this.

For instance, in *Hamlet*, Act III, scene iv, when Hamlet is trying to make his mother see the truth of her marriage to Claudius, and that Claudius is guilty of the death of King Hamlet, he needs her to understand so badly and to admit to what he sees as her sin that he wants to wring the truth out of her. This exercise brings out Hamlet's desperation.

If the scene is about the two characters wanting to get to each other for whatever reason, either love or anger, then both must be restrained.

The exercise brings out the passion in the language, and the need for understanding, without it in any way sounding over-done. It is an exercise which you need only do on part of a scene, but what you will experience is how the words become stretched out with the need to reach each other – and this added awareness will then inform the dynamic of the whole.

Reaching across

This is quite similar, though it has a different effect on the actor. As the actor needs to get across to someone else, the rest of the cast should walk between them. It can be two actors wanting to get close, or it can be one actor needing to get to the other, and the rest of the cast should prevent it, not by physical restraint, but rather by getting in their way and making it impossible for them to reach each other. The effect is both frustrating and confusing, for you cannot always see where the other person is, and you have to find them for everything is moving. This makes it less direct and more desperate. Again *Hamlet* comes to mind – the first part of Act I, scene v, when Hamlet is trying to reach the ghost of his father, but the ghost eludes him.

Building barriers

This can be very illuminating and is open to many possibilities: it is simply about building a barrier around one of the charac-ters, and this can be done with anything that is in the rehearsal space – chairs, tables, bags, etc. First, build a barrier round the actor involved, as bulky a barrier as possible, so that it is difficult to get through. The actor then tries to get out, but as he/she tries to pull down the barrier, the other actor builds it up again. It can include others in the scene if that is suitable. This can happen between two characters, or with a number of the cast involved.

I worked this exercise in a rehearsal of *Antony and Cleopatra*, Act III, scene xiii, and we built a barrier round Cleopatra. It worked like this: Antony catches Cleopatra, allowing Thidias, Caesar's friend, to kiss her hand and so believes she is aligning herself with Caesar and betraying him. He gives orders that Thidias be whipped and proceeds to rail at Cleopatra. Cleopatra, hemmed in by chairs etc., attempts to convince Antony of her loyalty to him, and while doing so she tries to break down the barrier and get to him. At the same time as she is breaking the barrier down, Antony and his men build it back up again – chaos and anger mixed – until finally she convinces him and he says, 'I am satisfied . . .' and lets her through.

The actors, in frustration, started throwing chairs about in order to get what they wanted, and it was very useful for them to find this wildness, this lack of reason in the centre of the scene, for the situation, both in personal terms and in terms of the war with Caesar, has become out of control.

They also discovered something about the arbitrariness of their decisions, perhaps asking the question, how do those in power make their decisions? At the end, of course, they make peace. The irony is here, as you will see:

CLEOPATRA   It is my birthday
                 I had thought t'have held it poor. But since my lord
                 Is Antony again, I will be Cleopatra.
ANTONY   We will yet do well.

Two other scenes come to mind which this exercise could work for: one is from *Richard II*, Act III, scenes ii and iii. They can be worked together. Richard, returned to England from the Irish wars, arrives at Barkloughly Castle, rejoicing to be in England once again. Later when Bolingbroke enters with Northumberland and all his followers, Richard appears on the walls of the castle. There is a parley, at the end of which Richard is duly forced to relinquish the crown. During the first scene we see Richard's followers building a throne, as high as possible, on to which Richard climbs: the throne is the symbol of Richard's sovereignty. But later, when Bolingbroke gathers his forces, he and his followers try to pull the throne down. Both sides, contending for power, concentrate on either building or destroying the throne until finally Richard surrenders and leaves the throne.

I worked this exercise also in rehearsal, and the throne became a very special symbol of Richard's fall from power, and it provided a shape for the whole scene.

The second scene is from *Measure for Measure*, Act III, scene i, between Isabella and Claudio. The duke's deputy, Angelo, has imposed the death sentence on Claudio for unlawfully getting Juliet with child before being married. Claudio's sister, Isabella, pleads with Angelo for her brother's life: Angelo will concede to her request only if she will lie with him. Isabella refuses. She comes to tell Claudio of Angelo's request and of her decision, and that he therefore must die. Claudio pleads with his sister but in vain.

The scene is a harrowing one, and to highlight Claudio's predicament and to up the stakes, a barrier can be built between them which Claudio tries to pull down, but as fast as he pulls it down it is built up again by others in the rehearsal. He cannot reach her for there is a huge gulf between.

These exercises can be used in as many ways as your imagination takes you, according to the needs and objectives of the scene, and because there is a good deal of movement involved it can be instrumental in giving a shape and a context to the scene as a whole.

The most important thing about this work is that, for the actor, it builds a concrete image to symbolise the difficulty the character is facing: it in fact concretises the dilemma.

Getting attention

This exercise is for two characters: one character needs to persuade another character to listen to advice and take action of some kind, while the other does not want to hear. So it is quite simply about one character walking away from the other.

The two characters should start the scene a little distance from each other. The objective of the first character, the persuader, is to make the other listen. The second character, the receiver, must keep his/her back to the other and walk away when the impulse takes them. The first character should keep following.

It is a particularly useful exercise in that it makes the character who is persuading force the other to take notice, and therefore to lay out the argument as clearly and persuasively as possible. The receiver can walk anywhere they like in the room – even walk out of the room. They can sit, hide their face, whatever fits their response. The aim of the speaker is to get them to turn and face them.

This exercise highlights the objective and gives a great sense of urgency to the scene.

Two scenes come to mind: the first from *Coriolanus*, when Volumnia is trying to persuade Coriolanus to put aside his pride and go to the people in the market place and ask for their voice. She has this extremely persuasive speech which for Coriolanus challenges his sense of honour. She is in fact teaching him to lie:

VOLUMNIA   Because that now it lies you on to speak
To th' people, not by your own instruction,
Nor by th'matter which your heart prompts you,
But with such words that are but roted in
Your tongue, though but bastards and syllables
Of no allowance to your bosom's truth.
Now this no more dishonours you at all
Than to take in a town with gentle words,
Which else would put you to your fortune and
The hazard of much blood.
I would dissemble with my nature where,
My fortunes and my friends at stake required
I should do so in honour. I am in this
Your wife, your son, these senators, the nobles;
And you will rather show our general louts
How you can frown, than spend a fawn upon 'em
For the inheritance of their loves and safeguard
Of what that want might ruin.

And after Menenius speaks, she continues:

I prithee now, my son,
Go to them with this bonnet in thy hand:
And thus far having stretched it – here be with them –
Thy knee bussing the stones – for in such business
Action is eloquence, and the eyes of th'ignorant
More learned than their ears – waving thy head,
With often thus correcting thy stout heart,
Now humble as the ripest mulberry
That will not hold the handling, say to them
Thou art a soldier, and being bred in broils

Hast not the soft way which, thou dost confess,
Were fit for thee to use as they to claim,
In asking their good loves; but thou wilt frame
Thyself, forsooth, hereafter, theirs so far
As thou hast power and person.

It is a very rich speech, eloquently argued, encompassing the
homely image of 'the ripest mulberry' with images of a soldier –
'bred in broils'. And the exercise would highlight this reluctance
of Coriolanus to do what she asks, and would therefore feed
Volumnia with the pressure to go on.

The scene is long, for Coriolanus needs much persuasion, but
there is this wonderful piece of irony which comes at the end:
Volumnia has gone and Coriolanus is left with Menenius, his
friend, and Cominius, a Roman general:

COMINIUS	Away! the Tribunes do attend you. Arm yourself
	To answer mildly; for they are prepared
	With accusations, as I hear, more strong
	Than are upon you yet.
CORIOLANUS	The word is 'mildly'. Pray you let us go.
	Let them accuse me by invention, I
	Will answer in mine honour.
MENENIUS	Ay, but mildly.
CORIOLANUS	Well, mildly be it then – mildly.

Coriolanus, III.ii.

The second scene for which the exercise would work well is
from *Henry IV Part II*, Act II, scene iii. It takes place between
the Earl of Northumberland, Lady Northumberland and their
daughter-in-law, Lady Percy, who is also Hotspur's widow.
Northumberland is preparing to join Bolingbroke to fight Prince
Henry: Lady Percy tries to dissuade him from joining the rebels.
This speech is fed by her grief at Hotspur's death: it is very long,
and to keep its energy and drive we need to find the different
shifts of thought which keep refuelling it, and by doing this
exercise, i.e. trying to reach Northumberland and coming to him
from different angles when he moves away, it would clarify how
each of those shifts takes us into a different place in her mind.

Manipulation

This is about trying to force a character to do something against their will – thus attempting to disempower them. This, in turn, forces a resistance.

It could be by one character trying to take the other's clothes off – the actor, of course, resists but that resistance will release the resistance in the language. Or it could be one character trying to manipulate another by making them lie down and be comfortable – disempowering them, in fact.

How you interpret the exercise has to come from the need of the scene.

There is a particular scene in *King Lear* where this exercise could be very helpful – in Act II, scene iv. Lear has decided to dispense with his kingdom and henceforth to live with his daughters, Goneril and Regan. They agree to this, but in return stipulate that he must be rid of his retinue of knights. It is a long and painful scene in which Lear goes to each daughter in turn to beg for their hospitality for him and for his knights.

As Goneril and Regan proceed to reason with Lear and try to bend him to their wishes, they try to make him comfortable; they get him to lie down, put pillows behind him, wrap him up, take his shoes off, etc., in order to take his authority away. But this sense of disempowerment in Lear suddenly erupts into 'O reason not the need . . .' and thus feeds the moment when he throws everything off and leaves them to go outside into the storm.

I tried this out myself in the workshop production I did of *King Lear* at The Other Place and what it did was this: because the actors playing Goneril and Regan had to improvise ways of making Lear comfortable, they also found that sense of improvising their persuasion tactics. They had to find ways of making him agree, and this gave the scene much more subtlety than I think it often has. They were no longer the 'wicked sisters', rather they were trying to make some sort of order out of an impossible situation – albeit for their own ends. It made the actor playing Lear, who had been trying to manipulate his daughters, suddenly realise that it was he who was being manipulated, which thus precipitated his outburst and made him so suddenly rebel. Now all these ideas would come as you talked through the scene, but to do it actively in this way allows you to hear and experience it in a quite profound way.

I have illustrated all this work only with Shakespeare, and this is because it can be illustrated so clearly by the very size of the events and the language. But all the exercises can be done just as easily with text from other periods, and will open us up to the hidden undercurrents of feeling that are at the centre of the work.

10 Landscapes of the Mind

I suppose every play is a mixture of both the present and the past, for what is happening in the present, i.e. the action, is being informed by the past. And I think some of the most interesting work you can do on text is to uncover these layers. I have called this 'landscapes of the mind' because I want to emphasise how thoughts are constantly on the move and being informed by different areas of the self, different areas of the character's experience.

In real life we react unconsciously to these inner shifts of thought: we may be having a discussion with someone, but our minds are never still. As we listen we are sifting through what is being said and reacting to it in terms of our imagination and in terms of past experience, and possibly in terms of our feelings, and all this is colouring our judgement. Or we may simply be thinking what we should do next. In other words, we are there in the present in that particular spot, but our minds are not still, and how we react is continually being informed by our imagination and by our experience.

In rehearsal, the actor and the director will look into all the reasons why a character thinks and acts as he/she does, both in psychological terms and in terms of the needs of the play, the story, and this has to be the basis of the work.

So having delved into the reasons for the character's thoughts and actions, what is exciting for the actor is to discover how the text can actively take us into those different spaces in the character's mind, and how each thought has a slightly different texture and dynamic. That is where we have to take the audience. And it is exhilarating to do this, for we hear the thoughts as movements rather than something static which has to be spoken through: we find their dynamic. For language is not just about making sense, it is about where it takes you.

This chapter is in two parts: the first is 'Imagination/Memory', which looks at quite straightforward exercises to help us place the different areas of thought which go to make up a speech. The second I have called 'Haunting/Loneliness', and it is about physical ways of expressing the need to be heard.

IMAGINATION/MEMORY

This consists of four sections:

    (i)   Inner v. outer landscape.
    (ii) Spaces in the mind.
    (iii) Drawing.
    (iv) Imaging.

The first two exercises focus on the movement in the thoughts, and where they go in the mind: they are quite similar and can be swapped around according to what you want to highlight. They are quite simply about moving to different places within the rehearsal space to find the different angles of thought, either of time or of place.

EXERCISES

Inner v. outer landscape

This focuses specifically on the switches between the present moment, i.e. the action of the play and what is going on in the character's mind. In choosing when you move you will come up against ambivalences and feel that you have taken wrong decisions, but that does not matter because it will alert you to the possibilities.

Set it up like this:

Within the rehearsal space mark out two areas: it can be one space with a line down the middle, so you will be walking from one side of the line to the other, or it can be two separate spaces in different parts of the room. Use one area for when the character is speaking in the present, furthering the plot in some way. Move to the other area when you are not in the present – when the thoughts take you to another part of the mind, perhaps to a past experience, a philosophical viewpoint, an intuition, etc. So you speak the thoughts to do with the present in one area, and when there is a shift in the thought, stop speaking and move to the other area. It is very important that you do not speak when you are moving, but when you move it has to be quite swift in order to keep up with the thought.

By physicalising these changes of thought, and hearing their different textures in this way, you not only uncover things that you may not have noticed before, but you hear how the inner landscape is both feeding and provoking the action, thus making sense of the whole. But the the centre of the exercise is this: because you are moving you are keeping the dynamic of the thought alive.

An excellent example of this is Brutus's soliloquy in *Julius Caesar*, as he contemplates the murder of Caesar. I have mentioned this already in terms of how a soliloquy is argued through, but here if we take it that his decision has already been made somewhere within himself, and that he is now justifying that decision, then the terms by which he argues, and the images he selects, take on a particularly charged tone. He is constantly moving between the action itself, and his justification of it in terms of his own philosophical viewpoint. It has many layers:

```
BRUTUS    It must be by his death; and for my part,
          I know no personal cause to spurn at him,
          But for the general. – He would be crowned.
          How that might change his nature, there's the question.
          It is the bright day that brings forth the adder,
          And that craves wary walking. Crown him! – that!
          And then, I grant, we put a sting in him
          That at his will he may do danger with.
          Th'abuse of greatness is when it disjoins
          Remorse from power; and, to speak truth of Caesar
          I have not known when his affections swayed
          More than his reason. But 'tis a common proof
          That lowliness is young ambition's ladder,
          Whereto the climber upward turns his face;
          But when he once attains the upmost round,
```

He then unto the ladder turns his back,
Looks in the clouds, scorning the base degrees
By which he did ascend: so Caesar may;
Then, lest he may, prevent. And, since the quarrel
Will bear no colour for the thing it is,
Fashion it thus: that what he is, augmented,
Would run to these and these extremities:
And therefore think him as a serpent's egg
Which, hatched, would, as his kind, grow mischievous,
And kill him in the shell.

Julius Caesar, II.i.

It starts with a statement – 'It must be by his death . . .' – yet you could argue that even this has a certain ambivalence to it, for it could also be underpinned by a question. It is not until he says 'How that might change his nature . . .' that he starts to find his resolve. It is then that he finds the image of the adder, which not only takes him into another area of his mind, but also provides the hinge to his thinking. As he goes back and forth, contemplating 'th'abuse of greatness' set against the good qualities of Caesar, he uses a philosophical argument about how power can change people's natures, and he then turns to analogy to prove his point. At first the analogy is simple, a homely wisdom about climbing a ladder. Then the more he convinces himself and the more involved he becomes with the argument, the more charged his analogies become, using that of a 'serpent's egg', until finally Caesar and the serpent's egg become interchangeable, ending with 'And kill him in the shell.' His mind is made up – he is in the present moment. But during the speech he has gone back and forth between the decision of the moment and his inward vision.

It is a great soliloquy because Brutus has such a large vision, and as he argues his dilemma through he reaches into those different parts of his mind, his past experience, his awareness of human nature, all of which feed the present action. We know that he is wrestling with his conscience and that everpresent question – when do you say 'no'? – something which is central to all political action and certainly central to Shakespeare's world.

Another wonderful, though quite different speech to look at is the nurse's speech in *Romeo and Juliet*, Act I, scene iii. This is specifically about the present and the past, and is packed with detail. It comes when Lady Capulet is about to tell Juliet of her father Capulet's plan for her to marry the County Paris – a good match. Knowing how delicate the situation might turn out to be, she begins by asking the nurse to leave, but then seeing how upset the nurse is and perhaps thinking that after all she might be helpful, she relents and asks her to stay. The scene starts off with the following dialogue:

LADY CAPULET   Thou know'st my daughter's of a pretty age.
NURSE   Faith, I can tell her age unto an hour.
LADY CAPULET   She's not fourteen.
NURSE   I'll lay fourteen of my teeth –
And yet, to my teen being spoken, I have but
    four –
She's not fourteen. How long is it now
To Lammastide?
LADY CAPULET   A fortnight and odd days.
NURSE   Even or odd, of all days in the year,
Come Lammas Eve at night she shall be
fourteen.

Romeo and Juliet, I.iii.

This launches the nurse into a long speech in which she remembers Juliet as a baby, and incidents in Juliet's childhood, memories which also involve her own husband. The whole spectrum of her life is there.

It is so often done – mistakenly, I think – by emphasising the comedy in the way she keeps switching from one thought to the other, back and forth in time. There is a lot of humour in it, of course, but that humour comes out of a real look at her life and a realisation that one part of it is coming to a close. It is also about a woman who has never been in charge of her own life, who has always been a servant and who has built her life round the one she serves – Juliet. To do this exercise of moving between past and present through the speech highlights this whole centre of her life, and how she remembers it, and her need to place it for herself.

Spaces in the mind
The focus here is on finding the structure and movement of the whole thoughts and how they are reasoned through, and the

different places you go to in your mind to find them, and how the one thought feeds the next. It is still about moving between thoughts, but this time moving on the sentence breaks – at a full-stop, a semi-colon, a question mark or an exclamation mark. This clarifies the logic.

The actor crouches in one part of the room and starts the speech. When you come to a stop, run to another part of the room, crouch and continue. You must not speak when you are running. If for any reason, you find it diffficult to crouch, then of course it can be done standing. I like the crouching because it gives the actor a sense of belonging to that space and I think increases the urgency of the running, but you can vary the movement in the exercise according to the needs of the speech.

However you choose to do it, crouching or standing, running or walking, the important thing is that you do not speak during the space between thoughts, and that you get to the next thought/space as quickly as possible.

The central reason for the exercise is this: because you are in one place for one thought, your mind stays on that one thought to its end – in other words, you do not pre-empt the next one. Then by moving to a fresh space for that next thought, you find it from a slightly different viewpoint and this gives you its shift in texture and rhythm. It tells us where our thoughts take us, and therefore how we reason things through in order to survive: in other words, how our minds tick. It is that moment when you find the thought that matters.

Now if it is not suitable to move quite so athletically, then you can find different movements, such as rolling to one side and then to the other. All that is important is that you go to a different place in your body and a different space in your mind, for it is that which informs your imagination.

It would be interesting to work this on Juliet's speech in Act IV, scene iii, as she contemplates taking the friar's distilling liquor. Her mind is racing between all the possibilities: is it really what the friar promised, a potion that will make her seem as dead though she is alive, or is it in fact a poison? Can she trust the friar or not? Each thought occupies her totally for the time it takes to speak it: and each thought sparks off a new thought, each one increasing in urgency, until in desperation she drinks the liquor. To do this exercise on the bed, the bed being her only source of stability, moving to different parts of it as her imagination takes her, would help the actor find that heightened sense of awareness of life and death that is filling her, and would also, by the very movement, help to create that sense of urgency that she feels.

This exercise works for any speech that is seeking some kind of expression of, or answer to, the character's feelings or point of view or need for action; and, of course, the temperature of each speech will be different.

Here are two of very different blood heats: first, a speech by Troilus from *Troilus and Cressida*. It comes near the end of the play when Cressida has been given to the Greeks in exchange for Antenor, one of the Trojan leaders. It is the scene where Calchas, Cressida's father who has defected to the Greeks, hands his daughter over to Diomed, one of the Greek leaders. Ulysses and Troilus have secretly got into the Greek camp and found where Calchas' tent is and they watch from a distance as Calchas gives his daughter to Diomed. Troilus watches Cressida talk to Diomed, and his blood is hot:

TROILUS   This she? No, this is Diomed's Cressida.
            If beauty have a soul, this is not she;
            If souls guide vows, if vows are sanctimony,
            If sanctimony be the gods' delight,
            If there be rule in unity itself,
            This is not she. O madness of discourse,
            That cause sets up with and against itself!
            Bifold authority, where reason can revolt
            Without perdition, and loss assume all reason
            Without revolt. This is, and is not, Cressid!
            Within my soul there doth conduce a fight
            Of this strange nature, that a thing inseparate
            Divides more wider than the sky and earth;
            And yet the spacious breadth of this division
            Admits no orifex for a point as subtle
            As Ariachne's broken woof to enter.
            Instance, O instance, strong as Pluto's gates!
            Cressid is mine, tied with the bonds of heaven.
            Instance, O instance, strong as heaven itself!
            The bonds of heaven are slipped, dissolved, and loosed;
            And with another knot, five-finger-tied,
            The fractions of her faith, orts of her love,

The fragments, scraps, the bits, and greasy relics
Of her o'er-eaten faith, are bound to Diomed.

Troilus and Cressida, V.ii.

It is a difficult speech and has to be unravelled, like Ariachne's woof, but in its very difficulty we hear the tortuousness of his feelings: he cannot reconcile his heart and his head. Therefore, to go to different spaces for each of those thoughts tells us of the effort he is making to put his feelings into words.

Henry is also working something out in this next speech – Henry V's soliloquy at the end of Act IV, scene i, but though angry, his blood is cooled by his reasoning. The scene takes place during the night before the battle of Agincourt. Henry is walking through the camp and comes upon a number of his soldiers; he is hooded and they do not recognise him. There follows quite a long scene where the men, Bates and Williams, have a debate with Henry regarding the behaviour and responsibility of the king as they see it and, in passing, blame him for their present plight. Henry attempts to defend the king's position. Finally, Williams picks a quarrel with Henry and throws down his glove, challenging him to a duel when they next meet. They exchange gloves to be worn in their hats for recognition. Henry, of course, enjoys the prospect of surprising Williams when they do eventually meet and Williams realises that he has challenged the king. Nevertheless, he takes the quarrel seriously and it sparks off these thoughts:

KING HENRY   Upon the King! Let us our lives, our souls,
                  Our debts, our careful wives,
                  Our children, and our sins, lay on the King!
                  We must bear all. O hard condition.
                  Twin-born of greatness, subject to the breath
                  Of every fool, whose sense no more can feel
                  But his own wringing! What infinite heart's ease
                  Must kings neglect that private men enjoy!
                  And what have kings that privates have not too,
                  Save ceremony, save general ceremony?
                  And what art thou, thou idol ceremony?
                  What kind of god art thou, that suffer'st more
                  Of mortal griefs than do thy worshippers.

Henry V, IV.i.

And so he continues to debate the whole issue of kingship: you feel it is the first time he has faced what it is like to be a king and what it entails. As he begins to explore all the issues which confront him he goes to different places in his mind and is surprised by what he finds, and in the process he comes face to face with himself. He starts in anger, but he also has that authority within him which allows him to be philosophical – it is both passionate and cool.

Drawing

This is quite different, but very interesting: it is still about imagination and perhaps memory but in an indirect way. It is a very simple exercise which involves drawing something on paper. It can be done with one actor on a particular speech, which is recounting something very precisely, or on a dialogue between two characters during which they discover a shared feeling, and perhaps some kind of coming together during the scene. It is a gentle exercise, but very revealing.

EXERCISES

We will focus on solo work first. All the actor needs is a piece of paper and a pen or pencil, and as you work through the speech draw a picture. The picture needs to be very specific, e.g. the first house you lived in; one part of the rehearsal room that you are in; what you see out of the window. Each of these drawings will evoke something different in your mind. If it is a drawing of where you lived in the past, that will evoke a memory. If it is of your own home now, that will evoke other feelings. If you are drawing what you see, that will make you very precise. If it is in the distance, that will bring something else to it.

But what is interesting is how the precision of drawing, whether it be of something from memory or of something in the present, forces you to find the words that you are speaking with equal precision. In other words, the more you look for the details in the picture, the more specific the words you are speaking become.

I have no answer to why this works, but I suspect it is because you are engaging another part of your mind to inform the words.

What I like so much about this exercise is that it focuses the mind on the detail within the text so that there cannot be an overlay of emotion. If, for instance, you were working on the speech of the hostess as she recounts the death of Falstaff, a speech we have already looked at, it would reveal the detail with which she spells out his death, that detail which is so vivid and yet so spare. The actor would then hear how it is the spareness of Shakespeare's writing which makes it so moving, and its power is lost if it is overlayed with emotion. Another speech which is similar in effect is Gertrude's account of Ophelia's death:

> QUEEN   There is a willow grows askant the brook,
> That shows his hoar leaves in the glassy stream,
> Therewith fantastic garlands did she make
> Of crowflowers, nettles, daisies, and long purples,
> That liberal shepherds give a grosser name,
> But our cold maids do dead-men's-fingers call them.
> There on the pendent boughs her crownet weeds
> Clambering to hang, an envious sliver broke,
> When down her weedy trophies and herself
> Fell in the weeping brook. Her clothes spread wide,
> And mermaid-like awhile they bore her up;
> Which time she chanted snatches of old tunes,
> As one incapable of her own distress,
> Or like a creature native and endued
> Unto that element. But long it could not be
> Till that her garments, heavy with their drink,
> Pulled the poor wretch from her melodious lay
> To muddy death.
>
>   *Hamlet*, IV.vii.

Gertrude gives us a much fuller picture of Ophelia's death than the hostess does of Falstaff's, even so, it is the objectivity of that description that is powerful, and it is that objectivity which impacts on the listener.

And one more instance, which is quite different, from *Othello*: Desdemona is both puzzled and distraught about Othello's behaviour for he has very abruptly told her, 'Get you to bed on th'instant. I will be returned forthwith. Dismiss your attendant here. Look't be done.' She senses something is very wrong, even dangerous.

There follows a very poignant scene between Emilia and Desdemona together which focuses on men's jealousy; Desdemona saying that she would not be unfaithful for the world, nor does she believe any woman would. Emilia, in trying to ease Desdemona's fears, replies with the following speech, which is also about her own fears of Iago:

EMILIA   Yes, a dozen: and as many to th'vantage as would stir the world they played for.
But I do think it is their husband's faults
If wives do fall. Say that they slack their duties,
And pour our treasures into foreign laps;
Or else break out in peevish jealousies,
Throwing restraint upon us; or say they strike us,
Or scant our former having in despite –
Why, we have galls, and though we have some grace,
Yet have we some revenge. Let husbands know
Their wives have sense like them: they see and smell,
And have their palates both for sweet and sour
As husbands have. What is it that they do,
When they change us for others? Is it sport?
I think it is. And doth affections breed it?
I think it doth. Is't frailty that thus errs?
It is so too. And have not we affections,
Desires for sport, and frailty, as men have?
Then let them use us well: else let them know
The ills we do, their ills instruct us so.

Othello, IV.iii.

It has a most wonderful rhythm, and you feel it is the first time she has expressed these thoughts, and that they come from somewhere very deep inside her: and she has to take us there. It treads a fine line between objectivity and feeling, and therefore to do this drawing exercise, particularly to focus on a past memory, helps the actor find that inner perspective – a wisdom fed of necessity. In other words, it takes away all sentimentality.

Now for work on dialogue, and this can be done either:

229

(i) with each actor drawing his/her own picture, thus focusing on his/her own character's particular way forward in the scene; or

(ii) with both actors creating the same picture.

The choice has to be arrived at out of the situation in the play.

For the first one, both actors have some paper and a pencil each, and each draw what they see out of the window. This reinforces both their separateness and their common aim.

It is very good, for instance, for the scene which we have already mentioned between Goneril and Regan at the end of the opening scene in *King Lear*. They are discussing how to handle Lear – his erratic behaviour, 'the infirmity of his age' – plus you feel there is little trust between them, and that as they talk they are also feeling each other's motives out. It is a wonderfully cool piece of dialogue coming at the end of that tempestuous scene with all its earth shifts: it is spare and factual, and though it is in prose it has a music all of its own. To use this exercise on that dialogue brings out the ambivalence of their feelings; they need each other yet they will act independently. Their minds are already somewhere else, off to their own castles – yet they need that alliance.

For the second option, spread a large piece of paper on the floor, and draw a picture together. The subject, of course, has to be set beforehand. This is good for any scene where the two characters draw closer together: it could be between two lovers finding trust in each other, or two conspirators. Whatever, it is something which engages them with a common purpose which grows as they make the picture.

A scene which comes to mind is that between Rosalind and Celia near the beginning of *As You Like It*, after Duke Frederick has banished Rosalind from the court for what he believes to be her subversion. They are both crestfallen with the news, but gradually the idea comes to Celia that they should leave the court together and make their way in the world. As the idea takes hold, they decide to go into the Forest of Arden, taking Touchstone, the court jester, with them. The scene starts off quite cool, but as the idea takes hold, their imaginations start to work and they get excited about their prospective adventure. The scene is quite short and factual when you consider how radical their decision is. However, if they were to draw a shared picture together, imagining the forest and what they might find there, its hidden dangers and its delights, I believe it would contribute so much to their shared imagination – and in the end to the substance and reality of the text.

Other variations: for a more public scene a large piece of paper can be pinned to the wall, on which the speaker can draw the map of a country, or an imaginary city – something with some scope to it and which connects with the scene. One thinks of Burgundy, near the end of *Henry V*, trying to reconcile the kings of France and England, or of Enobarbus describing Cleopatra in her barge – he would have to attempt a drawing of Cleopatra. Whatever, it is a liberating thing to do and one that stimulates the imagination, and in some way places the text and gives it a form.

Imaging

It is always useful at some point during rehearsal to work on a few speeches physicalising the images: as we interpret a text we look at the images, and we take time to imagine them, but still this keeps them in the mind. At some point I believe we have to see where they take us in our body; for when a character finds an image it is related to something in themselves. In the Brutus soliloquy the analogy of the ladder comes from his thought, but finding the images of the adder and the serpent comes from somewhere different – they are charged with his feelings about those creatures. And for those few moments that is where he exists as a person: they are his centre. So at some point in rehearsal this should be explored.

This exercise can be done either with the whole group on one speech, or with one actor on their own text. As the actor goes through a speech, they must physicalise each image as they speak it. If it is done with the whole group, then one person has to read out one phrase at a time which the group then repeats, and as they repeat it they have to physicalise the imagery within it. It is important that in the process of speaking the text, the phrase given is not too long so that it can be remembered easily by the group. This exercise is quite difficult to do at first, for it is not about describing the image, rather it is about experiencing it in the body and finding its reality – earthing it, as it were.

Take this speech of Juliet:

JULIET   Gallop apace, you fiery-footed steeds,
Towards Phoebus' lodging! Such a waggoner
As Phaeton would whip you to the West
And bring in cloudy night immediately.
Spread thy close curtain, love-performing night,
That runaway's eyes may wink, and Romeo
Leap to these arms untalked of and unseen.
Lovers can see to do their amorous rites
By their own beauties; or, if love be blind,
It best agrees with night. Come, civil night,
Thou sober-suited matron, all in black,
And learn me how to lose a winning match,
Played for a pair of stainless maidenhoods.
Hood my unmanned blood, bating in my cheeks,
With thy black mantle till strange love grow bold,
Think true love acted simple modesty.
Come, night. Come, Romeo. Come, thou day in night;
For thou wilt lie upon the wings of night
Whiter than new snow on a raven's back.
Come, gentle night. Come, loving, black-browed night.
Give me my Romeo. And when I shall die,
Take him and cut him out in little stars,
And he will make the face of heaven so fine
That all the world will be in love with night
And pay no worship to the garish sun.
O I have bought the mansion of a love
But not possessed it; and though I am sold,
Not yet enjoyed. So tedious is this day
As is the night before some festival
To an impatient child, who hath new robes
And may not wear them.

Romeo and Juliet, III.ii.

Juliet waiting for Romeo: it is an amazing piece to physicalise for just in that first line, 'Gallop apace you fiery-footed steeds/ Toward Phoebus' lodging', although we know she is talking about the sun, it tells us how her blood is racing. And so just by galloping round the room when you are speaking it, we get some idea of the movement, the sexuality, which is stirring within her, so that later she has to ask the night to 'Hood my unmann'd blood.' But where she takes us in her imagery is pure magic – orgasmic I should say.

For thou wilt lie upon the wings of night
Whiter than new snow on a raven's back.

And after 'And when I shall die', which is a euphemism for having an orgasm, she takes us to the relative calm of 'Take him and cut him out in little stars', followed by those rather more prosaic, anti-climactic images:

O I have bought the mansion of a love . . .
To an impatient child that hath new robes
And may not wear them.

This of course is a particularly good speech with which to illustrate the exercise, because it is so full of overt sexuality, and by doing it we bring out the wildness and freedom Juliet has found in this awakening. Plus also what is good is that the movement the speech asks for is quite rough and sudden, taking away any over-poeticism; again, it earths it. This is an excellent piece to use in a group: it needs to be worked several times in order to fully experience both the sexuality of the movement and the spirituality of the imagination.

Of course, not every speech lends itself to movement in quite the same way, but even on a gentler speech I think this area is worth exploring. Try it on only one or two speeches just to touch on the specificity of the image, for it must come out of a real investigation into the imagery and its cost, and not out of an easy enjoyment of the movement.

HAUNTING AND LONELINESS

Both the following exercises are about expressing some kind of 'aloneness', and about defining something for yourself which no one else will understand. They are in some way about the need to be understood.

EXERCISES

This first is about the extreme loneliness you feel when you know that no one else will either listen or understand: it is about the need to be understood. It needs to be worked with the group.

The group walks round the rehearsal space quite briskly. The actor speaking, as he/she works through the speech, tries to make contact with a member of the group. The aim for the actor is to make someone stop and listen so that each phrase can be spoken directly to one of the group. However, each member of the group, when the actor approaches, turns and walks away. Thus the actor cannot make anyone listen.

We know it is a game which has been set up, but the feeling of frustration which the speaker experiences when nobody will listen is oddly real, and thus very potent: it informs something about that inner need to be understood, and so the words become that much more defined and charged.

And that need is quite a common one, for we all know what it is like to have deep feelings which cannot be understood. This speech from Isabella, from *Measure for Measure* illustrates the point well.

The soliloquy comes at the end of the scene where she has begged Duke Angelo to spare her brother's life: he has agreed, but with the proviso that she sleep with him. We have already looked at Claudio's speech in the later scene between him and Isabella, when she tells him of her refusal to Angelo's request. Here she speaks of her dilemma:

ISABELLA   To whom should I complain? Did I tell this,
            Who would believe me? O perilous mouths,
            That bear in them one and the selfsame tongue,
            Either of condemnation or approof,
            Bidding the law make curtsy to their will,
            Hooking both right and wrong to th'appetite,
            To follow as it draws. I'll to my brother.
            Though he hath fall'n by prompture of the blood,
            Yet hath he in him such a mind of honour
            That, had he twenty heads to tender down
            On twenty bloody blocks, he'd yield them up,
            Before his sister should her body stoop
            To such abhorred pollution.
            Then, Isabel, live chaste, and brother, die.
            More than our brother is our chastity.
            I'll tell him yet of Angelo's request,
            And fit his mind to death, for his soul's rest.
                            Measure for Measure, II.iv.

The hard fact is of course that Claudio will not understand either: she is alone with her conscience.

Another speech that the exercise would serve well is that of Camillo in the second scene of *The Winter's Tale*, when he refuses to do Leontes' bidding, i.e. to get rid of Polixenes who he believes to be his wife's lover:

CAMILLO   What case stand I in? I must be the poisoner
               Of good Polixenes: and my ground to't
               Is the obedience to my master, one
               Who in rebellion with himself will have
               All that are his too. To do this deed,
               Promotion follows. If I could find example
               Of thousands that had struck anointed kings
               And flourished after, I'd not do't; but since
               Nor brass nor stone nor parchment bears not one
               Let villainy itself forswear't. I must
               Forsake the court. To do't, or no, is certain
               To me a break-neck. Happy star reign now!
                                          The Winter's Tale, I.ii.

And now for two modern pieces, totally different: first a speech from Edward Bond's *Lear*. The play is partly a deconstruct of *King Lear*, but it is not only that, for it gives a view of current human existence, and gives a whole new philosophical angle to Shakespeare's play. It is a wonderful piece of writing and to do this group exercise on it highlights Lear's need to find himself: the result is very powerful indeed.

LEAR   The king is always on oath! [*He stares in the mirror.*] No, that's not the king ... This is a little cage of bars with an animal in it. [*Peers closer.*] No, no, that's not the king! [*Suddenly gestures violently. The USHER takes the mirror.*] Who shut that animal in that cage? Let it out. Have you seen its face behind the bars? There's a poor animal with blood on its head and tears running down its face. Who did that to it? Is it a bird or a horse? It's lying in the dust and its wings are broken. Who broke its wings? Who cut off its hands so it can't shake the bars? It's pressing its snout on the glass. Who shut that animal in a glass cage? O God, there's no pity in this world. You let it lick the blood from

235

its hair in the corner of a cage with nowhere to hide from its tormentors. No shadow, no hole! Let that animal out of its cage! [*He takes the mirror and shows it round.*] Look! Look! Have pity. Look at its claws trying to open the cage. It's dragging its broken body over the floor. You are cruel! Cruel! Look at it lying in its corner! It's shocked and cut and shaking and licking the blood on its sides. [*USHER again takes the mirror from LEAR.*] No. No! Where are they taking it now! Not out of my sight! What will they do to it? O God, give it to me! Let me hold it and stroke it and wipe its blood! [*BODICE takes the mirror from the USHER.*] No!

Lear, II.i.

The second, a little back in time but perhaps giving another, very personal, perspective: it is from *A Streetcar Named Desire* by Tennessee Williams. Blanche, near the end of the play, is in a world of her own and conjures up an imaginary scenario with a rich lover which she tries to make Stanley believe in. He, of course, knows it is all a fantasy. She believes no one understands her:

Blanche: A cultivated woman, a woman of intelligence and breeding, can enrich a man's life – immeasurably! I have those things to offer, and this doesn't take them away. Physical beauty is passing. A transitory possession. But beauty of the mind and richness of the spirit and tenderness of the heart – and I have all of those things – aren't taken away, but grow! Increase with the years! How strange that I should be called a destitute woman! When I have all the treasures locked in my heart. (A choked sob comes from her.) I think of myself as a very, very rich woman! But I have been foolish – casting my pearls before swine!

A Streetcar Named Desire, Scene X

This is a heart-rending speech, for she is totally cut off from any reality and no one will listen. There is total isolation.

This second exercise is about the character defining something about a person or a situation that is haunting them, and about which they are trying to seek an answer. There are two characters: one, the character who is speaking, the other – either the character who is the subject of that speech, or the actor who is representing the situation or action that is haunting them. The speaker crouches in one spot and starts to speak: as they start, the second actor quietly comes up and stands just behind them. When the speaker feels the other near, they must run to another part of the space in order to escape. This format is repeated throughout the speech, the second character at intervals coming up and standing just behind them, and the speaker then running away.

The speech that at once comes to mind is Ophelia's soliloquy: we have looked at the form of this already, and how its shape and rhythm tells us so much about her condition, but now let us look at it in terms of this exercise:

OPHELIA   O, what a noble mind is here o'erthrown!
              The courtier's, soldier's, scholar's, eye, tongue, sword,
              Th'expectancy and rose of the fair state,
              The glass of fashion and the mould of form,
              Th'observed of all observers, quite, quite down!
              And I, of ladies most deject and wretched,
              That sucked the honey of his music vows,
              Now see that noble and most sovereign reason
              Like sweet bells jangled, out of time and harsh,
              That unmatched form and feature of blown youth
              Blasted with ecstasy. O, woe is me
              T'have seen what I have seen, see what I see!
                                          Hamlet, III.i.

Ophelia, haunted by her encounter with Hamlet, tries to define for herself what has happened to him: but somehow you feel she will never escape his spell and that this is the beginning of her disintegration as a person. What the exercise does is concretise the object of her thoughts, and this heightens her own vulnerability, for he will always be there at the back of her mind.

The second option is that the second actor represents an action of some sort, and it works in exactly the same way. Take for instance Macbeth contemplating the murder of Duncan: if, as he works through that soliloquy, the second actor represents the actual deed of the murder, the fact that in a sense his whole thinking is about running from that deed, then the speech acquires a surreal quality. The more he runs, the more out of control his thoughts become – he is on the edge.

These last two exercises are very useful in that they physically define something, first about the need to be understood and the terrible isolation one must feel when nobody listens or seems to want to understand – a plight not necessarily confined to the world of drama – and second, about that sense of something which the character is running away from, and which he/she does not want to face – the ghost that will haunt them.

11 Alignments and Symbols

This chapter is totally practical: it is about work on scenes and it is in two parts. The first part of the chapter is called 'Politics', for it is about the changing alignments between characters as they move through a scene, the politics of the situation within the scene, and about survival: it is basically about winning – and I like that.

The second part of the chapter is called 'Concretising Thoughts', for it is about how we can use an object to symbolise a thought in order the better to grapple with it with our minds. I find this a very useful exercise for, however metaphysical the thought may be, if we use a symbol to represent it we will find its centre and how real the thought is. Children have wonderful metaphysical thoughts about time and the world and the stars: I am not necessarily talking about these, but I am talking about thoughts which go beyond the concrete facts and take us into the world of enquiry, giving us pleasure. These thoughts are, after all, central to our lives, and it is the actor's job to excite the listener with them, for they also inform the life of the character.

POLITICS

I have divided this section up into four parts:

    (i)   Finding relationships
   (ii)   Conspiracy
  (iii)   Oneupmanship
  (iv)   Playing games

EXERCISES

Finding relationships

In every scene there is a movement of some sort which is to do with how each character relates to another character, and how that relationship changes as the scene progresses: whether they are in sympathy and want to get closer, whether they draw back momentarily, or whether they want to move right away. This movement is part of any scene, be it romantic, conspiratorial or confrontational.

First – we need a table and chairs: there need if possible to be at least twice the number of chairs as there are characters. Each character should sit on one of the chairs – keeping spaces between them. During the scene each character can move one chair at a time either away from, or towards the character who is speaking – i.e. according to how he/she reacts to what that character is saying. This should carry on until the end of the scene. During the scene one character may get angry and want to push another out of the way to get to the speaker: this must be resisted – but the feeling should be remembered.

What is interesting about this exercise is that it reveals very subtly each character's reaction to the other, i.e. whether they are drawn towards them or feel in retreat, plus what prompts that reaction. Here are three scenes which I will lay out as examples:

First – the opening scene in *King Lear*, which we have already looked at in some detail. Moving round the table in the way I have described helps to pinpoint the rivalry between Goneril and Regan, plus Cordelia's possible withdrawal, as they wait to hear how Lear will solve the division of his kingdom.

It could be set up like this: Lear and his three daughters sit round the table, with perhaps Cornwall and Albany standing behind their respective wives, and the Fool, though not specifically in the scene, standing behind Cordelia. As Goneril and Regan, in turn, each tell him of their love and duty, the one who is not speaking would try to get close to him, wanting to push the other out of the way. As each sister moves to another chair, their husbands also move with them – for their interests are also at stake. While at the same time Cordelia, who does not want to have anything to do with this, retreats. At the end of that scene Cordelia has two alternatives: either to get as far away as possible and disassociate herself from all these dealings, or to get as close to her father as possible with the aim of trying to make him come to his senses and see the truth for what it is.

The second scene is that between the conspirators in *Julius Caesar*, Act I, scene ii. Caesar has just come from the Capitol where he has been offered the crown three times, and each time he has refused it. But when Cassius, Brutus and Casca come together at the end of the scene, after Caesar and his train have gone out, they each sound each other out about their thoughts on Caesar's aspirations and ambitions and their attitude towards him, for they each fear that this new-found power of Caesar's will lead to disaster. In the scene none of them comes out directly with what the bottom line of their thinking is, i.e. the possible murder of Caesar, but as they work round each other they gradually build a trust. By moving nearer to, or further away from each other as they talk we highlight the circuitous path they are travelling – it is after all a dangerous one.

The third scene, and one which could not be more different, is from *As You Like It*, Act IV, scene i, and is between Orlando, Rosalind and Celia. This is the central scene between Rosalind and Orlando where they philosophise on love, and where Rosalind, in disguise, continually challenges Orlando's truth in his declaration of love, in other words – she puts him to the test. Celia watches all this, and, though hardly speaking, we feel her deep concern for Rosalind at this point. This exercise would highlight not only the arguments that both the lovers put up in their efforts to justify their feelings, but also it would point up Celia's involvement with the situation, and her realisation that Rosalind is in love, and what that might mean to their friendship. It would confirm her identity in the scene and make her presence active.

It is an extremely useful exercise to do on any scene, classical or modern, in that it makes us realise the fragility of our relationships, and what they depend on. It is of course in the end about the underlying motives within a scene, but what it does do is actively focus our minds on the listening, and on the changes in the moment, so we are not pre-empting the result.

Conspiracy

Again, this is a simple exercise, but is quite surprising in its results for it emphasises the very real sense of danger that underlies the plays. The bottom line is this: the actors in the scene must not let anyone else in the play hear what they are saying.

A space should be laid out in the centre for the actors to play the scene; a chair placed at each corner of that space. Down each side of the space there should be marked a path between the chair at the front and the chair at the back. The actors, however many in the scene, should place themselves in the centre of the space and start to play the scene. During the scene, two actors chosen from the group, one on each side of the acting area, have to walk up and down at random on the path marked between the front and back chairs. When they are between the two marks, the actors in the centre must stop speaking and wait for them to get out of sight: when the path is clear, they may carry on with the scene.

What is fascinating about this is first, the randomness of the actors walking and therefore how the players have to stop at random and wait, and in that waiting there is a tension, and that tension feeds the urgency of the next piece of dialogue; and secondly, the actors have to be constantly on the watch for those intruding, and from this we get a very real sense of the danger in the scene.

What this does is give the actors another awareness, an awareness of the outside world: also because they have to stop and wait at unexpected moments, they cannot pre-empt their response. It makes the actor aware of the 'other', i.e. the world outside their character and gives an added tension. It is also very illuminating for those watching.

The following two scenes make excellent examples: this first from *Richard II* is when Richard has gone to Ireland to fight, and Northumberland and Bolingbroke are gaining power in England:

BUSHY   The wind sits fair for news to go to Ireland,
         But none returns. For us to levy power
         Proportionable to the enemy
         Is all unpossible.
GREEN   Besides, our nearness to the King in love
         Is near the hate of those love not the King.
BAGOT   And that is the wavering commons; for their love
         Lies in their purses, and whoso empties them
         By so much fills their hearts with deadly hate.

BUSHY	Wherein the King stands generally condemn'd.
BAGOT	If judgement lie in them, then so do we,
	Because we ever have been near the King.
GREEN	Well, I will for refuge straight to Bristol castle,
	The Earl of Wiltshire is already there.
BUSHY	Thither will I with you; for little office
	Will the hateful commons perform for us –
	Except like curs to tear us all to pieces.
	Will you go along with us?
BAGOT	No, I will to Ireland to his majesty.
	Farewell. If heart's presages be not vain,
	We three here part that ne'er shall meet again.
BUSHY	That's as York thrives to beat back Bolingbroke.
GREEN	Alas, poor Duke! The task he undertakes
	Is numbering sands and drinking oceans dry.
	Where one on his side fights, thousands will fly.
BAGOT	Farewell at once, for once, for all, and ever.
BUSHY	Well, we may meet again.
BAGOT	I fear me, never.

Richard II, II.ii.

There is a fearful sense of fatality in the scene which of course lends itself to the exercise, so that the listener is excited by the suspense and tension created as the actors wait for the space to be clear in order to continue the dialogue.

This next scene from *A Midsummer Night's Dream* is quite different in that it is about two lovers planning their escape together; however, just because there is a romantic quality to the scene it is necessary that the underlying danger is heard. We must remember that Hermia's very life is at stake if she goes off with Lysander – the least that will happen is that she will be confined to a nunnery:

LYSANDER	How now, my love? Why is your cheek so pale?
	How chance the roses there do fade so fast?
HERMIA	Belike for want of rain, which I could well
	Beteem them from the tempest of my eyes.
LYSANDER	Ay me! For aught that I could ever read,
	Could ever hear by tale or history,
	The course of true love never did run smooth:
	But either it was different in blood –
HERMIA	O cross! – too high to be enthrall'd to low.

LYSANDER	Or else misgraffèd in respect of years –
HERMIA	O spite! – too old to be engaged to young.
LYSANDER	Or else it stood upon the choice of friends –
HERMIA	O hell! – to choose love by another's eyes.
LYSANDER	Or if there were a sympathy in choice,

War, death, or sickness did lay siege to it,
Making it momentary as a sound,
Swift as a shadow, short as any dream,
Brief as the lightning in the collied night,
That in a spleen unfolds both heaven and earth,
And – ere a man hath power to say 'Behold!' –
The jaws of darkness to devour it up.
So quick bright things come to confusion.

HERMIA   If then true lovers have been ever cross'd
It stands as an edict in destiny.
Then let us teach our trial patience,
Because it is a customary cross,
As due to love as thoughts, and dreams, and sighs,
Wishes, and tears – poor Fancy's followers.

LYSANDER   A good persuasion. Therefore hear me, Hermia:
I have a widow aunt, a dowager,
Of great revenue; and she hath no child.
From Athens is her house remote seven leagues;
And she respects me as her only son.
There, gentle Hermia, may I marry thee;
And to that place the sharp Athenian law
Cannot pursue us. If thou lovest me, then
Steal forth thy father's house tomorrow night,
And in the wood, a league without the town –
Where I did meet thee once with Helena
To do observance to a morn of May –
There will I stay for thee.

HERMIA   My good Lysander,
I swear to thee by Cupid's strongest bow,
By his best arrow with the golden head,
By the simplicity of Venus' doves,
By that which knitteth souls and prospers loves,
And by that fire which burned the Carthage queen
When the false Trojan under sail was seen,
By all the vows that ever men have broke –
In number more than ever women spoke, –
In that same place thou hast appointed me
Tomorrow truly will I meet with thee.

LYSANDER   Keep promise, love, Look – here comes Helena.
A Midsummer Night's Dream, I.i.

It is great to work the exercise on this scene for it adds another dimension to their love – that of the risk they are willing to undertake for each other.

I can think of so many scenes which this exercise will work for, not only in the more obviously political plays such as the histories, but also in the comedies where so often there is a covert plan which has to be set up – for instance the scene at the beginning of *As You Like It* between Rosalind and Celia as they plan to leave the court. But perhaps the most anarchic scene of all is that between Macbeth and Lady Macbeth as they plan the death of Duncan: this exercise would help to signal the danger, the density and the suddenness of their thoughts.

Oneupmanship

This exercise is simply about scoring points: it works on the same principle as that which we used to mark the ladders of thought in chapter seven.

It needs to be a scene between two or three characters, and should be set up like this: the characters should space themselves in the middle of the acting area: we need a sheet of paper in the middle – plus a couple of pencils. Mark the paper into columns so that each character has their own column. Work the scene through, and each time the actor feels that he/she has made and won a point, they must put a tick in their column: this both energises the thoughts, and is exciting to do, ie. – to win.

This exercise works well for so many scenes in that it points up the mental agility of the characters, the duelling of ideas, and the pleasure that is had from finding the right thought at the right moment and expressing it well: Shakespeare's audience relished that sense of sparring with words, and the speed and immediacy of the thoughts.

Many of the scenes that we have already looked at can be worked in this way, e.g. the scene between Leontes and Camillo in *The Winter's Tale*, or the scene between Petruchio and Katherina in *The Taming of the Shrew*, or the short exchanges between Beatrice and Benedick in *Much Ado About Nothing*. It would work for the central scenal between Troilus and Cressida when they each swear their love for each other, he in male, soldierly terms, and she in a much more philosophical way, aware of the passing of time and of the traps that lie in wait for a woman. It also works wonderfully for the early scenes in *Romeo and Juliet*, (the witty exchanges between Mercutio and Romeo, or between Benvolio and Romeo). I have even worked it in rehearsal on the opening scene of the play with the exchanges between the servants of the Montagues and the Capulets as they come together to pick a quarrel: when they started fighting, each time one of them scored a hit they had to tick their side of the paper, and this spiced the whole scene, for the dialogue and the duelling sparked each other off and became integral to each other. The result was that it became not only extraordinarily sharp and witty, but also serious and charged with real anger. For the exercise does not only feed the wit, the mental sharpness, it also feeds the emotional source.

We have already looked briefly at the quarrel between Brutus and Cassius in Act IV, scene iii of Julius Caesar, repeating the words that sting and fire each other up, but if we take this one stage further with this exercise we see how each new thought takes them into a different phase of the argument, and ups the emotional stakes: as each finds a new point to beat the other with so their gall rises, and the outcome has to be either in blood or in forgiveness. I think it is a wonderful scene, and it is only at the very end we hear from Brutus that Portia is dead:

CASSIUS	I did not think you could have been so angry.
BRUTUS	O Cassius, I am sick of many griefs.
CASSIUS	Of your philosophy you make no use,
	If you give place to accidental evils.
BRUTUS	No man bears sorrow better. Portia is dead.
CASSIUS	Ha? Portia?
BRUTUS	She is dead.
CASSIUS	How 'scaped I then the killing, when I crossed you so?
	O insupportable and touching loss!
	Upon what sickness?
BRUTUS	Impatient of my absence,
	And grief that young Octavius with Mark Antony
	Have made themselves so strong; for with her death
	That tidings came. With this she fell distract,
	And, her attendants absent, swallowed fire.

CASSIUS	And died she so?
BRUTUS	Even so.
CASSIUS	O ye immortal gods!

[Enter Lucius with wine and tapers]

BRUTUS	Speak no more of her. Give me a bowl of wine.
	In this I bury all unkindness, Cassius.

[He drinks]

CASSIUS	My heart is thirsty for that noble pledge.
	Fill, Lucius, till the wine o'erswell the cup:
	I cannot drink too much of Brutus' love.

After the turbulence of the scene, this outcome has such power and such compassion, and that is all in the spareness of the writing.

Playing games

This is very similar, and works to the same ends, though possibly it does not elicit quite the same emotional drive, but it does keep the mind active and on the moment.

As you work through a scene the actors have to play a game: it can be a game of noughts and crosses, or snap. The concentration on the game, and the need to win, sharpens the mind and brings its own excitement with it – for the exercise is about winning both the points in the game and the points in the argument. As a variation, particularly if the scene is quite rough, and has several people in it, you can play a game of tig, or something similar – whatever comes to mind.

These exercises are particularly good for modern text, for in no way are they pointing up any kind of heightened perception, rather they can be done on quite minimal and spare writing. This following piece is very interesting for, though quite minimal in expression, it has a very stylised form: it is from Caryl Churchill's *Serious Money*. Durkfield, a trader, and Merrison and Zackerman, two bankers, are talking. I think the subject speaks for itself:

Durkfield: There's guys don't want me in their club.
I don't give a rat's ass.
Those guys would have looked the other way
And let the cattle trucks pass.
(I don't want to play golf with those bastards. I
don't even play golf. I can play without hitting a ball.)

I'm good at my job.
I stay on the floor with the guys.
Screw the panelling, screw the Picassos, I am not
    interested in office size.
    (You like lunch, you have lunch.)
I run the best trading floor in New York City,
And traders make two dollars profit for this company
    for every dollar made by you bankers.
And you treat us like a load of shit.
You make me your equal, I'm meant to say thanks
For what? Thanks, Jack. Come off it.
I make this company eighty million dollars and
    bankers pocket most of that profit.
Bankers get on the cover of Time.

Merrison: Brother, can you spare a dime?

Durkfield: I do OK, sure, I'm not talking greed.
I'm talking how I mean to succeed.
    (My father came to this country – forget it.)
Which of us does this company need?
I'm talking indispensable.

Merrison: And my father? You think I'm some kind of patrician?
I was sweeping floors in my uncle's delicatessen
So don't –
The company needs us both. Be sensible.
There's two aspects to the institution.
Nobody means to imply they underestimate your
    invaluable contribution.
I need to understand what you're saying here so let's
    set a time we can have a further talk.

Durkfield: You don't seem to get it. You're sitting in my chair.
Walk.

Zac: And the guy walked.
    (He walked with twenty million dollars but he
    walked.)

Serious Money, I.

To do one of the above exercises on it would underline the hidden code of competitivenes and business practice that is their world. The writing has such a wonderful and surreal quality, highlighted by its very stylised form.

I think it is important at some point in rehearsal to play some games: it not only enlivens the language and takes it off the printed page, but it also arouses that sense of competition which is in all of us, and which is part and parcel of finding a good argument – and the need to survive to the best of one's ability.

CONCRETISING THOUGHT

I think this whole area is central to the work – and the imagination. For it is, as I said at the beginning, about making the thoughts specific and real for the moment. The section is divided into three parts:

(i)   Making an object symbolise the thought
(ii) Building an altar or a structure to represent the character's feelings or desires
(iii) Finding the centre line

Whatever the play, the period or the style, there is always something in the writing that makes us think of another reality, another set of thoughts, which will be different from our own and not part of our experience. The actor has to find that reality and these exercises are useful for that very reason – i.e. to help the actor specify the exact form and shape of the thought – perhaps this is metaphysical in itself.

EXERCISES

Making an object symbolise a thought or a concept

Choose a scene between two or three actors: find an object, e.g. an apple, a small purse, a cup – something which has a certain substance to it, and use that to represent the centre of the thought. Put the object on a table between you, and when you are dealing with that thought put the object in front of you. When the next character takes the thought on they then take/grab the object and move it to their own side of the table. You can use a table, or a particular space in the room depending on the size of the scene itself. Move the object in whatever way you please – you may want to keep it but the other character wrests it away from you, you may want to nurture it – the possibilities are endless. You will find that the argument opens out in very surprising ways.

This following scene between Queen Isabel and Bushy makes a very good example: on the surface it appears a little dry and over-reasoned, but as we personalise the thoughts in this way the grief takes a shape and becomes incredibly real. Richard has gone to the wars in Ireland, and Northumberland's subversion in England is taking hold.

BUSHY	Madam, your majesty is too much sad.
	You promised when you parted with the King
	To lay aside life-harming heaviness,
	And entertain a cheerful disposition.
QUEEN ISABEL	To please the King I did. To please myself
	I cannot do it. Yet I know no cause
	Why I should welcome such a guest as grief
	Save bidding farewell to so sweet a guest
	As my sweet Richard. Yet again methinks
	Some unborn sorrow ripe in fortune's womb
	Is coming towards me, and my inward soul
	With nothing trembles. At something it grieves
	More than the parting from my lord the King.
BUSHY	Each substance of a grief hath twenty shadows
	Which shows like grief itself, but is not so.
	For sorrow's eyes, glazèd with blinding tears,
	Divides one thing entire to many objects,
	Like perspectives which, rightly gazed upon,
	Show nothing but confusion; eyed awry,
	Distinguish form. So your sweet Majesty,
	Looking awry upon your lord's departure,
	Find shapes of grief more than himself to wail,
	Which looked on as it is, is naught but shadows
	Of what is not. Then, thrice-gracious Queen,
	More than your lord's departure weep not – more
	is not seen,
	Or if it be, 'tis with false sorrow's eye,
	Which for things true weep things imaginary.
QUEEN ISABEL	It may be so; but yet my inward soul
	Persuades me it is otherwise. Howe'er it be
	I cannot but be sad – so heavy-sad
	As, though on thinking on no thought I think,
	Makes me with heavy nothing faint and shrink.
BUSHY	'Tis nothing but conceit, my gracious lady.
QUEEN ISABEL	'Tis nothing less. Conceit is still derived

From some forefather grief. Mine is not so,
For nothing hath begot my something grief,
Or something hath the nothing that I grieve –
'Tis in reversion that I do possess –
But what it is that is not yet known what,
I cannot name; 'tis nameless woe, I wot.

Richard II, II.ii.

The object in this case represents grief: and this object can be passed back and forth between Bushy and the Queen, and they must use it in any way that seems appropriate for the moment. As you concretise the thought it becomes totally linked with the grief itself – and this becomes very moving. But also, and this is important, because you are using something to represent the thought, you are being objective about it, and this saves us from being sentimental.

This exercise could also be used on the scene near the end of *Henry IV Part II*: Hal, believing King Henry to be asleep, picks up the crown which is lying on the King's pillow, and takes it into another room. When the King stirs, he sees the crown has disappeared. The King is angry and calls for Hal: left together, the two have a long scene which is centred on the responsibility and cares of kingship, in the course of which they find reconciliation and the gradual bonding of their love for each other. If the crown is used as a symbol on which the discussion centres the whole thinking becomes real: it symbolises their realisation that only they know what that pressure and that reponsibility of kingship is – it makes the thought active rather than descriptive. This makes their bonding more complete and more profound.

I think this strategy of symbolising an idea, a concept, is most valuable for it keeps us specific to the matter in hand – we cannot gloss over it or romanticise it. To do this exercise, for instance, on the scene between Isabella and Claudio in *Measure for Measure* as they wrestle with the whole idea of Claudio's death versus Isabella's loss of virginity would be very powerful. It could be done with two objects, one representing Claudio's death and the other Isabella's rape: I think this would make the argument from both sides very rigorous and harsh, and thus make the situation unbearably real. In the same way, in the central scene between Hamlet and his mother in Act III, scene iv, when he is trying to make her see the truth surrounding his father's death, to have an object in the middle which represents the figure of the dead king would give their dialogue a horrible reality.

Building an altar or structure to represent feelings and ideas

The object here is for the actor to build some kind of construct with whatever there is in the room. This, like the drawing exercise which we looked at earlier, brings together two areas of the imagination: for the words you are speaking are stimulating your imagination, while at the same time, the invention of the object and finding things to build it with, shapes how you find the words and gives them a sense of being found in the moment. If the choice is to build an altar or perhaps a statue, then it is about something which is to do with the inner soul of the character: if the choice is to build a structure, then it means that you are trying to work something out in your mind – whatever, the action of having to find things with which to build stimulates the need to find the words.

Set it up like this: make a clear space in the room. With whatever there is in the room – chairs, tables, bags etc. – the actor has to build his/her structure in the centre. Again this is about making your thought, your image, your feeling concrete in some way – making it something which is tangible.

I remember working this with an actor rehearsing *Othello*, and the result was very moving. We were working the speech where Othello finally resolves to kill Desdemona: she is in her bed, and as we worked through the speech he built an altar to her. This speech would seem at first to be an unlikely choice for the exercise, for Othello has already set his mind on killing, yet what the exercise did was point up both his deep love for her and set it against his belief of her sexual transgression: it concretised the dilemma that came from these two parts of his consciousness. Now the exercise obviously has to be done out of the actual rehearsal set-up: but if we see Othello struggle to build his image of her which retains something of his ideal still there in his mind, we become aware of the anger and confusion which has taken hold of him, and which can only destroy. The very task of building the structure helps to identify this for him.

OTHELLO   It is the cause, it is the cause, my soul:
           Let me not name it to you, you chaste stars!
           It is the cause. Yet I'll not shed her blood,
           Nor scar that whiter skin of hers than snow,
           And smooth as monumental alabaster:
           Yet she must die, else she'll betray more men.
           Put out the light, and then put out the light:
           If I quench thee, thou flaming minister,
           I can again thy former light restore,
           Should I repent me; but once put out thy light,
           Thou cunning'st pattern of excelling nature,
           I know not where is that Promethean heat
           That can thy light relume. When I have plucked thy
               rose,
           I cannot give it vital growth again,
           It needs must wither. I'll smell it on the tree.
           [*He kisses her.*]
           O balmy breath, thou dost almost persuade
           Justice to break her sword! One more, one more.
           Be thus when thou art dead and I will kill thee,
           And love thee after. One more, and this the last.
           So sweet were ne'er so fatal. I must weep.
           But they are cruel tears: this sorrow's heavenly –
           It strikes where it doth love. She wakes.

                                            Othello, V.ii.

Or it can work for something infinitely more simple – Viola
building an altar to love: Viola, disguised as a boy, is in the
employment of Orsino, Duke of Illyria, and has been sent by
him to woo the Countess Olivia, who spurns him and does not
want to know of his love. When Olivia, attracted to Viola, asks
how she would woo, Viola replies with the following:

Make me a willow cabin at your gate,
And call upon my soul within the house;
Write loyal cantons of contemnèd love
And sing them loud even in the dead of night;
Hallow your name to the reverberate hills
And make the babbling gossip of the air
Cry out 'Olivia'! O, you should not rest
Between the elements of air and earth,
But you should pity me.

                                     Twelfth Night, I.v.

It is her altar to love, and ironically we suspect that love is for Orsino, so it has many layers.

There are many speeches which this exercise would serve: Berowne's speech about love in *Love's Labour's Lost* which we looked at earlier – that is an obvious one. But something less obvious would be Angelo's soliloquy in *Measure for Measure* in Act II, scene ii, after his first encounter with Isabella: he has become infatuated with her and has to rationalise his lust for her and weigh it against his own puritanism, and the law that he has already laid down which would result in the death of Claudio. The activity of finding ways to express this through a structure would give the thoughts a form and shape – something concrete which he has to contest physically.

But the exercise can also be used to express a philosophical idea, for instance Jacques' famous speech in *As You Like It* – 'All the world's a stage . . .', because it is so eloquent and flows so effortlessly it can easily become a kind of palliative. But if the actor playing Jacques speaks it through once while attempting to build a structure, perhaps a tower or even a pyramid, with anything that can be found in the rehearsal space, in trying to find the means to do just this while speaking those thoughts, we may perhaps perceive something of the time and of the rigour of mind which has gone into forming this particular perception of life, perhaps its absurdity, and of the need to express it in exactly the right way. It is an extraordinarily objective view, that of the outsider, and constructing something in this way places that objectivity.

The exercise can be useful in so many ways, to express grief for someone dead, or to express something which is to do with an ideal – an ideal state of being, or simply to express love or anger – speeches of both Antony and Cleopatra come to mind. The purpose is to both objectify, and be part of, the underlying emotion or desire at one and the same time.

Finding the centre line

I think every play has what I call a centre line, and by that I mean the thought which expresses the bottom line of the play: and this centre line is in its way a symbol of the whole. I think this is also true of a character: there is a line or a thought somewhere which expresses something at the very heart of the character, and I believe we have to look for it, because it somehow centres the work for us.

There is no specific exercise that can be done for this: but it is useful at times during rehearsal to get a view from each actor regarding what they perceive the centre line to be. This may change during the course of rehearsal as you get deeper into the play, but it is worth keeping at the back of our minds.

For *Hamlet* of course the centre line is palpably clear:

To be, or not to be, that is the question.

and the whole of the play is in one way or another working that central question out. For me *King Lear* has three centre lines:

What is the cause in nature that makes these hard hearts . . .

this second, from Lear, as he looks at Edgar, believing him to be a beggar:

Thou art the thing itself. Unaccommodated man is no more but such a poor, bare, forked animal as thou art.

and the last from Gloucester, blinded, on the cliff's edge:

So distribution should undo excess
And each man have enough.

Each one enquires into the essence of being.

And this final centre line from *Timon of Athens*: Timon has left his court, with all the flatterers and the courtiers grubbing for his money, to go into the wilderness and dig his hut, and finally his grave. Apemantus, the philosopher, comes to seek him out and tells him:

The middle of humanity thou never knewest, but the extremity of both ends.

Each play has at the core a thought, a concept, from which all else springs, and I think if we are aware of that centre, it helps us to identify with the play, to root down in it if you like, in order that we can find its extremes.

12 Working the Space

Every theatre space is acoustically unique, it is therefore vital that time is given to explore the particular sound qualities of that space so that each actor experiences for him/herself how best to fill it: and each actor will experience this differently. This work allows the actor to find his/her right level for that space, which in turn gives a sense of reassurance and takes away any feeling of pressure to force the voice in any way, i.e. it allows him/her to sit down in the voice and so get the best vibrations.

Sometimes a company is lucky enough to be able to rehearse quite a bit in the actual performance area, but that is rare. It is therefore essential that as we approach the end of a rehearsal period, sufficient time is allotted to work specifically on the tone quality needed for that particular acoustic, i.e. the pitch, the resonance, the muscularity and the volume, so that the subtleties of communication that have been found in rehearsal are not suddenly eroded by this new, and possibly alien, playing area.

As I have said every space is different with different resonating properties, and these can be deceptive for they depend on a number of random factors:

   (i)   Size – seating capacity.
  (ii)   Shape – height, depth and width.
 (iii)   Building material – the material with which the walls are built and how bright that is acoustically.
 (iv)   The space and shaping of the set – even in a space that is familiar the shaping of the set and the material used can alter the sound focus quite considerably.

Regarding size: in a large space, for instance, it is not necessarily a big increase in volume that is needed, but rather an awareness of how the vibrations of the consonants reach to the edges of that space, and how the voice can be lifted through. Also, the actual pitch used affects the sound, for each space has its own resonating quality, and it is useful to find the basic pitch which works for it. Contrary to what we may think, sometimes a very full and low-pitched voice over-resonates in a space and this can overlay the actual speaking of the words, the muscularity, with the result that the speech becomes unclear – i.e. we hear plenty of good tone but not the clarity of the words.

Regarding the shape: a great deal depends on the width and depth – a house can seat around the same number of people, but if the shape is wide but shallow it will need a different focus from one that is narrow but deep. Oddly, the deeper, more conventional theatre space is easier to work, for the focus is more contained; whereas if the space is wide – as in many modern theatres – the voice can be more difficult to place. And always the actor has to take height into consideration, so that those sitting in the upper areas feel included. It is vital that each actor finds the right basic pitch plus the muscularity needed to reach through the space – to its very rim.

A small theatre can be deceptive, for although it does not depend on volume in the same way, each space has its particular vagaries and often a small space has little resonance and may be more dead acoustically, requiring the actors to make up for this with their own vocal resonance. Of course it is the consonants that will carry and reach to the edge; however, if the language is naturalistic and throw-away in style, then we have to be particularly alert to the consonants so they do not drop at the ends of phrases – for the language is always particular even in its naturalism. If you are doing a classical play in a small space, then you must find a way of keeping the spaces in the language and the size of the imagery, yet making it proportionable to the area you are playing – all the things we have been looking at.

We must also take into account that in a studio space very often the seating is on three, or even four sides, and this of course means that the actor is inevitably backing at least one part of the audience.

I think I can probably best illustrate the practicalities of these differences in size and shape by my own personal experience with the Royal Shakespeare Company, for our theatre spaces are so varied: in Stratford for instance, where the Main House has a capacity of around 1700, the upper balcony, i.e. the third level, is good acoustically; it faces straight down on to the stage and there is little problem with audibility up there. In the dress circle, the second level, audibility is also good, as is the front two-thirds of the stalls: but the dead area here – the area we have to watch – is the back of the stalls. This is partly due to the fact that the theatre is deep and there are twenty odd rows in the stalls, so that if you are sitting in the back you feel far away from the stage; but the other factor is that it is under the quite deep overhang of the circle and this diverts and deadens the sound. While in our London theatre, the Barbican, although it seats roughly the same number as the Stratford house, the space is wide and relatively shallow, and although the depth of the seating is nowhere near as deep as it is in Stratford, i.e. the back wall is much nearer the stage, its very width makes it tricky to play – and we have to be very conscious of reaching through to every part with the muscularity of the language.

This is where the spatial awareness factor comes in, for the bottom line is this: if we, the audience, cannot see the actor clearly, this psychologically affects the way we hear – we feel we cannot hear. The actor therefore has to have that third awareness, that third ear, so that however intimate and quiet the scene being played is, he/she is aware of where it has to reach. Achieving this is always to do with intention, for it is about allowing the voice that moment to register with the audience so they can place it – and they can place you the speaker. Of course it also has to do with making sure that at some moment you allow each part of the house that split second to register your face: if in a large auditorium, you will have to allow those at the very back of the balcony to see you for that moment, so that when you are speaking they feel included. That bond, that sense of inclusion, has to be established

All this applies to the Swan Theatre in the same way. Although it seats only about 450, it also has its particular characteristics which have to be allowed for:

259

(a) The stage juts out quite considerably, so the people on the sides are often limited in vision, and –

(b) the height of the theatre related to its overall size makes the upper balcony very steep: the actor must be continually aware of this (subtly, of course) and allow for it.

The Other Place, the studio space, is currently relatively straightforward, for the seating is head on, and the acoustics are good and everything can be seen easily. However, it can be deceptive, and we always have to check on the audibility at the sides and back.

Now all this the actor knows, but each play is different, and the set-up for each play is different, and time is always needed to explore and discover the right vocal sensation, the right weight, for both the space involved and for the particular work in hand.

EXERCISES

In the space

First – a session of good voice exercises as in Chapter Five. Lie on the floor feeling spread and open. Open up your ribs and breathe out to counts of 10 and 15 – first without sound, and then humming – feeling the vibrations in your chest. Then focus on the stomach breath, finding the centre and singing out very gently on vowels. Continue by standing in a circle, again centring the voice, feeling the vibrations of the space by humming etc., and also touching out the vowels into the centre. It is essential to begin with these exercises for it is both reassuring for the actor plus it helps to build an awareness of the space. This should last no more than ten minutes for the important thing is to find the vocal balance which is right for the space.

Now for work on text. First the director or voice specialist needs to choose a piece of text – this could be a poem or passage we worked on in Chapter Six, or anything that you feel is suitable for the play in rehearsal – that feeds it in some way. We follow the same pattern of work, allocating a line or so each – however you feel, it is best broken up and divided. Allow time for the group to get familiar with their own section – begin by working it round in the circle. Then take it into the space – first running through the auditorium, jumping, or making a gesture on the individual lines. The group should then go to different parts of the space: if it is a formal theatre, i.e. a 3-tier space, then some actors should go to the top balcony, some to the circle, and some to the back of the stalls. When everyone is placed and standing still, speak the text round in order: as you do this, experiment with the pitch and volume, and take particular notice of the consonants and how they carry. Tell the story in the text in any way you want – it is important that, in finding the clarity of the language, you do not slow it down at all. Each time you go through it take a moment to assess the result. Finally, and this is the point of the exercise, speak it through as quietly as possible, not as a whisper but very quietly, making sure each word can be heard clearly, yet keeping the pace of the story: experiment with this a couple of times until you find exactly the right tone and muscularity that is needed to fill the space in this minimal way. In this way we will find the lowest common pitch, but of course with all these exercises we have to remember that when the audience is in, the sound is soaked up considerably more.

When all this has been done it is good to play a scene with the particular actors in different parts of the space – keeping the sense of intimacy in the scene within the distance imposed. It is then important to play a selection of scenes, or parts of scenes, on stage in situ, with other actors placed in different parts of the auditorium listening – this will tell us where the difficult areas are and therefore what adjustments we have to make to get the focus right.

An exercise I find particularly useful is this: the director should choose a poem (it is always good if it has some relevance to the work, but it should preferably be something which is unfamiliar to the cast). The printed text should be cut up into lines or suitable sections, and each section given to an actor, making sure each person knows the order in which they come. Each actor then goes to a different part of the space and, when ready, reads his/her section out in its right order, without knowing what the rest of the text is about.

The reason I like this exercise is that because each actor is familiar only with their own section and not the whole text, it makes us, the group, aware of just what is needed in order to make a text clear – i.e. something we do not know – and therefore just how much we have to lift the text through and give the words their exact value to make it understood. I think we have to continually remind ourselves of the fact that in rehearsal we get familiar with the sound of a text and what it means, but an audience is hearing it for the first time – this awareness must be always with us.

A text I particularly like using is this poem of Gunter Grass – 'The Jellied Pig's Head': it is in the form of a recipe, and so it is quite suitable to be read in sections: yet it is also anarchic, and unexpected, so it has to be very clear.

Take half a pig's head
including ear and cheek,
have the halved snout, the root of the ear,
the brainpan and the cheekbone chined,
together with two split trotters
from which the blue inspection stamp
should first have been removed,
with a clove-studded onion, a large bay leaf,
with a child's-handful of mustard seed
and a level tablespoon of medium rage
place them all in boiling salt water,
taking care
that in the large pot every part
is barely covered with water
and the flap of the ear, which otherwise would stick,
is not pressed down flat on to the bottom.
 Boil gently for an hour and a quarter,
 remembering that after the first boiling-up
 it is advisable to scoop off with a ladle
 the frothy brownish-grey excretions
 from the inner part of the snout, the conch of the ear
 and the halved, empty brainpan,
 so as to obtain a pure
 though not very savoury brawn,
 particularly as the rage, which so easily curdles to protest,
 tends to communicate in white particles with the froth
 unless constantly stirred from the start.
Meanwhile chop up four onions
and two peeled

and cored apples,
preferably small,
cut up two salted gherkins –
never dill, mustard or vinegar pickled gherkins –
into tiny cubes,
pound in your mind as though in a mortar
a heaped collarbone pit of black pepper
and, addding a ginger root,
as well as a little grated lemon peel,
leave the remaining rage
to simmer impotently over a low flame.
    As soon as – after a trial jab at the cheek –
    the meat of the head is tender,
    the back teeth are loose in the gums
    but still rooted,
    and the most jelly-conducive parts of the skin
    around the ear and the split edges
    of the added trotters begin to peel off,
    take all the components
    as well as the clove-studded onion
    and the bay leaf out of the pot,
    search the bottom with your ladle
    for bone splinters
    and the easily loosening front teeth,
    also for the grit-like grinding sand
    of the ear conch, and leave it to cool
    on a platter,
    preferably with the kitchen windows open
    and the pupils of your eyes contracted,
    while the broth should be left to simmer
    over a low flame.
Now proceed to detach
the soft parts of the snout,
the cheek, including the eye embedded in it,
and the layers of flesh beneath them,
from the bones.
    We recommend that you do not
    leave out the soft
    and firmer gristle
    or the jelly-like covering of the ear
    that can easily be scraped off with the back of a knife
    from the ear flap proper,
    since those very parts,

    like the lamellated gums
    and the horny
    root of the tongue that leads to the windpipe and oesophagus
    impart to our brawn
    that special and passionate brawn flavour.
Also, you should not fail
to let your hands, which during the work
have been covered again and again
with a film of jelly, drip dry
over the steaming broth,
because in that way the process of natural jelling
is aided once more;
for our jellied pig's head is to set
all by itself and communicated rage,
that is, without power and gelatine paper.
    Then cut up the fat and meat
    detached from the bones, not omitting the gristle,
    and together with the chopped onions and apples,
    the minutely cubed gherkins,
    the pounded black pepper,
    and an ample pinch of capers, place them in the broth.
Together with tarragon vinegar
stirred in by the spoonful, according to taste –
we recommend a not too sparing use
because vinegar tends to weaken when cold –
bring it all to the boil once more,
only now, after brief hesitation,
adding the rage
which meanwhile
has well thickened
over a low flame,
without the drained ginger root,
and then proceed to fill
a stoneware dish previously rinsed with cold water.
    Place this in a cool,
    if possible draughty place
    and for the next night
    invite well-disposed guests
    who will appreciate
    a home-made jellied pig's head.
Thrifty postscript: people who don't like waste
should cook the coarse gristle and bones
as well as the split trotters

once again, for spice
adding Marjoram, celery, carrots
and, providing more rage remains in the house,
a knife-tip of that,
so gaining a tasty soup
which, with turnips, barley, similar miseries
or dried peas
can replace for families with many children
a simple but nutritious meal.

I have included this purely as an example: it is possibly a little long, and certainly could only be worked with a large group. But what I wanted to show was that whatever we choose needs to be a little unexpected, a little off the wall, in order to catch the listener unawares, and so make us that much more sensitive to what is needed to catch the ear of the listener, and to draw them. There are of course countless poems which would be suitable in this way – classical or modern. Among the modern work T.S. Eliot is great to do because of the way the lines are broken up, each one containing its own layer of understanding, and so it tells us much about the spaces needed for the language to drop in. Another excellent source is W.H. Auden. As well as so much wonderful modern English and American work there is great material from poets like Pablo Neruda, 'To The Foot From Its Child' for instance, or Brecht or Gunnar Ekelof – just some of my favourites.

When all this work has been done I like to finish it off as follows: get the group to come together on the stage or playing area. Get into a circle and hum – again feeling the vibrations together – the vibrations in the chest, the head, the body: While you do this move the hum to different notes. When everyone has found a good resonance through humming, keep the hum going fairly quietly and then one at a time, and randomly, each one in the group should sing a line from the play over the group hum: this focusses us again on the play, plus it gives a sense of freedom and group involvement in the language. The line sung can be any line from the play and not necessarily the one belonging to the actor singing – plus the group can sing the line back if you like – but keep the hum going all the while. I like this exercise because it is freeing and gives a sense of collective enjoyment in the language.

To sum all this up then: we need to take full account of the space and each actor has to assess its resonance and size for him/herself, for it will affect each one dfferently. The bottom line is this – we need to feel the space belongs to us.

Afterword

Language gives life to our thoughts, and just as thoughts come to us suddenly and in their own time and rhythm, so how we speak them must be part of that creative process. And just as the actor, when working on a part, spends time exploring the thoughts and how they inform character and motive, so we must also explore how the words expressing those thoughts sound of themselves: and here I am not talking about the speech sounds of a character, i.e. the dialect, but rather how the thoughts erupt into language, and how the very speaking of them changes us.

I suppose what I am asking for in this book is a rethink of the rehearsal process so that the language becomes part of that process, not just by working its meaning and its implications, but by exploring how the word itself, however demotic it may be, is part of the imaginative life of the play. In heightened poetic writing we know that there are rhythms that have to be observed and imagery that has to be discovered and made alive: but even here we need more than just an awareness of those rhythms and that imagery, for all words spoken on stage are just as much part of the creative life of that stage as its visual life, and they must touch us in an active way. If they are beautiful then they must lift us, if they are violent we must feel their outrage: we must not be passive to them.

This book is specifically about work in rehearsal and as such I hope it will be equally useful for both directors and actors. I have assumed that the initiative will be taken by the director. However, I did not want to complicate the book by repeatedly referring specifically to either the director or the actor – I think that would be confusing – so I have most of the time reverted to the generalised 'you' and 'we' – I hope this will make itself clear. But of course my wish is that there is also a Voice Teacher involved in the work, as there should be in every company, who will not only bring their own particular understanding to the process, i.e. how the individual actor connects with a text, but they will also contribute to the work and open it out in their own particular way. Our job, and here I refer to myself as well, is to listen and respond creatively. The bottom line is this: that the issues in the book are taken on board by the director, and so given their proper time and value.

Now to be practical: I have concentrated on Shakespeare because of his universality: i.e. he is known and studied in so many countries and so many languages that one does not have to go into detail about plot and character, or particular societal values, which I think in the end would confuse the issues of the work itself. However, I do want to stress that all the exercises can be worked on any text of whatever period – Jacobean, Restoration, Victorian – right up to the latest modern work – they will always help to release something in the text; something unexpected. You simply need to pinpoint the need of the scene and the need of the actors so that you find the exercise that fits. Having said this, if a particular exercise does not seem to help it will usually point the way to another that will, plus perhaps show you the way you need to go. The exercises are to be viewed as a starting point, for as you get into them you can bend them round to fit the work in hand and let your imagination take you to what best will suit the specific need of the moment, and of the scene.

One other thing: it is not easy to write about the spoken word, and to describe the nuances of sounds and rhythms you may discover, so the exercises take a lot of words to explain them fully. Try not be put off by that, for once you have grasped the basic principle of an exercise, you will find it quite straightforward to set up and put into practice. Also of course they take you out of the rehearsal situation, and once you start to act the scene for real you have to let them go; however, what you discovered during the exercise will stay with you and inform your thinking and your action. They are there to open out the options.

I want to finish by quoting three very different pieces of text: they may seem disconnected, but I think in the end they will add up and make sense.

The first piece is from an essay which someone sent me by chance, for which I am most grateful. It is called 'The Last Word' and is by Earl Shorris who is a contributing editor to *Harper's Magazine*: he first quotes the linguist Michael Krauss, director of the Alaska Native Language Center, as saying that:

> as many as 3,000 languages comprising half of all the words on earth, are doomed to silence in the next century.

Shorris later goes on to say:

> English, as it is generally spoken, appears to be losing more words than it gains. You need only to look at the thin thesaurus that came with your word-processing program to see how the English language is losing its internal diversity. Nonetheless, ailing languages can be resuscitated; words can be brought back. The advent of another Shakespeare could vastly expand the vocabulary again. Cultures change, and languages survive by metamorphosis and the aesthetics of their creators. Who now speaks in the language of *Beowulf*?

The next piece is from the play *Our Country's Good* by Timberlake Wertenbaker. The play is set in a penal colony in Australia in 1787. The officers who run the colony are debating the possibility of getting the convicts to put on a play – *The Recruiting Officer* by George Farquhar: not all are in favour. Here Captain Arthur Phillip, RN, Governor-in-chief of New South Wales, is arguing for the project – against some odds:

Phillip: Some of these men will have finished their sentence in a few years. They will become members of society again, and help create a new society in this colony. Should we not encourage them now to think in a free and responsible manner?

Tench: I don't see how a comedy about two lovers will do that, Arthur.

Phillip: The theatre is an expression of civilization. We belong to a great country which has spawned great playwrights: Shakespeare, Marlowe, Jonson, and even in our own

time, Sheridan. The convicts will be speaking a refined,
literate language and expressing sentiments of a
delicacy they are not used to. It will remind them that
there is more to life than crime, punishment. And we,
this colony of a few hundred, will be watching this
together, for a few hours we will no longer be despised
prisoners and hated gaolers. We will laugh, we may be
moved, we may even think a little. Can you suggest
something else that will provide such an evening,
Watkin?

Our Country's Good, I.vi.

What I want to say is that we must protect our language, for
although English itself will not disappear, in fact it increasingly
dominates the world for, to quote Shorris yet again:

it is the *lingua franca* of science, the Internet, the movies, rock and
roll, television and even sports.

We, in the theatre, have a duty to keep the imaginative side of
our language alive, the one that expresses feelings, doubts,
questions, and therefore real communication between people,
for it is only in this way that our understanding will grow.
Perhaps, as Shorris says, we need another Shakespeare.

And here my last piece, from *The Tempest* – from Caliban. It
is particularly telling because it comes from someone who
earlier in the play has said to Prospero:

You taught me language, and my profit on't
Is, I know how to curse.

It is about listening to what is around us, and about an
imaginitive response to what we hear: it is also about silence. I
think it is one of the most beautiful passages in Shakespeare,
and of course it is not without its own particular irony:

CALIBAN   Be not afeard; the isle is full of noises,
           Sounds, and sweet airs, that give delight and hurt not.
           Sometimes a thousand twangling instruments
           Will hum about mine ears; and sometimes voices
           That, if I then had waked after long sleep,

Will make me sleep again; and then, in dreaming,
The clouds methought would open, and show riches
Ready to drop upon me, that when I waked
I cried to dream again.

The Tempest, III.ii.

Bibliography

Shakespeare – please note that all the extracts bar one are taken from the Penguin editions, as that is what we use at the RSC. The one exception is *Timon of Athens*, which is taken from the Arden Shakespeare. Punctuation in Shakespearean texts does vary depending on the publisher, and different punctuation may confuse an exercise.

Atkinson, Max. *Our Master's Voices*. Routledge, 1984.

Bond, Edward. *Lear*. Methuen Publishing Company, 1983.

Brown, Stan. 'The Cultural Voice' from *Creating the Voice*. Self-published, 1998.

Churchill, Caryl. *Serious Money*. Methuen Publishing Company, 1990.

Eliot, T.S. *The Family Reunion*. Faber and Faber, 1939.

Grass, Gunter. 'The Jellied Pig's Head'. Penguin, 1969.

Kane, Sarah. *Blasted*. Methuen Publishing Company, 1995.

Mamet, David. *American Buffalo*. Methuen Publishing Company, 1994.

Shaw, George Bernard. *Mrs Warren's Profession* (from *Plays Unpleasant*). Penguin, 2000.

Shorris, Earl. 'The Last Word' *Harper's Magazine*. 1990.

Wertenbaker, Timberlake. *Our Country's Good*. Faber and Faber, 1996.

Wesker, Arnold. *Roots*. Penguin, 1959.

Williams, Tennessee. *A Streetcar Named Desire*. London, John Lehmann, 1949.

Index